A COUNTER-HISTORY
OF FRENCH COLONIZATION

A COUNTER-HISTORY
OF FRENCH COLONIZATION

DRISS GHALI

Translated from the French by Ciarán Leglas

VAUBAN
BOOKS

Originally published in France as *Une contre-histoire de la colonisation française*
by Editions Jean-Cyrille Godefroy, Paris, in 2023. Copyright © 2023 by Editions Jean-Cyrille Godefroy.

27 26 25 24 1 2 3 4

ISBN 979-8-9887399-6-8 (paperback)

Library of Congress Control Number: 2024947018

Front cover illustration, Jacques & Pierre Bellenger, poster, 1931 International Colonial Exhibition in Paris

Vauban Books
P.O. Box 508
Blowing Rock, NC 28605
www.vaubanbooks.com

"We do not love the truth if we love it only when it is flattering and agreeable; we must also love it when it is bitter and harsh, distressing and severe; we must love its thorns and its wounds."

MONTAIGNE

~

In memory of my grandfather, Sidi El Ouafi,
a Moroccan *goumier* captured by the Nazis in June 1940
and imprisoned for four years in a Black Forest stalag.

To my mother, who taught me French, she who was not
allowed to complete her education, in a country where
women are looked upon as nothing. I learned French in
her name, and I hope to be worthy of her instruction.

To Luciana, for her patience and tact
during my spells of discouragement.

CONTENTS

GLOSSARY

Agha: leader appointed by the Turks in Algeria, hierarchical superior to the caïd.

Cadi: Muslim magistrate.

Caïd: tribal chief holding administrative, judicial, and police authority.

Chiaus: (pejorative) office-boy or underling.

Coolie: worker, porter.

Douar: a Moroccan hamlet or village, consisting of tents or brick-and-mortar houses. In Algeria, this is usually called a *mechta*.

Fellah: peasant or farmer.

Goum: (North Africa) name given to indigenous soldiers recruited by France to quell resistance to colonization and maintain internal order. The term comes from the Arab "qoum!", meaning "get up!"

Habous: religious foundation.

Imam: the imam leads prayers at the mosque and guides the local Islamic community in the practice of their religion.

Khalifa: deputy representing the caïd or pacha.

Koulouglis: a person of half-Turkish, half-Arab extraction.

Makhzen: (a) name given to the Moroccan government, whose core is the monarchy, or (b), in Algeria, the name given to tribes that collaborated with the central Ottoman authority, helping it to maintain internal order and receiving arable land by way of compensation.

Mandarin: high-ranking civil servant of the Chinese Empire and Vietnam, generally recruited according to criteria of academic excellence.

Pasha: town governor responsible for administrative, judicial, and police matters.

Sharif: descendant of the prophet Mohamed. In the North African tradition, the sharif has the authority to arbitrate disputes.

Sheik: deputy of the caïd.

Ulema: plural of ālim, a scholar versed in theology and Islamic law.

Vizier: a minister in the Ottoman and Arab world. The **Grand Vizier** is the equivalent of prime minister.

Zawiya: both a place (a mausoleum or building connected to a mausoleum) and a political-religious actor (a brotherhood, sect, or secret society, as the case may be).

SOME KEY DATES OF FRENCH COLONIZATION

The First Colonial Empire: When America was French

1604: Beginning of the very difficult process of colonizing Guyana, with the dispatch of the first French settlers. In the centuries that followed, there would be several further attempts, all disappointing, with disease decimating the white population.

June 1635: Two settlers from France, Liénard de L'Olive and Plessis d'Ossonville, take possession of Guadeloupe.

September 1635: The freebooter Pierre Belain d'Esnambuc takes possession of Martinique. The island's original inhabitants, the Caribs, permanently quit the island fifty years later.

1642: The French begin to colonize Bourbon Island, later known as Réunion. A governor would be appointed for the first time in 1665.

1659: Foundation of the French Saint-Louis trading post in Senegal.

1661: Louis XIV takes the reins of the Kingdom of France and revitalizes the French presence in Canada. He seeks to breathe new life into the colony, which—under-administered, ill-equipped, and unprosperous—had languished since the 16th century.

1682: French sovereignty is proclaimed over Louisiana, an immense territory stretching from Canada to the Gulf of Mexico.

1754: French presence in India is at its peak, thanks to the efforts of Dupleix. It is also the peak of the first French colonial empire, with trading posts in continental India, the Indian Ocean (Réunion, Mauritius, Seychelles), the Caribbean, and North America.

1763: Catastrophe! France loses its empire as a result of the Seven Years' War. It cedes Canada and the eastern part of Louisiana to the English and gives the western portion of Louisiana to the Spanish.

1798: General Bonaparte seizes Egypt, where the French will remain until 1801.

1800: Spain surrenders Louisiana to France. Three years later, Napoleon sells it to the United States for a pittance (9.5 cents per hectare).

Hemmed in, France Acts on an Ad Hoc Basis

1815: Congress of Vienna. France is confined to its natural borders and is prohibited from pursuing policies of any ambition in Europe.

July 1830: The French capture Algiers, deport Dey Hussein to Naples, and expel Turkish soldiers to Anatolia. Oran is taken in 1831, Bon (Annaba) in 1832, and Constantine in 1837.

1844: Establishment of the French protectorate in Tahiti.

1847: Emir Abdelkader lays down arms. The northern portion of Algeria, from the borders of Morocco to those of Tunisia, is largely in the hands of the French. Kabylia retains its independence. In the south, the Sahara remains untouched.

1849: The French obtain the right to establish and administer a territorial enclave of 66 hectares north of Shanghai.

1852: Napoleon III transforms Guyana into a penal colony. By the end of the 19th century, up to 15 percent of the population will consist of convicts.

1853: New Caledonia becomes a French colony.

1857: Capture of Lalla Fatma N'Soumer, a prominent Kabyle leader.

September 1860: The French come to the aid of Christians in Syria and Lebanon.

October 1860: French and British forces plunder and raze the emperor of China's Summer Palace (Beijing).

1862: The French take Saigon.

1863: Cambodia becomes a French protectorate.

1870: Defeat of Sedan and loss of Alsace-Lorraine. End of the Second Empire.

1871: Major uprising in Kabylia.

The Emergence of the Second French Colonial Empire

1873: Abortive attempt to establish a foothold in northern Vietnam.

1875: The Third Republic is established.

1876: Acceleration of French colonial expansion in Senegal.

1880: Treaty signed between Pierre Savorgnan de Brazza and Makoko Iloo, chief of the Téké people, establishing French sovereignty over the Congo.

1881: Establishment of the protectorate of Tunisia (Treaty of Bardo).

1883: Annam (central Vietnam) and Tonkin (northern Vietnam) become a French protectorate (Treaty of Hue).

1883: Capture of Bamako.

1884–1885: Berlin Conference. France's rights to the right bank of the Congo River (now Congo-Brazzaville and the Central African Republic) are recognized.

1887: Creation of the Indochinese Union, consisting of Cambodia, Cochinchina (southern Vietnam, including Saigon), Annam, and Tonkin. Laos will later be included.

1891: End of hostilities in Senegal. The entire territory is now held by France.

1893: Capture of Timbuktu.

1893: Laos becomes a French protectorate.

1895: Tonkin is essentially pacified twelve years after the treaty establishing the protectorate.

1895: Formation of French West Africa, with Dakar as its capital.

1900: At Kousséri, in northern Cameroon, French troops under the leadership of Commandant Lamy defeat Sultan Rabah, thus overcoming the final obstacle to French domination of the Lake Chad region.

1904: Inauguration of the Dakar-Niger railway line.

1905: The Algerian Sahara is under total French control.

1910: Formation of French Equatorial Africa, with Brazzaville as its capital.

1912: Establishment of the protectorate in Morocco (Treaty of Fez).

A Brief Climax

1914: First World War begins.

1919: After the First World War has ended, Cameroon and Togo pass under French control (granted by League of Nations mandate).

1920: France takes control of Syria and Lebanon (League of Nations mandate)

1921: Construction of the Congo-Ocean railway line begins. Thirteen years of work and thousands of deaths will follow.

1925: Lyautey is relieved of his post as resident-general of Morocco due to the intensification of the Rif rebellion. Though this is a Spanish territory, it poses a direct threat to French Morocco.

1925–1926: Syrian revolt against French presence. Bombardment of Damascus.

1926–1927: André Gide travels to Chad and Congo.

1929: Albert Londres tours Sub-Saharan Africa, from Senegal to Congo.

1931: The Paris Colonial Exposition.

1934: End of the pacification of Morocco.

1939: Beginning of the Second World War.

1943: Independence of Lebanon.

January–February 1944: Brazzaville Conference.

1945: End of the Second World War, and gradual return of indigenous soldiers to the colonies.

1945: Insurrection in Sétif, Algeria.

1946: After mistakenly believing he could negotiate with the French, Ho Chi Minh goes underground and declares a national war of independence.

1946: Independence of Syria.

1947: Beginning of the Malagasy Uprising, which lasts two years.

Decolonization Is Easier than Expected

July 1954: France withdraws from Indochina (Geneva Accords). Vietnam is split in two.

November 1954: Toussaint Rouge (beginning of the Algerian War).

1956: Independence of Morocco and Tunisia.

1958: Guinea wins independence.

1960: Independence of colonies in Sub-Saharan Africa and Madagascar.

1962: Independence of Algeria.

The Empire Strikes Back

1981: The first riots in the French *banlieues* take place, in the Minguettes neighborhood.

1983: First large protests of inhabitants of the *banlieues*, called the "*marche des beurs*" (March of the Arabs).

1984: Creation of *SOS Racisme*.

1986: Death of student Malik Oussekine at the hands of the police in Paris.

1989: In a conversation with French TV network TF1, King Hassan II of Morocco declares that immigration "should not lead to integration."

2000: ICESCO (the equivalent of UNESCO for the Islamic world) publishes its "Strategy of Islamic Cultural Action in the West," including methods intended to impede the integration of Muslim diasporas in France and other Western countries.

2005: First "Intifada" in French *banlieues* following the death by electrocution of two young men, Ziyed Bena and Bouna Traoré.

2017: Then-candidate for the French presidency, Emmanuel Macron, describes colonization as "a crime against humanity."

2018: France signs the Global Compact for Migration in Marrakesh (Marrakesh Migration Pact).

2019: In Abidjan, French President Macron declares that "colonialism was a grave mistake, a serious misdeed of the Republic."

INTRODUCTION:
DO NOT MISTAKE YOUR ENEMY

"Each generation, in relative obscurity, must discover its mission, fulfill it, or betray it."

FRANTZ FANON

In what concerns France, the current generation's mission is to invent a new formula of government. A formula that suits an old country suddenly become multiracial and multireligious. A formula that embraces new demographic realities without tearing society apart. A winning formula that can bring power, collective happiness, and prosperity.

For the moment, and even if everyone pretends all is well, no such formula exists. The warning bells are sounding, but the crew are all drunk on the bridge, singing as one that the Republic has an answer for everything.

Whether of native stock or the product of immigration, the French are not fated to participate in a collective catastrophe. Yet the chances are high that those now between twenty and thirty years old will witness or even participate in the break-up of France. It is up to them to break the spell if they do not want to become a cursed generation, the one that saw danger coming and did nothing, the one that preferred to bite the hand that fed it rather than preserve the nation's heritage.

I am quite serious: the ingredients are there for a civil war or the slow unraveling of the French nation, pulled apart by petty egoism on every side.

To paraphrase Fanon, cited above in epigraph: the context is obscure, but the mission is clear. Indeed, it is obvious. The fact that there is no ready-made formula to resolve the problem makes it especially frightening. Hence the temptation to take refuge in the past and identify the guilty among those who are dead and gone. There is no risk in doing so, since a corpse cannot strike back. Instead, it appears silently before the court of memory, which holds session daily, weekends included.

Egged on by their elders, the youth of today sink their teeth into the corpse's rotting flesh. On one side, there are those who accuse their ancestors of colonialism; on the other, those who present themselves as victims of colonialism, even though they have never seen a colonist in their lives or experienced even a single day of foreign occupation. In both cases, these are lions in the making, behaving like hyenas.

They are pushed to this crime by powerful lobbies. These dispensers of hatred sing as one about the duty of remembrance. It is in their interest to set the colonial question ablaze. Like a cloud of locusts, they bring devastation wherever they go. They fertilize nothing and sow dissent and disorder between brothers and sisters.

The Establishment or at least a portion of it gives center-stage to professional whiners whose only job is being black or Arab. Protected from all real criticism, they think themselves talented, and appear on television drunk with their ideological "victory." These simpletons take themselves for Martin Luther King when in fact they are the system's protectors. They walk on stilts: take away their patrons and they come crashing down.

This book is an antidote to the poison distilled by these apostles of bad faith. It seeks to offer a dispassionate overview of French colonialism. It proposes to get to the bottom of things without losing its way in the quarrels of historians. It is written in the awareness that society is faced with decisive questions and seeks bold answers, answers that are clearly expressed, without the author cloaking himself in false neutrality.

It is driven by the urgent need to turn the page so that we may devote ourselves body and soul to what counts: the true mission of this generation.

Turning the page does not mean glossing over oppression and injustice, nor gate-keeping trauma. It is a matter of rising to the level of the facts so as to look them in the eye, instead of crawling on the ground like a wounded animal or looking down from above like some arrogant demigod. It is a matter of acting and thinking like an adult, as simple as that.

I do not care if I am called a collaborator or traitor. I prefer to fight the battles of my time rather than appropriate the struggles of those long dead and gone. My great-grandfather fought against France during the conquest of Morocco. He lost. The die was cast. His sons moved on. They worked, had children, and waited for the moment to revolt, which never came. Too bad. Among these children was my father, the only one to attend elementary school. He somehow wormed his way into the French high school in Marrakesh, which was forbidden to Muslims at the time, and from which he graduated in 1956, the year France announced its withdrawal from Morocco. He promptly went to work for the new Moroccan authorities. On a shoestring budget, he managed to work wonders in his field, audiovisual media. My father never imagined demanding reparations from France or blaming it for his problems.

I have no right to re-open wounds that my ancestors healed over.

This work may offend some historians, who will say that I do not have their diplomas, and thus lack their legitimacy. It may also offend activists on both right and left, who will not find here the kind of Manichaeism that would allow them to distinguish with the wave of a wand between good guys and bad.

Preemptively, I say to both parties that I am an ordinary citizen with no time to lose. For France must be saved. And yet neither the historians, nor even less the activists, have produced a narrative that might defuse the colonial question and neutralize its toxic effects. To fill the void and respond to this urgent situation, an ordinary man is justified in trying to make himself useful to his contemporaries by exploring, despite his limitations, a field as complex as that of colonialism. Fundamentally, this is nothing less than a question of reviving the ideal of the *honnête homme*.[1] Under the spell of two impostors—the worldly intellectual who produces poses and the specialist expert who produces noise—France has sadly drifted from this ideal. *L'honnête homme* is a generalist who gets to work and is not afraid of getting to the bottom of things. He is sovereign because he lays claim to and exercises his capacity to learn by his own lights. Like the entrepreneur, he privileges the action necessary to resolve problems and create value. To put it another way, *l'honnête homme* does not prosper from disorder but instead prefers to make himself useful.

---

1. Trans. In the seventeenth century, the figure of the "honnête homme" (literally, honest man) came to be seen as the ideal candidate for polite society. In addition to being well-read and worldly, he possessed taste, savoir-faire, politeness, and the social graces. At once gentleman and generalist.

Some Details Concerning my Method

In the interests of readability and simplicity, this book is limited to the French colonization project closest to our time, the one that swallowed up Indochina, the Maghreb, and a large portion of Sub-Saharan Africa. That project began with the capture of Algiers in 1830 and ended in 1962, but it continues to reverberate to this day.

Other territories were taken by France in earlier centuries, including Réunion, Guyana, and the Antilles. While this history may be fascinating in various ways, I will be at pains not to touch upon it, for the colonies acquired by the Ancien Régime were governed in a completely different fashion from those acquired after the Revolution. They were the product of a mercantile vision of the world, geared towards promoting the interests of merchants and planters. With the capture of Algiers in 1830, a different kind of colonization came to be, one that did not play fair and that concealed its true motives behind terms such as "the civilizing mission" [*la mission civilatrice*]. At least the kings of France had the decency to not misrepresent the true motives of their colonial policy. It is a point to which we shall return at length in this book.

I will be leaving aside the Syrian and Lebanese experiences, as they constitute a separate chapter in the overall history of French colonization. The French trading posts in India, minuscule and far from the global heart of empire, will also be off the menu. I hope the reader will forgive this bias.

The book is structured in chronological fashion, making it easy to follow.

- Part one: the myth of paradise lost
- Part two: the origins of a wild idea (1830–1905)
- Part three: a raw deal (1905–54)
- Part four: a formality called decolonization (1954–62)
- Part five: the empire strikes back (1960s to the present)
- Part six: What is to be done? Mourn the past or smile upon the future?

Our study extends beyond the 1960s. Colonization has been stirred into our immediate history and has resulted in new relationships of domination and solidarity, with incalculable (and uncalculated) consequences.

While preparing this book, I was at great pains to eliminate or at least attenuate my pro-French bias. I am not sure I succeeded. In any case, I changed my mind on more than one occasion, especially as regards Algeria, where I am much less indulgent towards France than I was when I started this project. Changing one's opinion is a luxury available to anyone with the time to study and do their research. Try it yourself and be not afraid to admit when you are wrong. May this book help you in that.

Finally, let us retain some humility when passing judgment on acts committed by other people from other times. While it might be desirable to develop a keen sense of Good and Evil, it would be out of place to keep scorecards for figures who exhibited a degree of courage, resilience, and cultivation beyond the common lot of mortals. Let us not lecture giants from the sidelines of History.

The terms *indigenous* and *native* will be used in their original sense, with no pejorative undertone. When I write *black*, *Arab*, and *yellow*, I refer to a race and a skin color, with no intention of demeaning or exalting anyone.

PART 1:

THE MYTH OF PARADISE LOST

THE BANALITY OF THE COLONIAL

> *"The world has always been divided between happy peoples,*
> *who forget in their prosperity the solid virtues which made*
> *their glory, and others whose harsher, less comfortable*
> *existence powerfully contributes to the development of*
> *appetite and ambition."*

PAUL BOUDET

Setting the Scene

Colonization is a subject ripe for misinterpretation and false certainties. For there was not one colonization, but many colonizations, each changing its aspect from one era and one region to the next. Iberian colonization, for example, had little in common with French colonization. Similarly, to colonize the Antilles in the era of Louis XIV was totally different from colonizing Indochina under the Third Republic. And even within a given colony, the experience of the colonized varied by geography. An inhabitant of the high plateaus of Tonkin had almost no chance of encountering a French civil servant, in contrast to his peers in large urban centers like Saigon or Hanoi. From one place to another, the pressures placed on the native could be entirely different. Over the course of forty-four years of colonization, the men of my village, Bhalil, twenty kilometers from Fez, barely encountered France. Conversely, their neighbors in Séfrou, three kilometers to the south, had a military garrison, a town hall, a tax office, and found themselves living side by side with Europeans.

It is therefore almost impossible to generalize about colonialism as a phenomenon. Everything depends on the empire (French, Spanish, British, Russian, Japanese . . .), the specific location, and the era (the departure of an honest administrator and his replacement by some angry little man is enough to reverse the outcome). Hence the difficulty of our task, and hence the temptation to indulge in Manichaeism.

That said, certain fundamental elements are easy to identify. They will serve as a general framework and antidote to the vertigo that threatens every observer placed before a phenomenon that is as varied as it is fluid.

Over the course of the second half of the nineteenth century, the white man took possession of Africa and a large part of Asia, casting his armies and peoples far from their metropoles. This was not the first time that Europeans had set about conquering the world. As early as the sixteenth century, the Iberians had taken possession of the Americas and several Asian territories. But it is the magnitude and intensity of this movement that so impresses: in the space of just twenty years, between 1880 and 1900, France, Germany, and Great Britain divided the bulk of Africa between themselves. The multiplicity of actors who participated in this "scramble" is also impressive: the United States got in on the action, taking the Philippines in 1898; the Italians were busy, too, as were the Belgians and the Japanese. While Japan was not part of the white world, it was the first non-European country to adopt the industrial and technological civilization conceived in Europe. This gave Japan the recipe for military and economic prowess and thus a decisive advantage over its neighbors. By the 1890s, Japan had a foothold in Taiwan and Korea, and we all know what came next: expansion into Manchuria, then into China in the 1930s, and so on.

Amid this breakneck binge, it is worth recalling a few crucial dates that punctuated the subjugation of a large portion of humanity: 1860, 1885, and 1898.

Acting in concert, on October 18th, 1860, the French and English razed the Beijing Summer Palace, the emperor's vacation home. This tragic episode marked the end of the Second Opium War (1856–1860), which saw the defeat of China. It was forced to cede a large swathe of its territory, open its ports to foreign trade, pay financial compensation, and allow Christian missionaries to operate in every corner of the empire. The conspicuous brutality shown by European troops reflected their extreme disdain for the enemy, for whom no honorable way out was even considered. It also revealed an enormous, unapologetic, and insatiable appetite for conquest and the booty, glory, and territory that it brought in its train.

Meeting at a conference in Berlin in 1885, the Europeans drew up the rules for partitioning Africa. Contrary to what is commonly held, Africa was not dismembered in Berlin, but the rules for its subsequent dismemberment were clearly and *brazenly* decreed. The challenge was to prevent the scramble for Africa from provoking tension or even armed conflict between the European powers. Some just controlled a small coastal fringe and had ambitions to annex regions in the interior without having to go to the trouble of conquering them, through a kind of preferential right. This was the case of England, Portugal, and France. The Berlin conference established that, in order to claim a territory, a nation must first effectively occupy it. The conference also established a mechanism for exchanging information among the European powers, obliging them to inform each other of any territory they had successfully occupied as well as of their treaties with local populations.

Finally, it is worth emphasizing that the United States, so quick to lecture France on anticolonialism after 1945, also joined in the race for colonial possessions. In 1898, the United States ran the Spanish out of Cuba, Puerto Rico, and the Philippines. It replaced a well-established Catholic and monarchist colonial power with one that was modernist, Protestant, and republican. A little later, it established a foothold in Panama (1914) and the Dominican Republic (1916).

But What Does Colonization Actually Mean?

Colonization is of course a universal grammar, understood by all peoples. Like sex, money, and violence, it is one of those languages that need no translation to speak to human beings and reach them where they are most human: their will to dominate and their readiness to obey he who is stronger.

Understanding what colonization means is quite simple. Wherever there is inequality between peoples, there is domination. Once two countries, two cultures, two communities come into contact, they immediately measure each other up and throw themselves into a struggle for power. The strongest or he who thinks himself strongest will always try to dominate and thus oppress the other. Oppression can take several forms: trade in which the terms are unfavorable for the weaker party, extortion (payment of tribute), dependence or vassalage, and of course plain and simple colonization.

Alterity calls for domination. As soon as I discover the existence of an Other, I assess my chances of dominating him. This moment well precedes any desire to know or study him. It is a sad fact of the human condition: the will to power precedes the thirst for knowledge.

The Arabs and Berbers conquered the Iberian Peninsula in the eighth century without knowing the least thing about its culture, traditions, or customs. Later, the Spanish and Portuguese supplanted the Amerindians, only later becoming interested in their civilizations and peculiarities. Similarly, Napoleon subdued the Egyptians before confiding the task of studying the pyramids and hieroglyphs to French scholars.

In the nineteenth century, the French, Belgians, British, Russians, and Germans thus rushed into those parts of the globe where they saw what they perceived as a militarily or economically inferior alterity, even when they had not the least inkling of its basic geography. This reflex was driven by the awareness of inequality: I seize that which is available and poorly defended.

As we shall see below, other factors of course played an important role in the formidable expansionist effort of France. But none of this would have taken place, no conquest would ever have been imagined, if the French knew that, on the other side of the sea, there were powers capable of repelling the would-be conquerors. This is why they were wary of advancing in Latin America, the preserve of the United States, which protected it from every ambition but its own. The only exception to this rule occurred in the 1860s, when, with the Americans too busy with the Civil War to keep an eye on their backyard, Napoleon III sent an expeditionary force to Mexico.

Technological, military, and financial advantage merges with a feeling of superiority. One considers one's civilization (religion, values, customs) superior to those of the peoples one has subjugated, finding in this domination a justification for colonialism. And it is true that African and Asian civilizations did not invent the industrial revolution or open the way to the scientific and technological revolutions. They never saw to the revision of individual and collective mentalities necessary for this. As a result, they were "responsible" for colonization, having rendered the societies under their protection *colonizable*. Even today, this revision has not taken place, for otherwise we would no longer be talking about "emerging" or "developing" countries. No matter how much aid and investment are poured into Niger, Pakistan, and Haiti, nothing grows, because the local civilization refuses to change. But civilization is sovereign and always has the last word. It does what it wants when it wants to. It also has its own rhythm, with its own peaks and troughs. Sub-Saharan Africa, weak and sufficiently divided for Europeans to subjugate in the nineteenth century, had in earlier times given rise to brilliant empires with endless gold reserves. Mali, Songhai, Ghana . . . many African empires had radiated far and wide, but their lights had long before gone out. As we shall see, the white man discovered poorly governed populations, wretched and incapable of forming a united front. Contrary to today's doxa, no marvelous empire was destroyed by the colonial advance of the nineteenth century, whether in Africa or Asia. Pockets of refinement were defeated and crushed, but there was nothing that suggested a political form capable of producing a solid economy, a robust army, or a determined population. In Indochina, the Court of Hue was certainly much more civilized than the French soldiers who laid siege to it in the 1880s, but it only controlled the walled compound behind which sheltered its splendors. In Morocco and Benin, similarly, the royal courts were the guardians of a remarkable tradition, though this had become no more than a pale copy of the political and cultural fire first lit by earlier generations.

Yes, of course, the European civilization of that era was superior. Does it remain superior now, at the time of this book's publication? There is reason to think it does not. China has updated its civilization; it is no longer inferior to anyone. On this subject, we might offer a thousand and one criticisms (human rights, the environment, etc.); it is nevertheless impossible to deny the moral and intellectual revolution carried out by the Middle Kingdom. It has replaced weakness and division with unity and power. It is far from impossible to imagine that, someday soon, China might colonize us. For human beings, colonizing is as natural as the air they breathe.

France Did Not Invent Colonization

Colonization is the original sin of humanity. There is no corner of the Earth that has not been touched by it at some point in its history. No one is an *absolute native*, the firstcomer on virgin soil: in the beginning, there was a power struggle, a dispute, a shove that expelled one and installed the other. Every deed of ownership contains the trace of some more or less subtle feat of strength buried in the debris of the past. 1500 years ago, the Anglo-Saxons expelled the Celts from England and pushed them towards Wales, Scotland, and Ireland. A little later, the Arabs eradicated Carthage and took its place in present-day Tunisia. And when the Americans invaded the Philippines in

1898, they realized that they were just the latest visitors to a country that had itself resulted from a Malay colonization that drove out its first inhabitants, the *negritos*. The latter were still around, the living relics of a defeated population carrying on in the mountainous regions, there where life was hardest, far from the rice plains and coastal trading posts.

No member of the United Nations can boast of being innocent of the colonial crime, which consists of dispossessing an earlier population of its territory and sovereignty. This theft is followed by the victim's eradication, expulsion, or enslavement. In the eighteenth and nineteenth centuries, the Peuls invaded the territories of the Fouta Djallon (present-day Guinea), establishing their sovereignty over a land where gentler and less determined people had lived. Reinforcing the humiliation, they imposed a tribute upon them and took captives, who were promptly dispatched as slaves to North Africa. In the mid-nineteenth century, European explorers in the Sahara came across these unfortunate men, women, and sometimes children. "A caravan of five or six hundred slaves, mostly young girls and children below the age of twelve, carrying on their heads the twelve-to-fifteen-kilogram loads placed upon them by their drivers, the Tibbous (Toubous of Tibesti). The slaves are all chained by the neck, and a lanyard joins the collar to their right hand . . ."[1]

Dominate and Settle

Colonization advances by two prongs: domination and settlement. Sometimes, domination precedes settlement; sometimes, it is the other way round. But in every case, colonialism sets in motion a transfer of political power and a transfer of population.

Colonization can proceed from below, silently. It is enough to send one's excess population to empty territories or those belonging to others. The Annamite kingdom (ancestor of present-day Vietnam) encouraged its renegades and other undesirables to settle in neighboring Khmer country. Eventually this process, which continued throughout the seventeenth, eighteenth, and a portion of the nineteenth centuries, became a *fait accompli*, resulting in the conquest of Saigon and part of Cambodia, both historical possessions of the Khmer people.

---

1. A scene recorded by Eric Vougel, a German traveler, who encountered this cursed caravan in Libya's Fezzan region. See: Yves Boulevert. *Explorations en Afrique Centrale* 1790–1930 (Y. Boulevert, 2019).

One can also colonize from above, with cannons and diplomatic treaties. This was the method of the Europeans, Japanese, and Americans in the nineteenth century. It was also adopted by the Egyptians, who, in collaboration with the British, conquered Sudan in the 1820s. Indeed, the Arabs pursued their colonial activities until quite recently. Zanzibar, off the coast of Tanzania, still bears the traces of Omani domination, which ended only in 1861.

When colonization proceeds from above, population transfer follows the theft of sovereignty. Once the new order is established, agents of the colonial ecosystem are dispatched: civil servants, settlers who take possession of the countryside, entrepreneurs and merchants to enliven the cities, clerics, and essential craftsmen (tailors, shoemakers, jewelers, etc.). In fact, there is always some degree of human penetration before the takeover, but it is usually reserved and circumspect. These are the merchants, diplomats, military advisers, and engineers who work with native authorities on major public works; there are also spies of every kind . . . Yet these contingents are miniscule compared to the waves that arrive after sovereignty has been transferred.

An empire can be thought of as a stock portfolio containing various assets, which can be divided into three main categories: settler colonies, extractive colonies, and strategic operating bases. Of course, a given colony might combine all three.

With the exception of Algeria, France never practiced settler colonialism. It could not do so because it lacked candidates due to low birth rates in the metropole. In Algeria, it thus called upon the Portuguese, Spanish, Italians, Greeks, and Maltese, among other peoples with a significant demographic surplus.

The colonial "concept" adopted by France was that of economic exploitation (the all-too famous "development").[2] Later on, we will see that, in the absence of any real wealth to seize, this exploitation was often nothing more than wishful thinking.

In many cases, the large colonies dedicated to economic exploitation, like Senegal and Indochina, started out as minuscule military observation posts

---

2. Trans. In 2006, MRAP, a French anti-racist NGO, demanded that the popular French dictionary, *le Petit Robert*, be withdrawn from circulation due to the manner in which it defined "*colonization*." According to MRAP, the use of the phrase "*mise en valeur*" [development] attributed a positive role to the act of colonization and was thus a provocation on the part of the publisher. See: https://www.lemonde.fr /societe/article/2006/09/05/polemique-autour-du-petit-robert-et-de-sa-definition -de-la-colonisation_809887_3224.html

doubling as waypoints for travelers. One could fill up with potable water in Saint-Louis, Dakar, and Haiphong, while also doing business in the surrounding kingdoms. These places offered veritable "balconies" overlooking Sub-Saharan Africa, China, and Malaysia, trading with which was for many the stuff of dreams.

Little by little and for reasons we shall clarify when the time comes, these various trading posts and fortified outposts served as jumping off points for a relentless drive inland, towards the mountains, forests, and deserts.

THE MAGHREB WAS A
WRETCHED DEATHTRAP

*"Many times, I witnessed how Moroccans returning from Algeria
envied the fate of their neighbors: it is so nice to live in peace!
Whether a little or a lot, it's so nice to enjoy it without a worry!
Safe roads, railways, easy trade, respect for property, peace and
justice for all, this is what they saw over the border."*

CHARLES DE FOUCAULD

To listen to the eminent specialists of the authorized media, Africa was a pure
and wholesome land before colonization, and it was France that corrupted it.
Algeria and the Arab world were oases of culture and humanism, and it was
France that transformed them into an intellectual desert. Indochina was on
the verge of sending a satellite into orbit before the French expeditionary force
permanently suspended the Annamite space program . . .

Oh jealous, venomous France, you who ruined the destiny of tens of millions of humans, broken for all eternity!

Oh France, mother of all evils, pitiless destroyer of virginity and innocence!

Oh malevolent power, who subjugated perfect beings linked with their kin
in the harmony and joy of diversity.

How easy it is to accuse you of every calamity, and how agreeable it is to
believe in the myth of the noble savage!

No offense to the dreamers and the naive, but History is stubborn. France
never interrupted any golden era where all was well in the best of all possible
worlds. Everywhere it set foot, the land was already ravaged by injustice and
scarcity.

The populations of the Maghreb, Africa, and Asia did not wait for the arrival of France to eat of the forbidden fruit and suffer its curse. The human condition in the "free world" was already what it is today: that of an apple long fallen and penetrated to its core by worms.

The truth is that the flaws of the precolonial world were no less scandalous than the crimes of colonization. Let us take a brief but earnest survey, beginning with the Maghreb.

Poverty, Arbitrary Rule, and Backwardness

If my parents and above all my grandparents experienced colonial oppression, my great-grandparents and ancestors endured the agony of the most abject backwardness.

The Moroccan of the first years of the twentieth century—that is, when Morocco was still a free country—was a person tormented by scarcity and filth. He spent his childhood and adolescence with head shaved so as not to attract ticks and lice. He lived in a tent or a rammed earth house vulnerable to parasitic infestation. He ate meat (mutton) once a year for Aid El Kebir. The rest of the time his diet consisted of rye bread, oil, and olives. His skin was cracked, and he had calloused feet, which were deformed from walking in ill-fitting shoes, if indeed he had shoes at all. His spine was bent by the weight he had had to carry from a young age: for women, huge basins of water between fountain and home; for men, haystacks or jute sacks filled with fruits and vegetables. He smelled bad, since he went to the hammam just once a month and relieved himself in holes frequented by vipers and scorpions. Like his donkey and his mule, he travelled many kilometers every day between field and souq,[1] where he sold his meager surplus when there was any to be sold, that is, when there had been some rain and the grasshoppers had spared his crops.

He was constantly afraid. Famine, locusts, leprosy and other skin conditions, typhus, and dysentery were all immediate threats against which he could do nothing or very little. Every Moroccan family had to bury its young: babies, children, young men and women, cut down by disease and inadequate care. There was no hospital to speak of in either town or country. Magic and superstition were the only recourse. And, of course, prayer.

---

1. Trans. A souq is an open-air market or shopping district in an Arab or Berber city.

He perfectly understood his place in society. His survival depended on submission. He kissed the hand of the dignitary who threw him some crumbs during religious festivals. He threw himself at the feet of the *caïd* who protected him from bandits and defended him before the judge (*cadi*), who in the case of a dispute would always favor the side that greased his palm.

He had no choice. Were he to decide to live with some dignity, he would be quickly brought to heel by the arbitrary rule that governed his society. Governance in Morocco was synonymous with plunder, injustice, and violence. On his own, the individual counted for nothing. Isolated, he would lose his land and cattle, his wife, and all his possessions. He needed a *patron* to ensure his protection when things got tough. Society was therefore organized around patron-client relationships, the only protection against a life of great indignity. The patron was a *caïd*, a tribal chief, a member of the ruling family. To stay in his good books, it was essential to make offerings, to celebrate with him (births, marriages), to mourn with him (bereavement, disgrace, poor harvests), and above all to work free of charge, on demand, gathering fruit from the master's grove or repairing his roads. There was simply no choice. Most of the time the state was minimal or simply absent.

At the beginning of the twentieth century, the Moroccan state was reduced to a bare minimum. It barely had the means to defend itself against foreign aggression or fund various sovereign functions, of which the most important was collecting taxes. Only the submissive and the humiliated, those whom the state had managed to subjugate, paid their taxes. Taxation was thus more a form of extortion than a contribution to public services. Anything that might alleviate suffering and render conditions a little less miserable was entrusted to the Habous, a religious institution that offered medical aid, fed the needy, and taught reading and writing. It was financed by the donations of the faithful. The state washed its hands of it and left it alone

While things were bad enough for men, women faced an even more lamentable fate. Women were nothing. Mere spoils of the razzias[2] that broke out now and then whenever a tribe had a bad harvest and decided to pillage its neighbors. The woman was merchandise bought with a dowry: a few kilos of sugar and a beast of burden were often sufficient. She was an eternal child, always under supervision: by her father until she reached the age of twelve and then by her husband for the rest of her life. Moreover, she did not know the identity

---

2. Trans. A hostile raid for the purpose of conquest, plunder, capture of slaves.

of her future husband until the last minute, when she was brought to the matrimonial home. It was in her interest to remain a virgin, otherwise she would be returned to her sender, with whom she would begin a new, wretched, bitter stage of life, trapped in the skin of a tainted woman no one wanted

Children did not exist as such. They were mouths to feed. They were left to themselves when the adults went to pick olives or harvest wheat and barley. They would sometimes fall into a ditch or split their heads open on the smooth stone steps of the village, for play was a necessity and children know no fear. When they were not sick or injured, they were dirty, soiled, their eyes watering from a bout of conjunctivitis.

In a state of such abandon, men and women found refuge in the marabout.[3] It was no accident that the country was covered in mausoleums surrounded by shade trees (umbrella pines, carob, or fig trees): Sidi Abdellah in Bhalil, Sidi Yahya in Gharb, Sidi Bouknadel near Salé, Sidi Bouzid near Casablanca, Moulay Idriss Zerhoune in the town of the same name, Moulay Brahim near Marrakech, and so on. Here one could find a momentary refuge in prayer but also a shoulder to cry on. In fact, the marabout himself, when he was still of this world, served as an intermediary between the weak and the powerful, the oppressed and the oppressor. Even the worst scoundrel feared his curse and desired his blessing (the famous *baraka*).

Such was the society that the French colonized in 1912. A hell for man and a bottomless pit for his dignity.

The fate of the Moroccan did not differ from that of the Algerian or the Tunisian. From Cairo to Marrakech, all North Africa was one great tract of unbroken wretchedness. Here and there, tiny pockets of civilization shone out weakly: Fez and a string of fortified Moroccan villages (such as Tétouan, Salé and Meknès), locked down at night to ward off looters, Constantine and Tlemcen in Algeria, Kairouan in Tunisia. Within these cities, a minority of scholars and bourgeois pursued, almost covertly, a gentle and refined way of life. They had come from Andalusia, which they had left in 1492 and, again and in greater numbers, in 1609 when the Catholics unceremoniously expelled all Muslims. They were also the representatives of old urban families that had studied the Arab religion and language from generation to generation since the tenth century. Internal diasporas exiled to the depths of the cities, taking refuge in their culture and imagination.

---

3. Trans. A Muslim holy man or hermit, especially in North Africa.

Every city had its ghetto, the *mellah*, a quarter where Jews were placed under house arrest, a confined area that authorities locked down whenever they saw fit. Unable to live elsewhere, Jews added floors to existing dwellings to make room for growing families and new couples. Outside the *mellah*, Jews were at risk, vulnerable to harassment from Muslims and attacks by bandits. The ghetto itself was not immune to popular insurrections, like that of Fez in April 1912, when more than a hundred Jews were massacred by the populace.

The Israelites of the Maghreb spoke Arabic and thought of themselves as Moroccan, Algerian, or Tunisian. Despite their contribution to the embryonic cultural life that survived in the cities, they were the punching bag of a population that vented its frustrations against its weakest members whenever authority faltered. All it took was absence or weakness on the part of the sultan (Morocco) or Turk (Algeria, Tunisia) for a pogrom to break out.

Several times a year, these pockets of urban, Andalusian, Arab, and Jewish civilization were witness to the arrival of caravans from the Sahara, columns of several hundred camels that had taken two months to make the journey between Timbuktu and Mogador, Fez, or Tripoli. They were loaded with human cargo: black children, black females, and black males who had been castrated along the way. The sorry spectacle of a black Africa sold as lots by Arab and Berber traffickers.

There was an Arab-Berber, Muslim, and Maghrebi slave trade that bled Sub-Saharan Africa dry just as much, if not more so, than the Atlantic slave trade. In the nineteenth century, North Africans took around 1.2 million black Africans, of whom a portion were "lost" along the way (a mortality rate as high as 20 percent) due to the terrible conditions of the desert crossing. The "taking" of captives involved buying them from African traders or horrific raids by Maghrebi horsemen and their black African accomplices.[4]

So many abominations committed in the name of the inveterate racism of which blacks were the victims. A racism that Islam could never attenuate, far from it. Certain Islamic scholars even justified slavery and the slave trade by the curse of Ham, an Old Testament tale reinterpreted to explain the eternal

---

4. Edouard Vogel, whom we encountered in the previous chapter, accompanied (as a prisoner) a raid along the Logone River, bordering Chad and Cameroon, in which "two thousand five hundred slaves and four thousand cattle" were captured. He adds that "some prisoners were mutilated: left leg cut at the knee, right arm at the elbow, the loss of blood causing death . . . Of the four thousand prisoners, not even five hundred arrived in Kouka" (in Bornu Province, present-day Nigeria).

condemnation of blacks to slavery. According to the Bible, Noah cursed his grandson Canaan, the son of Ham, in the following terms: "Cursed be Canaan; a servant of servants He shall be to his brethren." This episode, rewritten in the service of Arab and Berber supremacy, was enough to legitimate or even render desirable the plight of blacks in North Africa. There was no abolitionist movement in the Maghreb. Slavery was taken for granted and the cause of blacks was a lost one. "Slaves were considered a subcategory of livestock whose defining characteristic was the use of language and the practice of fasting."[5]

Until the beginning of the twentieth century, Morocco received between 1000 and 5000 black captives per year. In Fez, well-to-do families had their "provision" of domestic slaves of sub-Saharan origin. It was the same in the bourgeois milieus of Algiers, Tlemcen, and Tunis in the nineteenth century. Everywhere, the patriarchy, in addition to its women, had its black or sometimes even Caucasian slaves.[6]

In the imagination of the time, black women occupied the place of the concubine, a legitimate lover (authorized by Islam) who offered nothing but benefits: they could be acquired and disposed of at will without having to fear the ire of a father-in-law or the destruction of a family alliance. While in hiding, the rebel Bou Hmara, captured and killed in 1909 (he was fed to a caged lion), built himself a multiracial harem. It included about twenty black women. The "HR manager" of this harem was a black slave, a eunuch named Djilali Addoukali.[7]

A World with No Superego

Nothing about France's conquest of North Africa can be understood without taking into account the region's extreme instability in the nineteenth and early twentieth centuries.

---

5. This terse description comes from the historian and anthropologist Ernest Gellner and is quoted by Mohammed Ennaji in his study of nineteenth-century slavery in Morocco: *Slavery, the State, and Islam* (Cambridge University Press, 2013)—a work that is not afraid to lift the veil on the realities of servitude in precolonial Morocco.
6. The attraction to female slaves with fair skin (Georgian, Armenian, etc.) is a specialty of the Turkish world, of which the Regency of Algiers and that of Tunis fully took part.
7. Bou Hmara (1860–1909) almost overthrew the Moroccan monarchy by forming a tribal alliance that stretched from the East (Oujda) to the Rif. The story of his life, including his "sentimental" life, is engagingly presented by Omar Mounir in *Bou Hmara, l'homme à l'ânesse* (MARSAM, 2009).

Morocco was infested with highway bandits who demanded payment of the *mezrag*, a kind of toll if one wanted one's life to be spared. In certain periods, the sultan himself had to take long detours to travel safely. Some routes were a constant problem, such as that between Fez and Taza, 80 percent of which was in rebel hands between 1880 and 1885. The same was true of the road linking Fez and Marrakech and the crossing of the Rif, which was almost impossible between Tétouan, Chefchaouen, and Ouezzane.

Beyond banditry, insecurity was first and foremost a tribal phenomenon, rooted in the incessant struggles for territory and pastureland. It took the Zemmours, for instance, three centuries to advance 100 kilometers in their quest for fertile land and docile populations to extort. Departing from Tafilalet in the sixteenth century, they scaled the Middle Atlas from east to west, using terror and harassment to drive out the tribes that had preceded them. In the mid-eighteenth century, they began to settle in the plain below Oulmes before subsequently invading the forest of Maamora (north-east of Rabat). If the French had not interrupted them, the Zemmours would probably have realized their dream of reaching the port of Mahdia to pillage its warehouses and fleece its merchant caravans.

There is nothing exceptional about the history of the Zemmours. Such stories were repeated across Morocco, Algeria, and Tunisia. The tribal world was like a pot that never stopped boiling. It was constantly in a state of alert and ready to catch fire. Women and children were always on the lookout, ready to take down their tents and pack their meager belongings to follow the chief, the marabout, or the emir. Everyone travelled, livestock included. There was no question of not answering the call of the chief, his wars concerned everyone— that is, all his clients. And everyone, warriors and civilians, men and women, hoped the campaign would be over before harvest time. Once the harvest had been gathered, the fear of pillage mounted, for the location of the silos was known and represented a target of choice for tribes whose stores were empty.

Life was hell. It was no place for the kind and decent.

While the Frenchman had undergone what Norbert Elias called the civilizing process, the Maghrebi had for his part not been thus "polished." He retained the belligerent mentality typical of a permanent state of alert. Aggressiveness rather than temperance. Loyalty limited to tribe members instead of any notion of the common good. In truth, solidarity and faithfulness were above all understood as matters concerning the family, the village, or the clan. A given tribe might be torn apart by infighting and allow its sons to kill each other in interminable vendettas, but the discord ceased the moment an external enemy attacked any part of the whole. In this case, all came together and acted as one against the foreigner. Xenophobia was the oxygen of this world: one breathed it to live; without it, one perished. Once the foreigner had been defeated or driven out, discord reasserted itself.

Relations were thus fragile and conditional. Many tribes literally collapsed in times of famine, abandoning their children and old folk to the dogs and lions before reuniting (as if nothing had happened) upon the first rain. In a Darwinian world where the abyss was always just around the corner, such flexibility was an advantage for survival. It was accompanied by an equally flexible morality ready made to make the most of circumstances in a cynical and opportunistic fashion. The main thing was to survive.

Seizing the possessions of others was not a crime, but proof of superiority. Feeling no pity was a virtue, not a fault. Feelings were buried under layers of scar tissue and poorly healed fractures. With the exception of a handful of scholars and mystics, most inhabitants of North Africa were only familiar with the caricature of feeling offered by magical phenomena and religious fanaticism. In both cases, the senses were excited to the breaking point, the threshold of madness.

This *lack of feeling* authorized brutality. People harmed each other far more easily when the fate of their peers aroused no feelings of shame or sorrow.

The contrast with the mores of the French, who underwent a profound civilizing process over the course of the nineteenth century, was total. This did not mean that the French had become angels, but rather that they had internalized deep within themselves the notions of Good and Evil. This tremendous cumulative undertaking had begun under the Ancien Régime and was completed by the Republic. A collaborative venture between Church and school, its most eloquent result was to rein in men and women. Individuals came to respect the law spontaneously, their consent to the rules flowing from the source—that is, from themselves.

Contrary to what is believed, man was not crushed under the weight of external authority in North Africa. He had more room for maneuver than a Frenchman or German of that time. He was not the object of tight supervision by the state, educational institutions, the church, or the hospital. The *caïd,* the *pasha,* and the village chief left him alone so long as he did not disturb the basic units of family, clan, tribe, and so on. Homicides and assaults committed against strangers (wanderers, travelers, members of neighboring tribes) often went unpunished or were resolved by blood money paid in live-stock or silver. The more rich and powerful one was, the less need one had of blood money: one could kill with impunity, because the family of the victim would never dare claim reparations. Central authority was always too remote, far too remote to intervene in a timely fashion and restore justice. It delegated law enforcement to representatives who, in addition to often lacking initiative or any sense of urgency, were generally corrupt. For this reason, and though it may seem paradoxical, the individual was free. Or at least he considered himself to be free in the sense that he was not hindered, his only limit being his strength, the loyalty of his allies, and their readiness to fight.

Hence peoples' attachment to their way of life, which only grew stronger the farther one travelled from the cities, those refuges of merchants with soft bellies and polished fingernails. The higher one climbed, the deeper one plunged into the folds of the desert, the more freely one breathed. On the eve of colonization, the bulk of the Maghreb's population enjoyed great autonomy. They governed themselves.

The individual had no superego in the classical sense. He did not bend under the weight of internalized moral precepts. Morality was external to him like the feeling of hot or cold. Everything was relative.

Where was Islam in all this? It did not interfere with individual autonomy—that of men, I mean, (women were cloistered in the home). Islam did not do away with expressions of instinct, contenting itself instead with offering a loose-fitting superego, like a straitjacket that was so loose it did not limit movement.

It was enough to pray five times a day and observe the fasts and a few rituals. Nothing more. It did not seek to inhibit certain impulses, such as greed, jealousy, and malice. To do so would have gone against tribal mores, and the tribes needed these very qualities. In the Maghreb of that time, raising a man above such baseness would have handicapped him for the pitiless rhythm of tribal existence: a life of permanent scarcity (stubborn hunger, especially for meat), a world without nuance that only acknowledged two categories, the dominant and the dominated.

Islam had long ago been driven out of the civil and political domains so that the individual might "breathe freely," and also to allow him to use every weapon at his disposal to defend himself in a dangerous environment forged by arbitrary rule.

Unruly, but Incapable of Revolution

Such was North Africa before the arrival of the French: an incessant movement that was nothing more than treading water. Due to constant razzias and ambushes, tribal society lacked the resources needed to create, innovate, or federate. It was stuck in a state of backwardness, hostage to a sterile mentality halfway between courage and rapine.

From afar, the horsemen rushing full tilt down the slopes of the Atlas Mountains were beautiful, but up close they aroused pity, for they were prisoners of an eternal return: constantly in need and chasing loot, that is, the wealth produced by others. For lack of knowledge and technology, but also incentive, they created nothing. What was the point of working when warfare brought greater returns? Why bother improving yields if a neighbor could seize them by the power of the sword?

Accustomed to warfare, they had done little to develop their agriculture. They did what they needed to do for the purpose of planting, plowing, sowing, and harvesting on fixed dates, leaving the rest of the time free for other activities, such as attacking their neighbors.

In this way, the tribes' perpetual instability paradoxically lent to social stability, since turmoil prevents change. The Moroccan, Kabyle, and nomad from southern Tunisia of 1900 was the same as that of 1500. Can the same be said of the Parisian worker or the Breton peasant? Certainly not.

There was no desire for emancipation or for moral and intellectual improvement. What would have been the use if society had already achieved equilibrium and settled into its comfort zone?

Given this context, the calamitous state of people's minds and consciences on the eve of French colonization should come as no surprise. From Fez to Tunis, the overwhelming majority of the population was illiterate and superstitious. Millions of inhabitants were cooped up in a giant rest area and in a state of mental deadlock, preventing them from participating in the great march of humanity. No Arab country had experienced the industrial revolution or the transition to capitalism. Industry still boiled down to a dying world of crafts, and agriculture was an often futile struggle against the climate and locusts. With the exception of a few remarkable regions (such as the hinterland of Tétouan, a land of orchards and terraced crops), the rural world was plunged in darkness.

Girls did not *exist*; education thus did not concern them. Boys, especially city boys, attended Quranic school, where they memorized all sixty surahs by heart. A tremendous waste, as it deprived these tender minds of any opportunity to indulge the curiosity so typical of their age. The brightest were channeled into further studies in a zawiya (a religious confraternity). There, they would cram their heads full of Islamic jurisprudence, Quranic exegesis, and a few outdated principles of Avicenna's medicine until around age eighteen. The level of this education was very low; they were not exposed to the least notion of modern science and only read authors harking back to the golden age of Islam (Ibn Khaldoun, Averroes, Avicenna). Upon completing this cursus, these young men received the title of *talib* and went on to become imams in mosques or teachers in Quranic schools.

A tiny elite would go on to enter the prestigious universities of Kairouan (Tunisia), Al Qarawiyyin (Fez), and Al Azhar (Cairo). There, this cream of the crop would of course specialize in theology and Islamic law.

Skilled foreigners, meanwhile, were relied upon for specific technical needs (carpentry, architecture, civil and military engineering). It should not be imagined that this involved fact-finding missions to Paris or New York or flying in international consultants. In general, it was the corsairs of Salé and Algiers who supplied carpenters, engineers, chemists, surveyors, and doctors, all kidnapped from ships intercepted in the Mediterranean and the Atlantic. Several major architectural works constructed in the city of Meknes at the time of Moulay Ismail (1672–1727), for example, including its terrifying, labyrinthine subterranean prison, were the work of European captives. Given such practices, there was no need to call into question the educational system or the elites it produced: one could indefinitely prolong the status quo and plunge society into a formaldehyde bath while Europe adopted the printing press, went through the Enlightenment, and carried out the industrial revolution.

Dispersion and Isolation

In the precolonial Maghreb, people were isolated from the next village whose inhabitants they might see at most once a week when they were lucky enough to visit the souk. Roads were poor and dangerous, cutting them off from neighboring regions. They suffocated under the accumulated strata of ignorance and superstition. There were many taboos, from the "cursed" fountain that one should never approach to the places to be avoided at night for fear of *djinns*.

The Moroccan, Algerian, and Tunisian of the nineteenth century did not travel. He spent his life close to his place of birth or within the limited expanse of seasonal nomadic movements. What lay beyond was *terra incognita*. Of the mountain he knew only the side he lived on; of the river, only the banks on which he had planted poplars and apple trees; of the valley, only the portion he could cross without being robbed. He knew the part, but not the whole. He lived on the land but was not part of the country. The landscape was either familiar or did not exist.

Of the Middle Atlas he knew only the peaks nearest him: Mount Bou Iblan (3192m) in the region of Séfrou or Tazekka (1980m) in that of Taza. He did not connect them to a larger whole called the Middle Atlas, which itself belonged to a chain that rose in successive pleats from the southwest to northeast (Anti-Atlas, High Atlas, Middle Atlas, Algerian Atlas).

It was the European explorer who went to the trouble of naming these larger agglomerations, for he crossed them and thus needed to classify and describe them. Mountain ranges, plateaus, rivers, oases: knowledge of the land would be horded by foreigners, scientists and spies from Germany, Britain, Spain, and France.

It was a diminished reality. A shrunken world. To travel meant moving from one "pen" to another after crossing through lawless no man's lands, places where it was wise to always keep moving. Such were the lives of the men and women whom France would soon colonize in Algeria (1830), Tunisia (1881), and Morocco (1912).

This isolation fueled regionalist impulses: a localist spirit mixed with an idea of purity of blood and the *de facto* solidarity between suffering people who had always found themselves together without external aid, central authority being spectacularly absent in times of famine or disease.

Society did not exist in the sense one uses the term today, that is, as a self-aware social body in solidarity with its various parts. Before the advent of colonization, the area between the sea and the desert contained several social bodies, each elbowing the others to the rhythm of razzias, seasonal migrations, and civil wars.

The French played upon this dispersion to impose their rule while investing as little as possible in men and material. How many battles could be won by Arab and Berber troops raised only days earlier among tribes that would rather attack their neighbors than fight the invader?

Structural Fanaticism

In a fractured world where people were isolated by language, ethnicity, and custom, religion was nearly the only vector of unity. And not just any religion.

Not the religion of love or peace, but that of fanaticism, a mixture of irritation and anger. There was no unity in hope or common purpose. Rather, unity was found in common hatred for the enemies of the faith and support for the champions of the "true religion."

The only way to break the cycle of discord was to call for jihad. Otherwise, it was simply impossible to get individuals and groups to collaborate with one another. Collective thinking was only conceivable within the framework of *collective* "delirium," of passion inflamed: effort was the product of a surging fever that soon subsided, and one was well-advised to succeed on one first's attempt, for perseverance was not a realistic prospect.

Fanaticism was the grammar of political change. Without it, the status quo was guaranteed: extreme division between political players, alternation between raids and small ambushes, perpetuation of a central power that divided and conquered.

Every substantial leap forward was the result of some crackpot jihad. Between two bouts of fever, it was just one long succession of minor crises and catastrophes (famine, disease). History in North Africa was an endless to-and-fro.

In Morocco, not a single dynasty had taken power without declaring jihad and leading a holy war. Almoravids, Almohads, Marinids, Saadians, Alawites: Since the eleventh century, power passed from one hand to another by the sword and under the pretext of religious reform. A ruling dynasty would be accused of lack of piety, and it would be claimed that its replacement would restore the purity of the faith. A practice as old as time itself—and it worked!

If Abdelkader had not been a religious leader and had not resorted to jihad, he would never have united anyone but his own West Algerian tribe. The conquest of Algeria would have been much easier.

When the fever abated, the ties that bound were undone. Autonomy once again became the rule and the individual was free to do as he pleased, within his means and according to whatever his arbitrary will allowed.

Unity was a utopia endlessly pursued but rarely realized. In Tunisia, the Bey controlled the region of Tunis and the large cities, but the wild, inaccessible interior of the country only feigned submission and lived a life apart. In Algeria no power had managed to unite the country from east to west. In the sixteenth century, the Turks had never even bothered to try, contenting themselves with pitting one tribe against another to prevent the formation of any tribal federation capable of opposing them. Only Morocco pursued the dream of unity, achieving it several times only to see the whole edifice collapse like a house of cards after a few decades. The entire history of Morocco from the year 1000 can be summarized as a series of energetic attempts to unite the country around a central authority, inevitably followed by dilution under the impact of powerful centrifugal forces, whether tribal or maraboutic. The great sultans of Morocco were magnificent "Jacobins" who exhausted themselves in trying to convince local lords that it was in their interest to obey the leader in Fez, Marrakech, or even Meknes, depending on the seat of the imperial capital. When one speaks of the Sharifian Empire, it is as if in homage to the immense task accomplished by the great men who managed to unite so many "nations," each foreign to the others: Arabs, Andalusians, Sanhaja Berbers, Masmuda Berbers, Riffians, city people, country people, Fassis,[8] Slaouis,[9] and so on.

If Morocco was a death-trap at the beginning of the twentieth century, this was due to the retreat of the state (and thus of the sultan) in the face of tribal rebellion. Though the Moroccan monarchs of the nineteenth century spared no expense to reestablish their authority, none succeeded. The last monarch to control the country without tolerating pockets of resistance was Moulay Ismail, who died in 1727. It had been a long time, in other words: more than 150 years of more or less chronic disintegration separated the Morocco of Moulay Ismail from the "Swiss cheese" that the French took over in 1912.

There is thus every reason to conclude that the precolonial Maghreb was a preserve of hardened men ready to engage in jihad or rise in rebellion at the drop of a hat, men who knew how to fight but lacked the resources needed to advance towards modernity. It was a war machine incapable of securing well-being and prosperity. Before colonization, the Maghreb was a desert of human resources. The question that needs to be asked today is whether the French period or sixty years of independence have truly changed this situation.

---

8. Inhabitants of Fez. In the nineteenth-century sense, they were an Arab people mixing descendants of the original inhabitants of the city (founded in the ninth century) with refugees from various places. The latter included Tunisians, Jews from the Iberian Peninsula, and Andalusians (Muslims expelled in the seventeenth century).
9. Inhabitants of Salé. It should be recalled that Salé was an independent republic in the seventeenth century, its economy largely based on seaborne piracy.

AFRICA DID NOT EXIST

"The first rational explanation capable of accounting for Sub-Saharan Africa's role in the slave trade is to be found in the absence, in a world where ethnic barriers were powerful, of any sense of belonging to one 'African' community."

OLIVIER PÉTRÉ-GRENOUILLEAU

There was a major difference between West Africa and the Maghreb: West Africa had no sense of belonging to a common civilizational area. There was no Africa, but many Africas. "Negritude" was born in Paris in the 1940s. Before colonization, a man identified himself by his place of birth and ancestors, not by his race or connection to a continent. The black man was born of his contact with the white man. Africa was born of a head-on and undesired collision with colonization.

Poverty and Oppression

With all due respect to decolonial[1] activists, West Africa on the eve of colonization was not a marvelous world covered with verdant fields and speckled with sumptuous pyramids, manifestations of the labor and self-abnegation of civilizations that had attained the pinnacle of refinement. To the contrary, it was a world of hunter-gatherers, one in which man lived frugally by taking only what he needed from nature (and sometimes not enough to live comfortably). Africa was also a patriarchal land of subsistence farming. To put it

---

1. Trans. *"indigénistes"*

another way, and to leave no room for doubt: precolonial Africa was a land of very little added value.

Unable to produce wealth, Africa was incapable of furnishing even an inkling of dignity for its inhabitants. Eating one's fill, avoiding catastrophic weather, living in a place that sheltered one from animals and insects, not dying in childbirth, having good health: these simple things were all out of reach.

The human condition in West Africa before colonization was characterized by scarcity, oppression, and discrimination.

Scarcity affected everyone except a thin layer of political leaders and their allies, who were involved in either warfare (warrior aristocracies) or spiritual matters (marabouts in Muslim regions and sorcerers and shamans in animist regions).

As in other parts of the world, scarcity was unequally distributed by gender, age, and social status.

In Sub-Saharan Africa, hunger was first and foremost the experience of women.

Women were less well-nourished overall than men, both in hunter-gatherer cultures and in those that grew crops and raised livestock. They had limited access to protein, consuming significantly less meat than men. When they were allowed to consume it, they were generally given the less "noble" cuts (such as offal) or meat from animals deemed repulsive (such as sickly piglets). In certain hunter-gatherer societies, women were forbidden to eat the meat of the cassowary or wild pig, which was deemed of too high quality to be wasted on them. Among the Ntomba of Congo, the product of the hunt was stored in houses that only men could access and where they would gather to consume their meat.

Among the Serers of Senegal, men and women dined together, but men were served first and took the best cuts.

Among the Bassari of Eastern Senegal, pregnant or breastfeeding women were discouraged from eating meat by dietary taboos. They were led to believe that meat was harmful, transforming a dietary prohibition into something desirable and legitimate.[2]

2. Touraille, Priscille. *Hommes grands, femmes petites : une évolution coûteuse : Les régimes de genre comme force sélective de l'adaptation biologique.* (Éditions de la Maison des sciences de l'homme, 2008) Online : http://books.openedition.org/editionsmsh/9687.

Women were not emancipated in the sense that they could not do with their bodies as they pleased. Their sexuality was controlled in one way or another. In general, the village chief controlled pubescent girls by means of his veto over matrimonial unions. Of course, Congolese or Guinean women did not live cloistered lives like their Moroccan or Egyptian counterparts. They were not covered from head to toe, yet they still had no say over their lives and even less over that of the society in which they lived. Their voice was not taken into consideration when it came to making decisions that would affect the future of the community.

African women were dominated.

Domination structured human relationships. Everyone had his or her place, and more often than not that place was permanent and left no hope for improving one's lot. In precolonial Sub-Saharan Africa, there was no such thing as social mobility.

It was a world of castes, less complex than Hindu India but just as fixed and oppressive for those without the privilege of being born into the right station, that is, to a free mother within an aristocratic or distinguished family.

At this stage, it is difficult to remain at the level of generality, for, as I indicated above, Africa was diverse, dispersed, and plural.

Consider the case of Gajaaga, a region of Senegal populated by the Soninke.

In the nineteenth century, before the arrival of the French, there were three categories of inhabitants: *hooro* (lords), *nyaxamalani* (free individuals who lived under the protection of the lords and provided services to them in return), and *komo* (slaves). The *komo* were divided into two groups: those who were entitled to a family name and to preserve their lineage and those who were objects with no recognized line of descent.

These categories were relatively fixed. The *komo*, for example, could only marry other slaves or freed slaves.

Another fault line dividing society was that between the *debi n Renmu* (the natives) and the *riyanndo* (foreigners). No matter what they did, foreigners and their descendants would always be foreigners. They had no access to land and were not allowed any involvement in war and politics.

The elite, or *hooro*, consisted of a warrior aristocracy, a set of families tasked with defending the population against raids and the slave trade. The *hooro* also launched attacks on their contiguous neighbors, both for the purpose of taking loot and for that of imperial expansion, that is, seizing others' territory or obliging them to pay tribute in exchange for the right to continue living there in peace.

There were also marabouts, or Muslim religious leaders, among the *hooro*. In theory, at least, they were not meant to engage in war. Instead, they were at the service of warrior nobles, blessing their endeavors and supplying other high value-added services, such as dispensing justice and washing the bodies of the dead. It should be noted that the *hooro* warrior families of Gajaaga were generally animists, but this did not prevent them from living in harmony with the marabouts and vice versa.

This symbiosis went beyond the distribution of roles, taking the form of a genuine economic alliance. The marabouts and warrior nobles were united in the long-distance trade linking the Atlantic coast to the Niger River and Mauritania to Guinea. The marabouts operated trade networks and negotiated and organized caravans while the nobles provided essential merchandise: the slaves captured in raids on enemy territory. This division of duties allowed nobles to solely concentrate on politics and war while the marabouts deftly blended the roles of slave trader and religious guide.

The lower classes also participated in trade, but only to the extent that they sporadically sent shipments after their work in the fields was complete. These included cotton loincloths made by slaves belonging to the *nyaxamalani*.

The Scramble for Slaves

Slavery was ubiquitous in Gajaaga. Slaves were everywhere, at all levels of society. Slaves served in homes, worked in the fields, were in the service of lord and simple cobbler alike. They were part of the elementary unit of society known as the *ka*, an enlarged patriarchal family consisting of several polygamous households. Any given village generally contained several *ka*, each of which constituted a common space of production and consumption to the degree that its members worked the fields together five days a week, from 8 a.m. to 2 p.m. The rest of the time, they were free to work their own plots, as were their women, who had the right to cultivate the land without interference during these hours.

This arrangement was similar elsewhere in Senegal and the geographic area that would soon come to be known as French West Africa (AOF) and French Equatorial Africa (AEF).[3]

What explains this "appetite" for slavery?

---

3. *Afrique-Occidentale française* (AOF) and *Afrique-Équatoriale française* (AEF), respectively.

The French historian Olivier Pétré-Grenouilleau offers two keys for under-standing the phenomenon. The first served as an epigraph to this chapter, and I will cite it once again: "The first rational explanation capable of accounting for Sub-Saharan Africa's role in the slave trade is to be found in the absence, in a world where ethnic barriers were powerful, of any sense of belonging to one 'African' community."

In other words, the individual belonging to a different ethnicity on the other side of the river was a foreigner and represented an inferior form of humanity. As such, he was easily reified and reduced to the status of merchandise.

The second explanation concerns the mode of governance in Sub-Saharan Africa, a system far removed from what could be witnessed in Europe or the Arab world at this time. Let us turn once again to Pétré-Grenouilleau: "In contrast to the states of modern Europe (especially France), which had em-barked upon a truly enormous and costly campaign of administrative, police, military, and clerical control, the elites had little appetite for exploiting their own subjects and thus hit upon a system of domination that required little in terms of internal coercion. To maintain their power, the elites of Sub-Saharan Africa relied upon two activities that were no doubt less differenti-ated than in the Europe of that time: war and long-distance trade. Neighbors were thus fair game, especially when they seemed weaker because possessing less sophisticated social, political, and military structures."

The elites, in other words, exerted relatively little pressure on society. Their domination was not accompanied by bullying impositions, whether in the form of high taxes, forced labor, or extortion.[4] The masters preferred to spare those they "administered," instead lashing out at foreigners, that is, the mem-bers of other ethnicities. This predation took two forms: one peaceful (trade), the other belligerent (capturing slaves).

This book makes no claim to being a history of slavery in Africa. It is enough to underscore that Africa was bled dry by three distinct slave trades, each of which was simultaneously operating from the sixteenth century on-wards and whose driving force was to be found in African societies them-selves. These were the Atlantic slave trade (roughly 10 million victims between 1500 and 1900), the Muslim slave trade in North Africa, Turkey, and the

---

4. This is a fundamental difference with the Maghreb and especially the Morocco of the same period, where financial pressure could be absurd or even confiscatory. Hence the temptation of dissidence (*essiba*) to avoid paying taxes.

Persian Gulf (roughly 17 million victims between 700 and 1900), and finally the internal slave trade (14 million people reduced to servitude before 1850).

Freedom

When he was not a slave, the African was a free man, with fewer constraints placed on him than the European. As we saw above, he was not confronted with a determined bureaucratic state doing its best to control him, interfering in his health and hygiene, seizing his children and forcing them to attend school, and so on.

Indeed, quite a few Africans did not live under the authority of a state, kingdom, or empire at all. They simply belonged to a lineal society that occupied a given territory, with a similarly lineal society or state as its neighbor. There was relatively little pressure exerted on the individual, in other words: no police, no public records, no judiciary, and so on.

And when he had converted to Islam, the African was not at the mercy of *ulemas*, *imams*, and *cadis* telling him what to think, whom to sleep with, or what to eat. The African Islam of the nineteenth century (despite some slides into extremism that we will detail later) was much easier to live with than its North African counterpart, starting with the African man's polite but firm refusal to shut away his wife. In the Islamized villages of the Sahel, Africa is still Africa: vibrant colors, smiling men, women everywhere . . . The exact opposite of large Arab cities like Cairo and Fez, where the atmosphere is heavy with (especially sexual) frustration and mutual surveillance.

Senegal invented a *smiling Islam*, a successful attempt to combine the Islamic religion with the joy and bloom of life here on earth. Very active in the nineteenth century, the Tijani brotherhood offered an *everyday Islam* far removed from theological disputes and rooted in the African soul: an Islam that exuded goodwill, a religion that laid down its sword for a moment to take man in its arms and show him a path (*tarika*) towards God.

Frozen in Time

Precolonial Africa was "configured" to maintain the status quo. This was for a variety of reasons, including:

- The exclusion of the lower classes from the market economy, long-distance trade being the preserve of elites.

- Those same dominant classes never thought of accumulating wealth but rather wished to flaunt its distribution or destruction in festivities and religious rituals. It is no coincidence that much of the continent lacked magnificent palaces and royal residences. What mattered lay elsewhere: governance mobilized symbols and tools very different from those employed in Europe and the Maghreb. A corollary of this cultural trait was a low propensity to accumulate capital, a prerequisite for any and all economic transformation.
- The elites held a tight grip over the circulation and production of knowledge, ensuring that innovation be limited to the realms of magic, religious ritual, and traditional medicine. All other forms of innovation were censored.
- Sub-Saharan Africa was cut off from the rest of the continent by desert (the Sahara) and inhospitable coastline, especially in the western areas of the continent.
- Finally, and even more importantly, African societies were in equilibrium. They did not consider themselves to be in a state of crisis or decline.[5] People were doubtless convinced they were living in the best of all possible worlds or at least the only possible one. They did not hope for change because they felt no need for it. Only the European considered himself entitled to think for others and decide on their behalf that they must change their way of life or civilization.

An Africa Sick with Diversity

Nowhere else has diversity been a better companion to fragmentation.

Like so many other Europeans, the French found themselves confronted with ethnicities that hated each other, castes that oppressed each other, and a multitude of disputes ready to burst into flames.

If Africa was colonized, it was not only due to its technological backwardness, but also its political and social fragmentation. At no time did the French ever have to face a united front that transcended ethnicity.

This lack of solidarity resulted from the extreme diversity characteristic of African societies. There was no coherent social body, just a scattered archipelago,

---

5. This was yet another significant difference with the Maghreb, where there was keen nostalgia, at least in some circles, for the glorious era when the Mediterranean was an Arab sea and Andalusia a Muslim land.

with men clustering around a multitude of tribes and clans. One only had to walk a few kilometers to find oneself in a different universe, language, ethnicity, and civilization. The Ivory Coast alone counted more than 700 distinct languages, each of them the possession of a group that did not mix with its neighbors, even those closest to them.

In truth, France arrived in a conquered land. All that was needed was to set in motion the energies and passions that had made of it a myriad of mutually ignorant or hostile realities. Africa was a victim of its extreme diversity.

It is Africa's fault lines that explain why it was so easy for a handful of white men to dominate a sea of blacks. These fault lines included religious conflict between Muslims and animists. The Portuguese, in particular, skillfully played upon this to compensate for their lack of men and ammunition. To conquer Guinea-Bissau, they pit the Fula against the Malinkes, Muslims against vehement animists. Who was to blame? The Machiavellian Lusitanians or the Fula, so steeped in religious fanaticism that they willingly delivered the black man into the hands of the white invader? The fault was shared.

The Portuguese had no trouble getting Muslims, who had always been a demographic minority in Guinea-Bissau, to massacre their animist neighbors over an extended period. During the 1936 rebellion of the Bijagos, an archipelago off the coast of the colony's capital, Bissau, the Portuguese governor, lacking any regular troops of his own, ordered the Muslim Fula to massacre the animist rebels. Several thousand died as a result.

Under such conditions, it is easy to explain the enormous imbalance between Europeans and natives throughout the colonial period. The Belgian Congo counted no more than 2000 Europeans in 1900 and barely 30,000 in 1945.[6] What need for more white men if black men were willing to oppress their brothers on behalf of the invader?

In 1950, 2500 Portuguese with a few rusty rifles lived in peace alongside 535,000 natives in Guinea-Bissau![7]

Certain African societies had been on the way to transcending their divisions. In nineteenth-century Madagascar, the Merina had brought together all the peoples of the island under its rule. A structured monarchy with princes,

---

6. Piette Valérie. "La Belgique au Congo ou la volonté d'imposer sa ville ? L'exemple de Léopoldville," *Revue belge de philologie et d'histoire*, 2011.
7. Unobtrusive and powerless, the Portuguese excelled in the art of delegating the repression of natives to other natives. I highly recommend the work of historian René Pelissier on this subject (see bibliography).

a court, a nobility, governors, and a central administration had taken it upon itself to unify the territory and standardize its habits and customs.

The violent incursion of the French beginning in 1881 shattered this process, which perhaps needed just another forty or fifty years (and a bit of luck) to succeed.

INDOCHINA IN THE GRIPS OF GREAT REPLACEMENT

"Pity our country. The son of the Annamite commands the Cham like buffalo."

EIGHTEENTH-CENTURY INDOCHINESE POEM[1]

The French presence in Indochina dates from 1857. It was an entirely different world from that of Africa and the Arab Maghreb. It first and foremost stood apart from these two civilizations for the hold it exerted over the individual. Indochinese man toed the line, placing himself in the service of the community and a common good greater than himself. One found none of the unruliness and radical autonomy of the Tuareg and pastoral Fula in Vietnam, Cambodia, and Laos. In these countries, the human being was enmeshed in a web of constraints, at once familial, social, cultural, spiritual, and political.

Of the three civilizations that France colonized, Indochina was clearly the best "equipped," at least on paper, to reach modernity. It had already won the battle of domesticating the individual but lacked access to technology, a prerequisite for industrialization and thus power.

---

1. With touching charm, Paul Boudet evokes the sad fate of the Chams, swept aside by the Annamites and sidelined by history despite the sophistication of their civilization. Paul Boudet (1888–1948) was a graduate of the École Nationale de Chartes. In 1917 he was assigned Indochina, where he would establish the archival service from scratch and later found the National Library of Vietnam.

A Fluid Notion

Indochina: the name nicely captures the thing. A meeting point of two great civilizations: Hindu India and Confucian China. The former exerted its influence through present-day Thailand (Siam) and Cambodia. The latter left its mark on Tonkin, Annam, and Cochinchina, three territories occupied by the Viet (or Annamites, as they were called at the time) and extending like a curved spinal column from north to south.

While the terminology is useful, it is also misleading, for it tells us nothing about the submerged portion of the iceberg. It does not recount the history of the peoples, men and women, the princes and kings who were the respective vectors of these civilizations. When underscoring India's influence over Indochina, one must immediately note that this was only possible due to the dynamism of the Thais and Khmers. When it is said that China radiated to the south, one must immediately note that this was thanks to the expansionism of the Annamite people, who were a conduit for its culture and vehicle for its authority.

In the eighteenth century and first half of the nineteenth, Cambodia and Laos were losing steam. The Khmers, the region's largest population group, were unable to withstand the pressure simultaneously exerted by the Thais and Annamites. They lost the Mekong Delta, including Saigon and the neighboring provinces, to the Annamites and their Chinese allies.

To the east, the winds also favored the Annamites. They successively occupied two very different territories.

(A) The flat lands (25 percent of the territory): between 1700 and 1750, the plains and river deltas were gradually conquered and colonized by the Annamites. This is called the March to the South or *Nam Tiên*. Among its principal victims were the peoples encountered along the way: the genuine natives, including the Chams in the center and the Khmers to the south, in the area of the Mekong Delta. The Chams, an ancient and once splendid people, would end up losing everything and be dispersed to Cambodia and neighboring countries (Malaysia and Thailand, but also China).

(B) The mountains and highlands (75 percent of the territory): these ended up falling into the hands of the Annamites once their colonization of the lowlands was complete. This rugged terrain was originally occupied by fifty-one ethnicities of varying stages of development and which ethnologists typically divide into three main linguistic groups: the Tay-Thaï, the Hmong-Dao, and the Môn Khmer. The Annamites, an imperialistic people, called them "mountain-dwellers" or, pejoratively, "Mois" (i.e., "savages"). These first peoples were peasants perfectly adapted to the dense tropical forest. They knew how to exploit it sparingly and with respect. They were relatively isolated from the "encounter" between India and China that played out below them. After the Annamite advance, the mountain-dwellers scattered through the forest, making themselves more "discreet" in the hope that they would be left in peace. Mission accomplished, for, given their lifestyle, the Annamites were principally interested in areas suited for rice farming, most of which were located near the coast, far removed from the mountain peoples.

Colonizing the Colonizer

On the eve of France's entry upon the scene, Indochina was thus experiencing its own phenomenon of colonization. Power at that time was held by the Nguyen dynasty, which had led the Annamite people since the early nineteenth century. It had patiently dispatched deserters, the destitute, and official colonists to seize lands still in the hands of the Chams and Khmers—a Great Replacement in ethnic and cultural terms. The newcomers assimilated the long-established population. What remained was crushed under the weight of the victor's intolerance towards the mores of the conquered, leaving only a private, residual identity to be furtively imparted to children.

France's arrival disrupted a historic movement of territorial reunification and *vietnamification* (in the sense of a standardization of habits and customs around the Viêt or Annamite model).

On top of the Annamites came the Chinese, who excelled in trade. They put their contacts in their nearby homeland and the Chinese diasporas of Southeast Asia to good use. An implicit pact joined them to the Annamites: they helped them supplant the Chams and Khmers and were in turn given the right to settle in the thus "liberated" regions.

Upon seizing Saigon in 1859, the French discovered a large Chinese community established in the village of Cholon.

The Straitjacket

The individual man was merely a cog in this great machine, nothing more than a grain of sand to a community that demanded his loyalty and collaboration. He was hemmed in on all sides by a network of obligations towards his village (to which he owed mandatory labor) and the state (which could call him up for military service, a terrible ordeal in more ways than one).

And if he refused to respect the rules, he was excluded, which meant banishment. He became a wandering isolate, without identity or guardian. A lost soul.

Every year, thousands of outlaws (in the sense of non-conformists) took to the forest trails and disappeared into the "virgin" lands still in the hands of the Khmers, Chams, or other mountain peoples. It was a battle for survival: to not perish from hunger and despair, one had to despoil those weaker than oneself.

Those who played the game, by contrast, had a miniscule but still real chance of finding a place in the sun. To do so, they had to obey, conform, and kowtow. Among them were contenders for the highly selective mandarin exam, a door-opener for anyone hoping to join the bureaucracy that governed the country. Selection was based on merit, not nepotism or corruption. Once again, to have a chance of succeeding, one needed only work hard and obey the rules. The individual was brought to heel; at every moment and every street corner, he was taught discipline. A far cry from the "license" that prevailed in the Maghreb and Africa as soon as the Sultan or chief turned his back.

Yet all this discipline and esprit de corps was in the service of rice cultivation. There was no prospect of industrialization. No revolution in the arts and sciences was waiting in the wings. Vietnam was not Prussia. In a certain sense, it was a fragment of Chinese civilization clinging to the rice fields and forests of the peninsula. It would have to wait for China to awaken and carry out its modern revolution (well after the end of the Cold War) to finally enter the industrial era.

The Diversity of the Colonies

The Maghreb, Africa, and Indochina: three separate worlds with very little in common. In no way were they a paradise for man, his dignity, or his well-being. In no way were they in a position to generate the technological progress that Europe and North America experienced at the end of the nineteenth century.[2]

---

2. The appraisals expressed in this chapter may seem harsh. They undoubtedly reflect a value judgment at one point or another. As I am neither an historian nor a journalist, I have no need to feign neutrality.

These two conclusions are not a reason for France to have encroached upon these civilizations and subjected them to the shock of colonization.

The point is simply that one should not idealize the pre-colonial era. It was no Garden of Eden. Nowhere did France disrupt a perfect and harmonious order.

Colonization or no colonization, the Maghreb, Africa, and Indochina were sooner or later going to experience immense transformations leading to a capitalist economy and industrialization. These transformations were immense shocks capable of shaking society to its core, firedamp explosions that opened the way for development, even if it meant some would be maimed and others buried under the rubble. Sacrifices were inevitable; they were the price for entering modernity. No country has ever industrialized without transferring, in one way or another, a portion of its peasant population to the cities, where they are exploited by unscrupulous employers. No nation has ever built a modern state without overcoming feudal, tribal, and regional resistance, sometimes at the price of blood and tears. To understand what modernization entails, one need only recall the human cost of the French Revolution.

Africa, Indochina, and the Arab world had an unavoidable date with modernity. To deny this is as naive as it is dishonest.

PART II:

THE ORIGINS OF A WILD IDEA
(1830–1905)

THE ORIGINS OF FRENCH COLONIZATION: SLOW GESTATION AND RAPID DELIVERY

> *"There are neither silver bars to gather, nor any great bounty to reap; I see hardly anything to take but blows."*
>
> CAPTAIN PIERRE CUPET[1]

Everything or almost everything is known about the course of French colonization, its key dates and major events, but very little about its true motivations. While colonization is a meticulously mapped river, its sources are located far upstream, difficult to reach and cloaked in a shroud of fog.

The Point of Departure: A Quid Pro Quo

Official history teaches us that French colonization was intended as a civilizing mission. Once the indigenous people had been subdued and the colonies pacified, however, the French did not put this civilizing mission into practice. Apart from banning slavery and putting an end to civil wars, the French turned their backs on the colonized: no education, little or no medical care, no transfers of technology. Things only began to change in the aftermath of the Second World War, or just ten to fifteen years before decolonization.

This lack of interest in the civilizing mission is also to be seen in the fact that it was never defined. A motivation that might be confused with a sketch or mirage is an odd one indeed! What does it mean to "civilize"? To

---

1. Captain Cupet (1859–1907) took part in the exploration of the Indochinese Highlands at the end of the nineteenth century.

evangelize, Gallicize, bring the natives into modernity, or even make them "better men" in ethical or moral terms? The civilizing mission was never precisely formulated, that is, never set down on paper as part of a detailed, concrete plan of action, with budgets, deadlines, methods of evaluation, or a ministry to oversee it.

Official history also asks us to believe that France launched its attack on Africa and Asia in order to obtain trade opportunities and raw materials. Here too, there is reason for surprise, for French capitalism cold-shouldered the colonies from start to finish, preferring to focus on the metropole, Europe, Russia, and the New World. Elites and capital only entered the colonies tentatively and in homeopathic doses. In 1900, the colonies represented barely 5.3 percent of all French foreign investment.[2] In fact, colonial administrators and political circles in Paris always lamented the apathy of entrepreneurs and financiers as regarded the colonies. Where, then, is that desire, that thirst for profit, that greed about which Marxists and postcolonialists talk so much? But it was not just the elites who, with a few notable exceptions, so loftily ignored the colonies; the people also failed to get on board. With the exception of Algeria, Frenchmen were extremely scare in all of the colonies. Everywhere, the observation is the same: a human desert where Europeans are an ultra-minority. If the French really wanted to plunder the empire, would they not have settled there en masse? To plunder a territory, one must first go there. Yet the French had no need to emigrate, for they had everything they wanted at home, the metropole being underpopulated and in the midst of economic transformation. The industrial revolution, major infrastructure works (rail networks, in particular), and the growth of cities were all reasons to stay home.

Finally, the doxa holds that the third and final motivation for colonization was the pursuit of prestige. And why not? In the late nineteenth century, French, British, Germans, and Belgians were indeed in a race against one another to acquire colonies, a race in which the number of kilometers annexed was thought to reflect the "grandeur" and influence of a nation. But at the same time, France was still bleeding from the amputation of Alsace and Lorraine. What kind of international prestige could be expected after such an injury to its vanity? The question is worth raising, for it is difficult to lay claim to gran-

---

2. At the time, Russia represented 26 percent of the total, while Spain and Portugal represented 16 percent! See Giradet, Raoul. *L'idée coloniale en France: de 1871 à 1962*. Paris, La Table Ronde, 1972.

deur when one was just beaten at home and robbed of two historic provinces. Imagine a Miss World who is missing an eye or a cheek. Paul Déroulède, a nationalist parliamentarian and anti-German revanchist, responded thus: "I have lost two sisters, and you offer me twenty servants."[3]

There are thus many gray areas in the official account, leaving the observer who merely wishes to know why France committed to colonization unsatisfied. The usual answers to this question are either questionable (the civilizing mission, the economy) or brittle and flabby (prestige).

It is impossible to isolate a single factor or even a collection of factors that might offer a satisfactory explanation for French colonization. Faced with such an evasive, fluid, and extremely complex phenomenon, one might be excused for feeling dizzy. Things intersect, link together, and intertwine, ruling out any simple pictures or Manichaeism. The forces that drove colonization were a blend of interests, passions, individual and collective wills, and even in a certain sense the conspiracies of small groups capable of overcoming disagreement to collaborate with one another. We have already seen how seasoned monarchists and diehard republicans jointly campaigned to raise the tricolor over Algeria and Morocco. Luck played a role, too, for historical circumstances precipitated decisions and altered resolutions. It can thus reasonably be said that the cause of French colonization was a cumulative process, which step by step gave birth to the colonial empire.

This process goes far back, all the way to the bowels of the Ancien Régime, and in the nineteenth century found fertile soil for its incredible expansion. Drawing upon the best circumstances and accidents of that century, it burst through the ceiling and expanded across the world, like a plant gone mad after plunging its roots into soil stuffed with nutrients.

In historical hindsight, however, every stage of the process is explained by the preceding one and clears the way for the next. This confers a logical and spontaneous appearance upon what was a largely irrational phenomenon. This is because we tend to examine the process from its sharp end, that which is closest to us: the empire as it had or would soon come to be in the early twentieth century. And indeed, from this perspective, all seems to flow from the source: men financed and equipped by a powerful country were able to conquer and subjugate weak and divided countries. But if we take a transversal view and consider the expanse of time that began before 1830 and continued through

3. This is how Déroulède addressed Jules Ferry regarding the colonial question.

the twentieth century, it becomes apparent that what we are dealing with is in fact a shaft: a shaft made up of motives that, taken individually, explain nothing, but that, fused together as a whole, form an arrow capable of piercing even the thickest armor.

The process that gave rise to French colonization was marked by three key stages:

- From 1830 to 1870: The conquests made in this period were adventures, "great exploits" of the sort one may permit oneself when one is powerful. Colonization proceeded by fits and starts, opportunistically and without any overall vision.
- From 1870 to 1885: France was traumatized by the loss of Alsace and Lorraine. The republican left proposed colonization as a therapeutic policy to console the nation and repair its wounded pride. In five years, from 1880 to 1885, several countries were conquered, creating the sense of a *fait accompli* within the political class.
- From 1885 to 1905: Colonial soldiers and the colonial lobby created a favorable climate for expanding the empire and marshalling ever greater resources in its service. War weary, the opponents of the colonial idea ultimately resigned themselves to it or allowed themselves to be won over.

1830–1870: A Game, an Accessory of Little Importance

The colonies conquered between 1830 and 1870 were part of a movement of limited size and modest stakes. At the time, colonization was a policy of secondary importance, an *accessory* not meant to weigh too heavily on the nation's future or its finances.

In 1830, France set foot in Algeria and began a long and arduous conquest that officially concluded eighteen years later.[4] In 1844, it seized Tahiti, and, in 1853, New Caledonia. In 1862, France raised its flag over Saigon and Cochinchina, that is, the southern part of present-day Vietnam, where the Mekong River meets the sea. The following year, Cambodia willingly placed itself under the protection of France. On the other side of the world, France

---

4. We shall consider the conquest of Algeria below. As we will see then, it only truly ended in 1905, with the pacification of the Sahara. Emir Abdelkader's resistance came to a close in 1848.

expanded its holdings in Senegal, a colony inherited from the Ancien Régime and which by the 1860s encompassed the entire Atlantic coast, extending upstream along the Senegal River.

There was no roadmap or overarching idea guiding this movement. Rather, it was all trial and error, making a go of it, trying one's luck, without any destination in mind or idea of the risks that might be involved.

These conquests more closely resembled accidents than they did the outcome of any carefully conceived plan. They were the prerogative of a powerful country possessing the means needed to intervene far from its centers of power. Several factors spurred France to act—three, in particular. The first had to do with the prevailing mindset of the time, which made it acceptable and even desirable to plunder and dominate foreign peoples. Colonization was seen as a matter of course, just one reflex among others at the level of a country or people. The second factor concerns the general political framework in which French interests evolved between 1830 and 1870, a context marked by the disaggregation of the country's economic and military power from the room for maneuver available to it on the world stage. The third factor, finally, reflects the activism of pressure groups which, though small in size, had some influence and used it to cajole the political authorities.

The Nineteenth Century Was a Golden Age for the White Man, and Planet Earth Was His Garden

It is impossible to understand colonial expansion without taking into consideration the incredible disparities in development that separated the West from the rest of the world. Throughout the nineteenth century, Western Europe[5] and the United States were the stage for the most exhilarating and intense expressions of human genius. Everything was changing, transforming, seeming to get better and better: industry, medicine, science, arts, and culture. Everything suggested that the white man had found the recipe granting power and sophistication of a type never before seen in the history of humanity.

Hence the certainty, shared by all, as to the absolute and unquestionable superiority of European man over all others. Compared to him, there were only backward peoples, some of which were said to be "exhausted" (the

---

5. Ireland's level of development was of course not that of England or Prussia in the nineteenth century. The same held for the countries of the Iberian Peninsula.

Chinese, Indians, and even the Ottomans), others nothing more than "primitive" (all of Africa and a large portion of Asia).

The era was rich in outsized figures capable of feats worthy of the demigods of antiquity. Explorers, adventurers, geographers, entrepreneurs, and military men: every profession shone with exceptional human talent. One is here dealing with men who were "larger than life," men like Stanley and Livingstone, Victor Hugo and Flaubert, Eiffel and de Lesseps, Laennec and Claude Bernard, among other exceptional individuals. From the United States, a new country, to Europe, one encountered the same phenomenon: the "stuff" of humanity was exceptional. Take a young man like Savorgnan de Brazza (1852–1905), a naturalized French citizen of Italian origin, who alone conquered a large part of the Congo River Basin using nothing but seduction and negotiation. What courage it must have taken to plunge headlong, alone or nearly so, into such an unknown and dangerous environment! What skill must have been needed to convince kings and princes to become vassals of a distant power they had never seen! Such was the European man of the nineteenth century. He shared nothing with the deconstructed man with whom we have the misfortune of rubbing shoulders today. He was equipped to conquer the world and had all the qualities needed to do so: trust in himself and his lucky star, pride in representing the world's most advanced *race*,[6] courage, brutality, and a lack of scruples.

Courage came in various forms. There was that of the missionaries who, unarmed and unaccompanied, threw themselves headlong into China to convert the heathens. There was that of the soldiers who, several thousand kilometers from their headquarters, gave battle with spirit and determination. In them, there lived on something of the aristocratic spirit of past centuries, when the soldier fought for honor, when his was a calling, not a profession.

In the Mexican village of Camerón in 1863, sixty-three French legionaries squared off against 600 Mexican cavalry and 1400 infantry. They were of course beaten, but the eight survivors only agreed to surrender on condition that they be allowed to keep their weapons, and that their wounded receive care.

From outstanding courage to villainous brutality there is but one step. And, in this, his *golden century*, European man did not hesitate to take it, be-

---

6. "Race" is to be read here in keeping with the historical context as meaning people, civilization, and ethnocultural identity. One thus spoke of the French race, the German race, the Spanish race, and so on.

coming as savage as the savages he so despised. When the Egyptian Soleyman el Halaby assassinated General Kleber in Cairo on June 14th, 1800, the French responded by burning his right hand down to the bone. They then impaled him for four hours straight. A terrible, shameful torture, the hallmark of peoples who are fluent in the despicable language of domination, of which violence is the grammar. Savagery was not exclusive to the French. Americans spent a good part of the nineteenth century exterminating the Native Americans. Having brought this genocide to completion, they invaded the Philippines in 1898, where they practiced large-scale collective punishment. Such was the case in Samar in 1902. After the civilian population of that Philippine island failed to alert the Americans of an imminent rebel attack, 15,000 innocents were slaughtered in retaliation.

Cruelty was accompanied by deception, cynicism, and unscrupulousness. Peoples were sold and resold without consultation. Like the Poles, condemned to death *in absentia* at the Congress of Vienna (1815), which authorized Russia and Austro-Hungary to carve up their country. No one found fault with this, for such was the era. Raison d'État knew nothing of the right of peoples to self-determination, and power scorned feeling. Violence was lawful, it constituted an argument in its own right and was accepted as such. In the nineteenth century, European man did not hold back.

And why should he have done so, given that he was convinced of his manifest destiny? He had been chosen to be at the vanguard of humanity. With the privilege entrusted him by Providence came the "duty" to spread civilization everywhere that man found himself in the grips of barbarism.

Only a thin membrane separates the duty to act from the need to act and, as exhausted civilizations collapse upon themselves, it bursts. Through the cracks, one glimpses subjugated peoples awaiting deliverance. Over the course of the nineteenth century, contact was reestablished with Eastern Christians, the victims of abuse and discrimination in the Ottoman Empire (the sick man of that era). It was also "discovered" that slavery was practiced in Africa by Africans themselves and that millions of black men groaned under the blows and scorn of other black men. They had to be saved, as quickly as possible.

There was thus no shortage of pretexts for interfering in the affairs of others. To colonize was in no way illicit or reprehensible; indeed, it was a commendable undertaking.

In this context, the Russians were a case apart, their sensibilities being different. They dreamed of reaching the warm seas (Crimea, the Black Sea, and the Mediterranean) and dominating the frozen steppes from which the invaders who had both terrorized and fertilized them came (Central Asia, Mongolia, Siberia). Europeans, for their part, all looked towards mysterious Asia and shadowy Africa. These unknown horizons stimulated them and aroused their appetites, both intellectually and materially. Geographers and explorers hungered for new discoveries, and certain economic and political circles hungered after resources. Both parties shared the belief that the Earth was finite, that its limits would soon be reached, and that little time remained to profit from it.[7]

Each country was a case apart, cultivating its own particular dispositions and inhibitions. The British rightly feared overpopulation. Between 1821 (20 million) and 1901, their population had doubled (to 41 million).[8] In the same period, the French with difficulty rose from 31 million to 40 million.[9] For the British, colonization was an urgent matter if it was to export its surplus population, beginning with the dangerous classes that were forming around its industrial centers.

The Danes, Norwegians, and Swedes, great maritime nations with a proven colonial past, were too busy with their internal political reconstruction to participate in the rush for colonies. Norway, for example, dedicated the nineteenth century to freeing itself from the Danish yoke, more than enough to forget about any adventures under the tropical sun.

The Dutch, for their part, were preoccupied with Indonesia, which throughout the nineteenth century was a constant source of trouble. They had no resources to free up for the purpose of exploring elsewhere.

France, a Great Power Hobbled

The French were not like other Europeans. In the eyes of their peers, they had committed an unpardonable crime: the revolution of 1789. From London to

---

7. At this stage, enthusiasm and an impatient desire to act were exclusive to the elites or rather to a small portion thereof. Public opinion did not have the leisure to ponder these questions or consider the immense gap separating the power of Europe from the weakness of the rest of the world.

8. Meuriot, Paul. "La Population de l'Angleterre en 1901," *Journal de la société statistique de Paris*, volume 44, 1903 (online) : http://www.numdam.org/article /JSFS_1903_44_99_0.pdf.

9. Louis Henry, Yves Blayo. "*La population de la France de 1740 à 1860*". Population, year 30, n° 1, 1975 (online) : https://www.persee.fr/doc/Pop_0032-4663_1975_hos _30_1_15696#pop_0032-4663_1975_hos_30_1_T1_0071_0000

Moscow, Europe's monarchies had cut them off, as it were, from the European family. They pardoned her neither the death of Louis XVI nor the destruction of the traditional order. And they were even less inclined to forget the Napoleonic era, a colonial thrust as sudden as it was brutal, and which nearly devoured the entire continent. Europe had many things to reproach France. It thus monitored and punished her, putting her in a straitjacket too tight for her body.

In 1815, the powers that had defeated Napoleon gathered at the Congress of Vienna to settle their scores with France. The punishment lasted a century, only truly lifting in 1914. In the meantime, France spent many years wandering the desert, deprived of cherished territories (Savoy and the County of Nice, in particular), surrounded by buffer states tailor-made to contain it (Belgium, for example), and deprived of allies of any importance.

All efforts to break free of these shackles were doomed to failure or at most partial success: the Crimean War of 1853–56 (a partial success, with France not receiving the credit it believed was its due), the Italian Campaign of 1859 (another partial success, with Napoleon III managing to anger his allies, the Italians), and the Mexican War of 1861–67 (an absolute, irrevocable catastrophe).

It would not be until the final years of the nineteenth century that the winds once again began to favor France, bringing new alliances between France and Russia (1892) and France and Great Britain (1904).

For this frustrated power, constantly hindered by its peers, colonization offered an outlet. Indeed, colonization was not a novelty for France; the country had a longstanding colonial tradition. The Ancien Régime had built a colonial empire that contributed to its greatness and brought it some degree of wealth. The highly profitable "agricultural" islands of the Antilles and the vast expanses of Canada and the Mississippi were still a good—indeed, excellent— memory for France. So why refrain from imitating the great things accomplished by one's predecessors?

It was in this microclimate that the nation's contemporary colonial history got off the ground, with France's intervention in Algeria in July 1830. The decision to intervene in this country was taken in the context we have just outlined: France succumbed to the temptation to "make a move," one that was easy and relatively low risk, albeit unlikely to pay much in the way of dividends. With little legitimacy in public opinion, King Charles X wanted to cause a stir at little cost. In the process, he also hoped to raise France's prestige among its European peers, reminding them that it was still a power to be reckoned with. On the pretext of a diplomatic dispute, he dispatched an expeditionary force that defeated the Ottoman forces more easily than anticipated. Beyond that, there was no plan, no objective, no doctrine. We shall return to this point in the pages that follow.

We here find ourselves confronted with a *policy of opportunity*, of occasions to be seized without any thought given to the long-term consequences. In July 1830, no one had the slightest idea what Algeria was or what should be done with it. These questions were not even raised: action was taken to obtain an immediate political dividend (in a matter of weeks, the Dey was defeated and the Turks expelled). No thought was given the future because the future was not in Algeria; it was in France; it was in Europe. The world at this time was limited to Europe in the broad sense of the term, a territory stretching from the Ural Mountains to the United States. The rest of the planet was a playground, an area of intervention to be taken advantage of, when possible, but where there was no real intention of investing or setting down roots.

Reaction: response to a temptation, to a stimulus. In 1830, the opportunity to "chastise" a medieval potentate at little cost was the stimulus. Later, the stimulus would come from specialized circles working on behalf of "sectional" interests.

Colonization, a Hobby Restricted to a Small Circle

Certain turns of the rudder were suggested by pressure groups consisting of soldiers, missionaries, and long-distance merchants, the first advocates of the colonial cause.

Soldiers and, especially, sailors nurtured a nostalgia for the colonies of the Ancien Régime, possessions that had been lost in the upheavals of the eighteenth century (Canada, in particular) and the tumult of the Revolution and Napoleonic wars (like Mauritius). Officers dreamt of a rematch with the English and longed for glory. They also stressed the need for support bases for their ships, which were supposed to protect French trade.

The overseas territories were also a temptation in some religious circles, Catholic and Protestant alike. These were activists, in the noble sense of the term, who wished to lead the heathen to salvation. They established "missions" with headquarters in Paris, Lille, Lyon, and Bordeaux.[10]

The merchants of Marseille, Nantes, and Le Havre, for their part, talked up the potential of little-known markets or even those forbidden to French interests (that of China, for example). They complained about the lack of security (e.g., Indonesian piracy) and the competition from British merchants, who relied on a maritime network that had been developing since the eighteenth century: Cape Town, India, Burma, Singapore, and so on.

To varying degrees, these three groups influenced the decisions of public authorities regarding overseas territories. In Indochina, there was a convergence of interests among the military, Catholics, and merchants. France's first steps in this region were driven by the need to aid local Catholics being persecuted by the Buddhists. Whence the Franco-Spanish landing in Tourane in 1858, which four years later would result in total control of Cochinchina. The merchants immediately set to work, discovering once there that the Chinese had preceded them. But that is another story . . .

While this happened, the Navy planted the tricolor in the Pacific, hoping thereby to steal a step on the British, who were already masters of the Australian vastness.

In Senegal, coastal merchants, both French and Senegalese, were the motors of colonization. Competing with African traders from the interior who specialized in long-distance trade (the slave trade), they wished to supplant them and thereby gain direct access to the best markets. These merchants also feared the activism of the Portuguese, who had established a presence nearby in present-day Guinea-Bissau, as well as the advancing British, who were very active on the west coast of Africa. Such purely commercial logic combined with concerns over security, the colony's immediate environment being prone to recurrent turmoil. In the north, the Moors launched murderous raids from the coast of Saint-Louis. To the south and the east, successive jihads beginning in the eighteenth century threatened caravans, support installations, and the allies of the colony's merchants. Under Faidherbe's leadership (1852–1865), France expanded its colony as part of a "police operation," bringing security

---

10. 1822: creation of the Charitable Society for the Propagation of the Faith [l'Œuvre de la propagation de la foi]; 1854: creation of the African Missions of Lyon [Missions africaines de Lyon]; 1868: creation of the Society of African Missionaries [Société des Missionnaires d'Afrique] (known as the *White Fathers* [Père Blancs]).

and cementing the coastal merchants' dominance. In the space of a few years, the original colony, limited to a few towns such as Saint-Louis, Gorée, and Rufisque, came to encompass the entire coastline, plunging into the continent's interior along the course of the Senegal River.

Soldiers nostalgic and eager for revenge against the British, religious missionaries, and long-distance merchants saw colonization as a necessity, but they had neither the political influence needed to force the hand of the state nor any desire to commit France to all-out expansionism. Each dreamt of placing pins in the globe, but they had no plans for a French colonial empire that would take on responsibility for tens of millions of inhabitants.

The result was an uneven policy marked by acceleration and stagnation, and largely guided and driven by circumstances. No one cared, for it was a subsidiary matter. Colonization was nothing more than a subtitle in France's foreign policy. It added another arrow to its quiver. France's interventions grew increasingly diverse: it invaded China alongside the British (1857–60); it came to the aid of Christians in the East (1860–61); it spread its influence with the Universal Exhibition in Paris (1867); and it dug the Suez Canal, a marvel of engineering and a demonstration of French genius (opened in 1869).

The context would radically change after September 1870. What was once a "toy" in the hands of a small circle became a question of vital importance for the nation.

1870–85: From Trauma to Binge

In the summer of 1870, Napoleon III, poorly advised, decided to attack Prussia. The conflict quickly resulted in the defeat at Sedan in September 1870, with the emperor taken prisoner and a portion of French territory occupied. The regime collapsed, opening the way to a series of internal political upheavals, the most serious being the Paris Commune (March 18th–May 28th, 1871). At the same time, Alsace and Lorraine were officially annexed by the German Empire (Treaty of Frankfurt, May 10th, 1871). France had been amputated.

Raw Nerves

This cataclysm provoked two simultaneous crises, one institutional and the other emotional.

France's defeat was followed by fifteen years of political instability. From 1871 to 1875, the country hesitated between Bonapartism, monarchism (Orléanist or Legitimist), and republicanism. And while the 1875 constitution enshrined the republican system, subsequent elections continued to send to Paris substantial contingents of the Republic's enemies who wished (if one is to take them at their word) to seize upon the first opportunity to be rid of it. After 1885, the risk of a coup d'état or a restoration of the monarchy diminished, but the challenge to the regime—implicit, if no less powerful— persisted. The Republic had been born of the loss of Alsace-Lorraine; it was an abortion cruelly lacking in legitimacy.

France was divided into two camps, each presenting arguments that were valid in absolute terms and that resonated deeply with public opinion. There was no consensus or common ground. So enormous was the gulf separating them on fundamental issues, such as the nature of the regime and the role of religion in society, that right (monarchists, Bonapartists) and left appeared irreconcilable.

Hearts and minds were sorely tested. Public opinion was disconsolate. The loss of Alsace-Lorraine was a central issue for all social classes, a pain that extended far beyond military and political circles. France was in mourning. It had lost "vital organs," not distant possessions in the Antilles or the Indian Ocean.

Beyond the sorrow and shame, beyond the distress at the fate of the French forced to flee the lost provinces to rejoin the motherland, there was an awareness, indeed a recognition that the country had come down in the world. A certainty settled in that transcended ideological boundaries and portended the country's slow death, a death that would come sooner or later if nothing was done to avert it. The theme of decadence, political and intellectual, permeated public debate. The prevailing sentiment was that of a nation at risk of sinking and that had to act quickly and effectively if it was to survive. In truth, France's decline would not necessarily lead to its death, but rather to stagnation within the ranks of second-class countries. Deprived of the vigor and grandeur that had made for France's "panache," the nation was at risk, not of dying, but of shrinking.

At the same time, great empires were rising in the East (Russia, Germany) and West (the United States).

There was thus a flourishing literature of decline and of the fight against decline. Whether of Catholic or republican inspiration, it implicitly evoked the image of a France in dire straits, forced by bad luck and the jealousy of its neighbors to withdraw into itself, though it was born to reach the stars. France was a radiant plant that had been transplanted to a cramped pot. It inevitably withered, and nothing could console it for the loss of its natural soil.

This intense distress caused madness, pushing some to suicide. In 1885, the historian Alfred Rambaud, a contemporary of the defeat at Sedan, recalled the dominant state of mind in the following terms: the French were at risk of "seeing their warrior instincts turn to infighting, bloody intrigues, class hatred, even civil war."[11]

What was to be done?

Two possibilities emerged. The first: revenge and thus war. The second: meditation and thus respite, relief, introspection. The arguments marshaled in support of these two possibilities were equally powerful, but until 1880 circumstances dictated meditation. It took around ten years to rebuild the nation's army, recover the enormous economic potential that had been lost as a result of territorial amputation, and to restore public finances. Later, things returned to normal, meditation lost its appeal and was at risk of being mistaken for resignation and cowardice.

The Republican Left's Stroke of Genius

Capable of astutely reading the emotional (and thus political) landscape of its time, the republican left changed the terms of the debate. Desiring neither revenge nor meditation, it rejected the dichotomy. Instead, it proposed to conquer the world. This doctrine was broadly inspired and implemented by Jules Ferry, the two-time head of government between 1880 and 1885. It was also championed by Léon Gambetta, who was in power from 1881 to 1882, as well as by the leading lights of what was at the time known as the *republican party*, in opposition to the monarchists and Bonapartists.

The main benefit of this policy had something of the marketing slogan about it and was the work of Léon Gambetta himself, who presented it as a "restorative and proud national policy." It was a form of nationalism (*national policy*) practiced externally, upon contact with and at the expense of natives. There was no question of launching an attack on the blue line of the Vosges.[12]

---

11. Rambaud, Alfred. "Préface" in J.R. Seeley, *L'Expansion de l'Angleterre*, Paris, 1885.
12. Trans. The Vosges mountains, which at the time separated France from the "lost provinces" of Alsace and Lorraine, then under German control.

It had nothing to do with the German enemy, the main source of France's malaise. This imperialism saw itself as therapeutic since it would repair what had been broken at Sedan: self-confidence, the feeling of grandeur, and pride in being French.

How? By killing two birds with one stone. Colonial expansion harnessed the emotional shock of defeat, acknowledged it, and offered it consolation in the form of conquests and victories across the globe. It also promised to curb the decline that haunted all minds. Against this, it put forward three remedies that formed the official justification for French colonization mentioned above: (1) we colonize to increase our economic power; (2) we colonize to remain a great nation that must be taken into account in the new world order that is emerging, as well to provide our navy with the waypoints and bases it needs to retain its standing; (3) we of course colonize to civilize primitive peoples, which confirms our status as a superior people, far removed from the tribulations and frightful backwardness of the natives we propose to raise morally and materially.

Throughout, it was thus a matter of warding off decline. Colonization was a potion giving economic, geopolitical, and finally military power. The solution was comprehensive. If one was to believe its promoters, it was all upside, an original third way allowing the country to "do something" without risking a new conflict with Germany. And this something was not trivial: it was a project of great import, a reconciliation with the Destiny of France, which common sense regarded as exceptional by definition. Jules Ferry nicely summed it up:

> "The republican party has shown that it fully realizes we cannot offer France a political ideal in keeping with that of nations like free Belgium and republican Switzerland: that something else is needed for France: that she cannot just be a free country, but must also be a great country, exerting all the influence that is hers on the destinies of Europe, that she must spread this influence across the world and carry with her wherever she can her language, her mores, her flag, her genius."[13]

The genius of the republican left was also expressed in tactical terms. From 1871 to 1880, it guided the reconstruction effort, which demanded restraint on

---

13. Speech of July 28th, 1885.

the international stage. From 1880 to 1885 it oversaw the conquest of Tunisia, Annam, and Tonkin, intervened in Madagascar, and raised the tricolor in North Congo. It moved quickly on the grounds that competition among European powers was fierce, and that places had to be taken, there would be time later to reflect on what was to be done with them. And it is true that British imperial efforts had been in the ascendant since 1874 under the leadership of Prime Minister Disraeli. The same held for the Belgians, who had an eye on the Congo River Basin, and the Germans, who looked towards Africa and Asia for an opportunity to hinder the British. Urgency is a powerful tool for the clever prince and an excellent way to extract consent. One shelters behind the force of circumstances and takes advantage of any escalation. Action came first, explanations later.

It was only as he prepared to leave government in July 1885 that Jules Ferry presented members of parliament—and thus the sovereign nation—with the clearest, most condensed, and most complete explanation of the motives behind colonization. These were the three arguments outlined above. Before this speech, these arguments had of course made the rounds, but they dissipated in the clamor of voices and echoes of news that were the background music of decision-makers. They came as no real surprise when formally set forth by Ferry, but it is likely they had never been put to music in this way.

The strategy paid off, for it allowed the opposition to be lastingly disarmed. Once it had been conquered, it was indeed difficult to surrender a territory. Complicated, also, to forgo the tribute of French soldiers' blood. And it was impossible to vacate places that perfidious Albion might immediately gobble up. The deed was done, the die had been cast, and anti-colonialist parliamentarians found themselves subject to the rule of the *fait accompli*.

The decisive years between 1880 and 1885 were no walk in the park for the Assembly. The debates were raucous, the government reeled, but the colonial cause won "by a thread." Neither Clemenceau's far left nor Deroulède's traditionalist right were able to bar its way. They often held out admirably, but Providence chose to give imperialism the last word.

The genius of the left was also reflected in the designation of a new enemy: England. It was a shrewd maneuver to channel the passions of soldiers avid for revenge against Germany. In 1911, Maurice Barrès wrote of Gambetta: "He kept the imagination of the best officers far from the Rhine and brought us into conflict with England."

What virtues the republican left discovered in colonization! Consolation, a remedy against decline, and the diversion of the vital forces that might have troubled it.

1885–1905: The Triumph of the Colonial Lobby

Whatever one might say, it is men and women who colonize, not flags or banners. The soldiers who triumphed in Indochina, the officers who bravely penetrated the equatorial forest along the coastline of the Gulf of Guinea, these soldiers wrote letters to their families, they corresponded with their fellow soldiers and their friends in the provinces from which they came. The words of survivors with good news to relate found their way into the press, for victory sold papers, especially when the country needed to raise its morale. The "colonials," as they were called from the 1880s onwards, joined the chorus of praise spun by the republican left and the early advocates of French imperialism (missionaries, geographers, merchants, etc.). The colonial officer became the best publicist for the colonial idea since he had earned his legitimacy in the field: he fought against the mandarins of Indochina, got the better of the Chinese pirates who terrorized peasants along the upper course of the Red River, had personally laid eyes on the minarets of Timbuktu and the fantastic Amazons of King Behanzin of Benin. His words carried far, and his logic was irrefutable, for victory won people over and suspended all doubt.

And what did this colonial officer tell us? Well, it was always the same story, a kind of heroic and redemptive quest in which the soldier "formatted" by his instruction in France confronts extraordinary dangers and finds himself entrusted with duties well beyond his age and rank. He had no choice but to shake loose the tight frame of habit and routine and take the initiative, learning on the job from unforeseen events and sacrifices. Colonization was thus an apprenticeship, a kind of rite of passage or initiation opening the way to a higher state, that of a younger, more beautiful, more radiant humanity. The experience of conquest and the administration of subjugated peoples was a school that produced complete men, emancipated from the culture of specialization that traps the individual in a silo, imprisoning him and depriving him of responsibility. The colonial officer gradually presented himself as an elite soldier who thought for himself and allowed his subordinates to think for themselves as well, because passivity and conformism could be deadly on the banks of the Congo River.

Gallieni, the hero of the conquest of West Africa, Tonkin, and Madagascar, loved to tell his deputies: "In the name of good sense, our administrators and officers must defend the interests entrusted to them and not oppose them in the name of regulations." In any army, whether past or present, these are revolutionary words indeed.

France was seen as a prison. If he was to have a life worth living, a man had to take his leave of it, throwing himself into hostile territory overseas. It was an existence irrigated by manly action and noble intentions. The colonial France, the *New France*, that the colonial officer was helping to construct conquered to civilize; his was the noblest of wars. No one better theorized this virtuous war than Lyautey, who spent his whole life practicing it in Indochina, Madagascar, Algeria, and, finally, Morocco:

"The wars of Europe, those which we must wage when necessary for the preservation of our independence, always leave lasting ruin in their wake. Colonial war leaves only life and fertility in its wake . . ."

Colonial war was a kind of rejuvenation, a return to the true sources of French genius, which no longer had any outlet in the metropole. The army was reborn in the tropics and there renewed its human resources:

"When one has had the great honor of leading men in battle, and soldiers of France, he knows there is no more invigorating crucible for the race. The good become better and the worst become good."

The soldier opened the way, beating a path so that the colonist could follow. This expatriate also benefited from colonial rejuvenation, an admittedly painful regimen synonymous with danger and privation but that rendered stronger whomever it did not kill.

"For our race, this is what the Far West is for America, that is, an occasion par excellence for energy, rejuvenation, and fertility [. . .] You must be convinced, with legitimate pride, that the plant that grows here is not some diminished Frenchman, but, if I may say so, an *enhanced* Frenchman."

Addressing himself in these terms to the colonists of the Tiaret region (Algeria) in 1897, Lyautey had the audacity to speak freely, shining a light on his project to forge a "new man." One would think one was reading a Spartan warrior obsessed with the moral virtues and physical qualities of his city-state's inhabitants. Except that the words of Lyautey resonated across an entire empire. He considered the colonies an incubator of excellence destined to regenerate the metropole. The colony was a graft that would inevitably straighten the nation's spine, which was bent and for a time seemed on the point of snapping.

> "And I will never stop hoping that this colonial sap, returning from the periphery to the center, will restore its strength, that strength with which no organism can do without, which is and always will be the final argument and essential precondition of independence and of the very life of peoples."

It would have been impossible to put matters any more clearly.

Lyautey introduced a synthesis, one that was perhaps more convincing than what Ferry presented before the Assembly in 1885:

> "It is the superiority of colonial life that, thanks to the distance it grants, engenders a broader, more tolerant, more comforting view of things, and from this distance all rifts in the metropole seem less deep, less severe, and more susceptible to remedy."

Everything is there. Colonization would allow France to finally turn its gaze from the open wound left by 1870. From Tonkin to Congo, its victories offered consolation, as did the surplus of activity that occupied the mind and filled hearts with other and better concerns than the need to take vengeance against Germany. It offered an outlet for energies that would have stagnated in France, rotting away under the influence of boredom and bitterness. At a distance, as Lyautey writes, reconciliation seemed to be within arm's reach. There were no longer monarchists or republicans, Dreyfusards or anti-Dreyfusards, Catholics or radical anti-clericals. There were simply *enhanced Frenchmen*.

To read Lyautey, colonization was the panacea for the malaise afflicting France.

The Colonial Lobby

The ideology peddled in colonial discourse was amplified by a network of well-established organizations formed in the 1890s, well after colonization first began to accelerate in the first half of the previous decade (Tunisia, Tonkin, Madagascar, Congo).

It was in recognition of this fact that the press coined the term "the Colonial Party." A nice turn of phrase that aptly described the apolitical character of this collective entity, which brought together people of both left and right. After several years of activity—a decade, at most—the Colonial Party succeeded in making everyone forget that the colonial idea had been born on the left.

The Colonial Party was supported by three pillars. The first and most important of these was the Colonial Committee, a parliamentary group founded in 1892. At its peak (1902), it consisted of 200 deputies from both left and right. Outside of these properly political circles, there was the Committee for French Africa, founded in 1890. This was a club or think tank, as we say today, that sought to promote the colonial idea in the media, finance exploratory missions, and encourage scientific research in Sub-Saharan Africa. Other specialized committees would make their appearance a little later, including the Morocco Committee and the Committee for French Asia. Finally, there was the French Colonial Union, a private association in the service of business circles and consisting of merchants, financiers, and industrialists.

These organizations handled the "customer service" side of colonization. They spread the good news and managed the bad. They pulled the strings in the ministries and chambers to ensure that the colonization effort lacked for nothing.

At the time of their appearance, colonization was on the verge of winning the battle of ideas but was still vulnerable. Like a newborn child, it needed to be cared for if it was to grow and flourish. In concrete terms, this was a matter of allocating the necessary military personnel and financial resources to conquer coveted territories as well as to fully gain control of the territories that had already been swallowed up. Among the territories in the crosshairs was Madagascar, upon which the colonial lobby set great store. Since the early 1880s, France had had a very modest foothold in that country. In 1895, it went "all in," sending 15,000 troops to seize the capital, Antananarivo. In October of that same year, a protectorate was declared there, albeit at the price of very heavy losses from disease. Elsewhere, where conquest had already taken place, it was a matter of reducing the last pockets of resistance and banditry, a process that history would come to know as *pacification*. This was a delicate operation, midway between war and law enforcement. Since the enemy could blend in perfectly with the general population, it generally required several months of thankless toil. In Indochina, for example, pacification took ten years. For while the Court of Hue accepted French sovereignty in 1883, it was not until roughly 1895 that Tonkin (the northern province) was once and for all subjugated.

All of these operations, whether of conquest or pacification, cost dearly and came with their share of accidents, setbacks, and epidemics. The Colonial Party saw to it that, despite these incidents, political support for the venture never faltered.

The French "diaspora" in Algeria, which had always been generally supportive of republican principles, conferred an Algerian overtone upon this lobby.[14] Eugène Étienne—a well-connected man of action who opened doors and overcame obstacles of all sorts[15]—provided a valuable conduit for its influence in Paris. Under his aegis, the Colonial Party managed relations between the agents of colonization (military, civil servants, colonists), its promoters (politicians, active or retired), and the ecosystem (journalists, intellectuals) that gravitates around any major public policy. He provided a "family" of thought for an extremely diverse range of actors who, outside of colonial questions, had very little in common.

Each year, scholarships were awarded to deserving students to travel overseas and return with a report of the marvels they had witnessed. Explorers,

---

14. Of the 700,000 French living in the colonies on the eve of the First World War, 500,000 lived in Algeria.
15. A "pied noir" from Oran, Eugene Étienne (1844–1921) was more than just the spokesman for the Algerian colony in Paris; he would come to personally embody the colonial cause, its mindset, and its rhetoric. As a deputy and undersecretary of state for the colonies, he would lend considerable support to Lyautey, who sojourned in Algeria at the end of the nineteenth century to pacify the region known as Southwest Oran. The warm relationship between Étienne and Lyautey symbolized French "reconciliation" in the colonies: Étienne was a republican, and a rather uncompromising and anticlerical one at that, while Lyautey was the complete opposite, yet they got along wonderfully in what concerned the policy to be pursued overseas.

geographers, and intellectuals were invited to visit the empire and speak pub-licly about its potential and promise at formal dinners, banquets, and con-ferences in Paris and the provinces. The press was in on the game, of course. Indeed, the first president of the Committee of French Africa, the Prince of Arenberg, also happened to be the director of the *Journal des Débats*.[16] The good word was also spread via monthly bulletins, which reported on the voy-ages of some and the triumphs of others (4000 copies were printed of each number of the bulletin of the Committee of French Africa).

In 1895, the die was cast. In the space of fifteen years, beginning with the first government of Jules Ferry, France had increased the extent of its overseas possessions tenfold. It was enough to make one dizzy: 9,500,000 square kilo-meters and fifty million souls of all races and faiths. In 1887, the Indochinese Union was established, a political-administrative body covering Cambodia, Cochinchina, Annam, and Tonkin, with Saigon as its capital. In 1895, French West Africa was in its turn born, with its capital in Dakar.

This resounding success did not fail to excite the public's interest, nor, for that matter, its anglophobia. The British had borne the cost of France's colonial appetite, and in 1898 the two nations almost went to war over the Fashoda Incident, after the name of an insignificant village on the banks of the Nile (in present-day Sudan). Having arrived first, the soldiers of the Marchand col-umn, after marching eastwards from the Atlantic coast, were surrounded by the British descending from Khartoum.

Marchand resisted, requesting instructions from Paris. Ultimately, they arrived: he was to leave the place to the British. This caused immense turmoil in Paris, where the mob was eager to make the English pay for this latest in-dignity, just the last in a long series of quarrels and low blows.

The militants of the colonial idea, the *colonists*, had won their bet. Colonialism was now an integral part of France's "software," and one of its most fundamental reflexes was distrust of Perfidious Albion.

With public opinion no longer having anything with which to reproach col-onization, the hour had come for recalcitrant political parties to convert to its cause. The first to eat their words were the radicals. Positioned to the left of the

---

16. Trans. The *Journal des Débats* was a French weekly newspaper published between 1789 and 1944. Until its suppression following the Liberation of Paris in 1944, it exerted a powerful influence over the worlds of French politics, literature, and culture.

republicans, in the 1880s they had given Jules Ferry a rough time over the issue of Tonkin. When they came to power in 1902, they firmly adopted the colonial idea, putting themselves in its service. They prepared to swallow up Morocco, the last North African country to have kept a semblance of sovereignty. And when William II furrowed his brow and demanded first dibs (First Moroccan Crisis, 1905), the royalist right in its turn came around to the colonial idea. In what came to be known as the *Moroccan affair*, they found an opportunity to exercise their hatred of Germany while stealthily converting to the cause of colonization.[17]

From 1905 on, tensions began to mount in Europe, with many coming to believe that war was on the horizon, a war that would allow the French and Germans to finally settle their scores with one another. French industrial power had undergone a vigorous revival, and the French could now count on major European allies, including Russia and Great Britain. The debate over colonization was completely lost from sight as preparations were unconsciously made for the "great showdown" with Germany.

Conclusion: The Resounding Success of Political Will and Predestination

There was no single cause of French colonization, nor two, nor three, nor four. A process, at once spontaneous and willed by a small coterie within the elite, was set in motion and only grew stronger with the passing years. This process was the true cause of colonization. Its *escalation* between 1880 and 1885 forced the hand of all political actors and even public opinion, rendering colonization a *fait accompli* that one either joyfully accepted or resigned oneself to live with.

All of the credit for this goes to the republican left, which played its cards admirably, the most important of these being the shock caused by the loss of Alsace-Lorraine. It was able to convince France that it was necessary to respond to the trauma inflicted by the Germans in 1870 with another trauma, this one to be imposed on native populations. The republican left was very lucky, for its policy found soldiers admirably suited for the task and capable

---

17. On March 31st, 1905, without notifying anyone, the German emperor traveled to Tangier. He rode through the city on horseback and met with the Moroccan Sultan, assuring him of his support against French and English imperialism.

of quickly and effectively carrying it out. The element of luck is decisive, even when it defies all rational analysis. Yet in seeming to confirm that France had an inevitable appointment with colonization, that she could not escape this, it nevertheless expressed the direction of history.

This invisible hand of History parted the seas for the Frenchmen who threw themselves at Africa and Asia. But it could not bring about two miracles at once. For France had no idea what it was going to do with these colonies. It was as if dumbfounded by its rapid victories, which immediately demanded exceptional men to manage the millions of people it had just subjugated. Yet nothing, absolutely nothing was ready. The soldiers and administrators who arrived in the tropics had no roadmap or doctrine to fall back on. Their bosses in Paris had their heads full of ideals, preconceptions, and fantasies, and did not want to concern themselves with the business of logistics. At least not for the moment.

This fecklessness would have dire consequences for colonization. The sponsors of the colonial idea had written a play for the French in which all the lines were spoken by Frenchmen. The black man, the yellow man, and the Arab were mere extras who were so good as to lend their living space as décor for an entirely French tragedy. Lyautey said it and repeated it: the French had set off for the colonies to regenerate themselves, to be at peace with their vital energies, and to forget about the infighting that divided their nation. The native was ultimately of no intrinsic interest. He had the merit of being weak and divided, making his conquest relatively easy and the pretext of civiliz- ing perfectly plausible. His role was limited to observing and submitting. He watched as French genius spread from Antananarivo to Casablanca and suf- fered the rigors of humiliation and loss of sovereignty. No one lost sleep over his misfortune, for the colonial idea had no real empathy for him. It felt no responsibility for his well-being. Its responsibility was to France, to its gran- deur and its renewal.

What then was the point of making preparations to govern fifty million people, some of whom lived as far as 10,000 kilometers from Paris?

From the outset, French colonization was suspended over an abyss: the fate of the natives.

A TWISTED IDEA

"But after the battle, it did not take us long to see having defeated a nation is not enough to govern it."

ALEXIS DE TOCQUEVILLE

In a certain sense, the colonial idea was a twisted one, for it rested on nothing but French anxieties and only responded to them. We have seen above how the very origins of colonization bore the imprint of the great emotional burden occasioned by the loss of Alsace and Lorraine. The desire to colonize was first and foremost a largely impulsive response to this immense distress. And when one suffers intensely, one sometimes does foolish things.

In the case of France, it was like a waking dream. The "colonial dream," as Clemenceau called it, was something of a digression. A welcome digression that allowed one to momentarily escape an intolerable reality. A noble digression, too, for men like Lyautey, who in the tropics expressed what was best in France's genius. But it was also a dangerous delirium, a perilous detour on the part of the country's elites, who heaped immense responsibilities but no real returns upon France.

Outsized Ambition

The ultra-rapid growth of the empire between 1880 and 1895 caught public services and the country as a whole off guard. France had nowhere near the manpower or finances needed to take on such an enormous responsibility. The birth rate, which had been depressed since the Revolution, provided no demographic surplus to send to the colonies. The economy, while certainly expanding in the nineteenth century, had not prepared the French state for such external projection. From the outset, the empire would face shortages in its budget, civil service, resources, and military.

In French Equatorial Africa, there was a single district officer for a territory four times as large as the department of Bouches-du-Rhône.[1] In Algeria, outside of European population centers, finding a post office often required one to travel more than 60 kilometers. In French West Africa, 300 kilometers of veritable medical desert often separated one clinic from the next.

Could it have ever been otherwise when one recalls that the tropics were the white man's tomb? Even if France had had sufficient manpower to send to the colonies, it would have been decimated. Around 1830, the mortality rate for French soldiers was eight times higher in Senegal than in France due to malaria, sleeping sickness, yellow fever, and other ailments. Eight decades later, and despite advances in tropical medicine, the mortality rate for European soldiers (the armies of France, Great Britain, Portugal, etc.) in African and Asian colonies was twice that recorded in their metropoles.[2]

French colonies would be constantly under-administered, their territories very superficially covered by security forces, and their populations quite literally cast off, denied all contact with France.

The disunity and technological backwardness of the natives concealed the chronic under-administration of the colonies. Everyone had simply been too stunned by the extraordinary firepower of the French military. But a country is not governed by bayonets alone. It needs to be mapped, monitored, and studied in detail by agents of the state, its inhabitants (literally) taken in hand by nurses, doctors, and civil registrars, not to mention schoolteachers and religious personnel. It was thus that France, Italy, and Spain were governed. Africa, the Maghreb, and Indochina were no different, human nature being everywhere the same.

By the millions, Moroccans, Algerians, and Vietnamese would spend their entire lives without seeing a single French police officer, doctor, or school-

---

1. Trans. A department in southern France bordering the Mediterranean, with its administrative center located in the city of Marseille.
2. For an excellent analysis of the demographic aspect of colonization, I refer you to this article, from which I moreover drew this handful of statistics relating to soldiers' mortality rates:
   Etermad Bouda, "Pour une approche démographique de l'expansion colonial de l'Europe", *Annales de démographie historique*, 2007 (online): https://www.cairn .info/revue-annales-de-demographie-historique-2007-1-page-13.htm.

teacher. They knew their country was under French occupation but were never taken in hand by the colonial administration. Instead, they were confined to a hybrid reality where their way of life was preserved but their sovereignty nullified.

In Bhalil, the village from which both my mother's and father's families came, forty-four years of French presence boiled down to a single aviator who, in his free time, travelled from Fez, twenty kilometers to the north, to give lessons to the children of prominent villagers. The rest, all of it, was managed as before, that is, entrusted to a *caïd* who served as both mayor and chief of police.

The consequences of this chronic under-administration were many and immense. We shall return to them later. Perhaps the most important was that the conquest was superficial. The people's subjugation was never synonymous with support for the colonial order. People bowed their heads more from fear than from deference. From 1830 to 1962, the Algerian remained unchanged, subject to the same way of life as his ancestors. It would be the same for Moroccans, Tunisians, the Malgache, the Congolese, and the Vietnamese during their periods of colonization. France merely skimmed the surface of hearts and minds. It could break bones and tear flesh but would never have the privilege of touching the souls of the peoples under its supervision.

The Unbearable Lightness of the Colonial Idea

The implementation of the colonial idea was a casual affair. France had not trained men and women for the task at hand, and no plan of government or development had been devised. Worse, the territories to be conquered were often not reconnoitered in advance.

No One Even Thought of Creating a Roadmap

In record time, the French had brought the Second Colonial Empire into being without ever possessing a doctrine for the domination, exploitation, or advancement of native populations. More than a little paradoxical for an undertaking that postcolonialists today depict as the epitome of oppression.

It is hard to admit that the French elites of the time should have committed the country so lightly to an adventure as colossal and perilous as this. This irresponsibility can only be justified by reference to the pressure of irrepressible forces, deeply rooted in the French psyche, that burst every dam after the defeat at Sedan.

Nothing had been prepared. Everything was learned on the spot by dint of practical intelligence and the administration's ability to take a higher view of the situation, which compensated for political myopia. First-class civil servants like Paul Cambon in Tunisia, the inventor of the protectorate system, made up for the massive blind spots of the colonial project. Very rarely, well-informed politicians like Jean-Louis de Lanessan, a former radical deputy become governor-general of Indochina, sometimes brought off the miracle of establishing authority and "governance" without a "manual" for colonization.

If colonization was an art, then the French colonial project never attended art school. It was in the bush, under mosquito netting and far from the master's studio and protection, that its "artists" discovered their gift.

In 1805, a National School of Overseas France (*École Nationale de la France d'outre-mer*) was established in Paris. Its ambitions were limited, as it exclusively trained small cohorts of colonial administrators (fifty per year). Yet the task at hand was immense. To meet it, it would have been necessary to dedicate entire universities to the study of the cultures of Asia and Africa, to mapping religions and sects, to language instruction, and to the analysis of subsoils and biodiversity. In short, what was needed was to build from scratch the most sophisticated knowledge possible of the peoples to be "civilized" and their environments.

Serving in the colonies was not simply a matter of passing exams. It was also a state of mind open to the world, a capacity to take the initiative and subsequently seek appropriate instructions, and the ability to keep the cool head needed to use force sparingly without giving in to fear or pressure from colonists. Quite the opposite, in other words, of the sort of racism that renders one lazy and blind by virtue of explaining every difficulty by reference to the supposed ill-will of the foreigner.

A Leap into the Unknown

Colonial expansion was carried out blindly, conquest having preceded knowledge of the territories and their populations. The ignorance was shocking and unfathomable, but it is at least partly explained by the mystery in which so much of the world was then shrouded.

At the end of the nineteenth century, Morocco, though so close to Europe, was a hermetically sealed country. Only a handful of diplomats were allowed access, with a small number of expatriates, including doctors and merchants, under their protection. All or almost all of them lived in the coastal cities (Tangier, Rabat, Salé, Essaouira) or the capital Fez. At most, there were 200 to 300 people, all nationalities combined, who carefully avoided setting foot in the country's interior, where the authority of the Sultan was null and void. In rebel zones, or four-fifths of the territory, only Muslims and Jews were allowed, and then only if they had a patron (and, in some cases, an armed escort). Christians were *personae non gratae*.

Charles de Foucauld took the risk and slipped into Morocco in 1883 disguised as a Sephardic Jew. As a Catholic this was the only subterfuge he could devise to visit the country, where he wished to map the territory in a private capacity. His guide was Mordechai, a Moroccan rabbi whom he met in Algiers, a French city at that time. Despite all his precautions, Charles de Foucauld was unmasked in the Sous region and owed his life to the decisive intervention of a Moroccan noble, El Hadj Bou Rhim, who took him under his wing.[3] Separated from his Moroccan friend, he was beaten and robbed by the bodyguards he had hired to take him to Oujda.

The situation was hardly any better in Africa, which remained a vast blank space on maps of the world. At the turn of the twentieth century, the legend of Lake Liba, mentioned by Ptolemy eighteen centuries earlier, was still widely believed. This lake was reputed to cover an immense basin between the Sahara and the equatorial forest. It was only following the conquest that the myth was dispelled. In its place, one found desolate populations scattered between the savannas and the sands of the Sahel. No cereal crops to harvest, no gold to extract, no major trade to tax or divert. So why stay?

No one wanted to draw the obvious conclusions from these discoveries and leave. To this day, these regions are destitute and have little in the way of resources, with the exception of Ivory Coast's export agriculture (which thrived between two civil wars). Did France really need to produce its own coffee, cocoa, and cashews in Ivory Coast? Did the Swedes and Bulgarians,

---

3. "He was, for me, the most reliable, selfless, and devoted friend; on two occasions, he risked his life to protect mine." This tribute to Hadj Bou Rhim can be found in Charles de Foucauld's report of his journey to Morocco. See: *Reconnaissance du Maroc, 1883–1884*.

who never planted their flag in this country, ever lack for tropical produce? Of course not.

Even in Asia, the French were poorly informed as to what awaited them. They set foot in Tonkin in the early 1870s based on reports transmitted by French merchants, who assured them that local Christians would be well disposed towards them. Once the conquest began, the decisive uprising of Christians failed to materialize. France was forced to make two attempts to seize Hanoi, the capital of Tonkin. The second of these, led by Captain Rivière in 1883, was successful. There followed nearly fifteen years of difficult pacification in the inland territories, where France, poorly informed as to the actual state of the country and the morale of the Vietnamese, discovered two formidable enemies: rebellious peasants and pirates from China. Where was the payoff if the conquest itself required colossal sums to arm and equip troops over an extended period?

From the outset, the colonial idea was tainted. Its assumptions were false, its ambitions were excessive, and its methods were slapdash.

It did not take a rocket scientist to foresee its failure.

THE ALGERIAN "APPRENTICESHIP"

"Who knew then what France would like to do with Algeria, what it could make of it? For that matter, who knew the country that France's victory had placed in our hands?"

LÉON ROCHES

The conquest of Algeria sheds a bloody light on the origins of French colonization. It is its laboratory and counter-model: a sort of founding deed that all would like to erase from their memories, but which none can truly forget, for it is loaded with precious lessons.

In Algeria, every mistake that should have been avoided was made. No other colony was so flooded by carelessness, amateurism, and excessive violence. As France's first significant overseas territorial conquest of the nineteenth century, Algeria served as a testing ground. Military operations and political blunders caused Algerian society to quite literally explode, diluting it and grinding it down until it had become a sort of ungovernable "porridge."

During these decisive years, France would not just destroy; it also developed the know-how that would guide its subsequent colonial expansion. The soldiers who landed in Tunisia, Sub-Saharan Africa, and Indochina from 1880 onwards would seek to spare native populations as far as possible. With an eye to future collaboration in the exploitation of the country, they sought to keep them "intact." Finally, France would never again attempt to settle a territory. In contrast to the British, who created "replicas" of England from one end of the world to the other (southern Africa, Oceania), the French were content to add just a dash of their population to the colonies. In Sub-Saharan Africa, the French contingent in the colonies never exceeded 1 percent of the total population. In 1938, they were barely 0.2 percent of the total (or 60,000 people from Dakar to Djibouti, by way of Brazzaville). Indeed, in Algeria, France had learned to distrust colonists: if one was not careful, they could take an administration hostage and force it to govern in their interests.

For reasons of humanity but also self-interest, colonial expansion would always bear in mind the fiasco that was Algeria.

This "wisdom," however, was incapable of tempering the French appetite for colonization. For despite the colossal sums that had been burned through to take Algeria, French authorities would not lose their appetite for colonization anytime soon—proof, if any were needed, that this policy was above all essentially irrational. A sort of addiction to pain and suffering.

The Algerian Exception

The Algerians were caught off-guard by the French invasion. This was yet another particularity of their experience, for other populations had been "warned" of France's intentions.

To understand their reaction to colonization, we must first immerse ourselves in the political and mental landscape of Algeria in 1830. Any interpretation of the facts that fails to take account of states of mind, beliefs, and loyalties runs the risk of becoming just another morality tale about innocent victims and designated perpetrators.

On the eve of France's arrival, Algeria was deeply fragmented along ethnic, religious, regional, and tribal lines. There was no Algerian people and no Algeria, but rather a mosaic of populations living in relative isolation from one another and in permanent conflict. Disputes, discord, and recourse to violence dominated relations between the various communities, be they tribes, families, or religious associations. The individual as such counted for little, and above all defined himself according to one or more affiliations: race (Kabyle or Arab), location, tribe, religion (Jew or Muslim), and religious practice (i.e., membership in one of the many brotherhoods overseeing spiritual life and serving as intermediaries between God and man).

Uniting this fragmented world was immensely difficult, and only the most exceptional figures were up to the task. Emir Abdelkader (1808–1883) was one such, a man capable of bringing force upon the recalcitrant but also of galvanizing the enthusiastic. A true son of his country who knew how to use the raw materials then so abundant in Algeria: xenophobia and religious fanaticism. Christians were doubly hated as foreigners who came to plunder the country and infidels who perturbed the Muslim faith.

Without appealing to these two unhappy passions, it was impossible to unite the country's energies around a common goal. And even then, the taste for intrigue and spirit of vendetta ever stirring in people's hearts meant that anything done had to be redone the next day.

Algeria was also a land under foreign sovereignty, one that contented itself with governing according to the principle of divide and rule. No elaborate institutions, sophisticated councils, or pompous ideologies here; Islam, coercion, and cooptation were all that was needed. The sole ambition was to exploit the population without giving them anything in return.

The Regency of Algiers, the name given to the Ottoman political authority in Algeria, was a "low-cost" colony where the Turks spent little and governed much. Although their power was only nominal in certain places, they were always at the heart of the action, the arbiters of intrigue and overlords of all ambition. From the coast to the edge of the desert, no strong man could maintain his position without the blessing of the Dey of Algiers.[4]

Ottoman domination of Algeria was based on brazen social engineering in which carefully selected Algerians were tasked with oppressing other Algerians. The system was so effective that, in normal times, the number of Turkish soldiers deployed to Algeria never exceeded 3500 men.[5] Compared to the forces sent by France to assure its own control (100,000 soldiers in the 1840s), this was exceedingly small.

As the holders of power, the Turks lived in Algiers and such large cities as Oran, Constantine, and Tlemcen. They intervened directly in the administration of the backcountry around Algiers, where they had farms and country homes. In this predominantly Arab sector, the territory was divided among *caids* distributed across eleven administrative subdivisions known as *aoutan*. Security was provided by permanent garrisons and Arab tribes posted to sensitive locations. In the east, a portion of the Arab Arib tribe guarded the Constantine Road and kept their eyes glued on Kabylia. In the west, the Zemouls and Hadjouts kept watch. As compensation for their services, these "self-defense forces" were allowed to cultivate the fields of state-owned domains at no charge and were exempt from taxation. Finally, as a precaution,

---

4. The Dey governed the regency on behalf of the Sultan of Constantinople.
5. This number of course increased in the event of armed conflict or rebellion.

the borders of peripheral *aoutan* were artificially extended a few kilometers to the foot of the mountains, in this way placing the highland Berbers under the de facto authority of the lowland Arabs. A clever way of stoking interethnic tensions and preventing any union against the colonizer.

In the rest of the country, Turkish rule was administered indirectly and principally relied on two levers.

The Kouloughlis, mixed-race descendants of Ottoman soldiers (Turkish fathers and Arab mothers), were one of them. As supporters of the established order convinced of their racial superiority vis-à-vis the Algerians, they formed a separate caste. When they were not occupying leading administrative roles in Algiers, they were sent with their wives and children to man inland garrisons. There, they led the life of armed colonists and were known for their warlike virtues and flourishing agriculture.

The Ottoman's second lever consisted in a disparate assembly of antagonistic tribes—*makhzen* tribes on one side, *raya* tribes on the other—that the Turks restrained from devouring one another. The *makhzen* took precedence over the *raya*, who they forcibly obliged to pay taxes. When necessary, they subdued them by means of razzias, plundering them of goods, cattle, and women. Imagine that the French government closed the police station and tax office in your town and then entrusted the prerogatives of government to a gang of Chechens—it was something like that.

On a map of Algeria, one is struck by how the various tribes were positioned. The territory was a woven mat hemming in the most turbulent and least reliable elements. In the west, for example, the *raya* tribes were confined between *makhzen* tribes neatly arranged along two parallel lines running (in the north) from Oran to the middle of the Chelif Basin and (in the south) from Sebdou to the city of Saïda.

The highest ranking *makhzen* tribes were the Smella and the Douairs from the Oran region. They were referred to as the *great* or *high makhzen* because they had been formed specifically by the Turks for this role. Imagine an entire community devoted to military service: farmers, shepherds, artisans, notables, and warlords. In return for services rendered, the tribes of the *great makhzen* cultivated state-owned land. Elsewhere, the Turks delegated law enforcement and tax collection powers to tribes more loyal and aggressive than their neighbors. These were the *low makhzen*, who differed from their "high" counterparts in that they generally worked their own land and only mobilized when circumstances demanded it.

To guard against intrigue and thwart conspiracy, the various *makhzen* tribes were assigned different chains of command. On the high central plateau, the Oulad Aziz and the Oulad Antar, contiguous *makhzen* tribes, took orders from different leaders: in one case, it was the Agha of Algiers, in the other, the Dey of Oran.

There was nevertheless a gap in the Turkish system: Kabylia. In 1830, the region was self-governing under the leadership of the Mokranis, an aristocratic family who only formally recognized Ottoman authority.

The generalized fragmentation and division of social structures also affected man's conscience.

Seen from Paris, it was easy to believe that the Algerians were simply Sunni Muslims. But Algerian Islam was split between several religious movements that competed among themselves and with political power. Adept at secrecy, these groups formed bona fide parallel societies opaque to outsiders. Among these groups were the Qadiriyya, the Shadhili, the Darqawiyya, the Tijaniyyah, the Rahmaniyya, and the Senusiyya. Each offered its own *tariqah*, that is, its own path for communicating with God and obtaining His graces. Let the reader imagine religious confraternities with their own secret greetings, their own meeting places off-limits to worldly authorities, and their own fixed political views (for or against the Christians, for or against the Turks, for or against an alliance with the Sultan of Morocco, for or against Islam interfering in secular life).

What the Turks ruled over was thus a sort of political millefeuille, its layers only partly visible to the naked eye. They were the only ones capable of handling it without it breaking or requiring a fortune to hold together.

A fact-finding commission dispatched to Algeria by the Chamber of Deputies in 1833 summarized the Turkish colonization of Algeria as follows:

"The Turks know only the present, the sovereignty of the moment. They care little about tomorrow, and only govern the population in the interest of power, without thinking of those whom they govern, leaving them to their own devices."[6]

---

6. This assessment was made by Monsieur de La Pinssonière, deputy for Indre-et-Loire. They are quoted in an article by Xavier Yacono, who in the 1950s was an historian and professor at the University of Algiers. See Xavier Yacono, "La Régence d'Alger en 1830 d'après des commissions de 1833–1834," *Revue de l'Occident musulman et de la Méditerranée*, no. 2, 1966, pp. 227–247.

The French, for their part, would smash it all to pieces in less than 20 years. The Turks handed them a sick body, nearly a corpse, and they turned it into porridge.

The French would be surprised by the combativeness of the Algerians, a product of the hostility that coursed through the veins of a society of fighters in which everyone was at war or expected to be sooner or later. The mentality and values of the Algerians reflected the skills that allowed for survival in a brutal environment where the law of the strongest prevailed: agility and aggression on the one hand, unruliness and dissension on the other.

A Royal Whim

Twenty-one days. It took Charles X just twenty-one days to drive the Turks out of Algeria. Between June 14th and July 5th, 1830, the reactionary king won an easy victory and landed France in a quagmire from which it has never really escaped. For while Algeria has been independent since 1962, France was Algerianized in the years that followed and now counts between 1.5 and 4 million Algerians residing on its territory.[7]

On the pretext of avenging an offense against the French consul,[8] King Charles X sent 40,000 men to Algeria. Their mission was to secure the capitulation of the Dey of Algiers, thereby raising French prestige on the international stage and advancing the king's ambitions. In the eyes of French public opinion, the city of Algiers was a den of pirates who had scoured the Mediterranean for centuries, bandits specialized in kidnapping for ransom. Charles X hoped his exploit would help mollify the French in anticipation of a planned authoritarian crackdown. It would be a wasted effort, for the four edicts announced on July 26th (including one ending freedom of the press) provoked the July Revolution, a revolt of the people of Paris that would lead to the regime's downfall.

Rather than ordering a withdrawal, the new king, Louis-Philippe, maintained a military presence in Algeria, albeit with fewer troops and limited to Algiers, Oran, and Annaba.

---

7. The number varies depending on whether one relies on the estimates of French (1.5 million) or Algerian (4 million) authorities.
8. The infamous "Fan Affair" that took place three years earlier.

In 1830, the French expeditionary corps had no idea how to conduct a colonial war. Its eldest officers remembered the immense carnage of the Napoleonic wars, where the goal was to annihilate the adversary even if it meant devastating the country and its inhabitants. They had no experience of conflict in which the enemy was to be spared so that he might become tomorrow's partner and collaborator. Indeed, no European army of that time possessed that kind of skill.

France's war aims were a muddle. Apart from humiliating the Dey of Algiers, all was unclear. The French immediately expelled Ottoman civilian and military elites to Turkey.[9] An act of pure madness, for this decision brought down a system of governance based on balancing mutual antipathy. Expelling the Turks removed the dykes and ushered in all-out civil war among Algerians. Long-repressed resentments finally burst forth and the blood flowed copiously.

The Algiers of 1830 somewhat resembled the Baghdad of 2003, where American governor Paul Bremer announced that all members of the Baath Party would be irrevocably banished for life.

- The Kouloughlis were targeted by "native stock" Algerians. Desperate, they sought refuge with the French, offering their services as soldiers and administrators. Ignorant of Algerian realities, the French declined this offer.
- Deprived of the moderating influence of Turkish police, the Algerian tribes set about tearing each other to pieces.
- By late July 1830, opposition to the Christian occupation began to emerge and became increasingly virulent.

Lacking any doctrine or plan of conquest, French officers adapted by copying local methods. It was no time before they began practicing razzia, a technique which the Turks and Algerians themselves had implemented before them.

The recruitment of Yusuf (né Joseph Vantini) symbolized the rapid alignment of French practices with Arab ways of warfare. Yusuf was born Corsican and captured while still an infant by Barbary pirates, who sold him to the Dey of Tunisia. After converting to Islam, he learned Arabic and received a military

---

9. The Dey himself was deported to Naples. The janissaries and other Turks were transferred to Anatolia.

education. In 1830, he fled Tunisia under extraordinary circumstances and offered his services to the French in Algiers. Initially an interpreter, he wasted no time establishing a "private" unit of Arab horsemen, deploying them in spontaneous raids around Algiers. There followed a string of military exploits, with Yusuf having himself named Bey of Constantine in anticipation of his conquest of that city, which was firmly held by a Turkish governor allied with Arab tribes. He would end his career with the rank of general.

To ensure that the war was conducted properly, the French Army began recruiting Algerians, forming entire battalions exclusively consisting of natives. The famous *zouaves*[10] were established in August 1830, or barely a month after the fall of Algiers. They consisted of seasoned companies of light infantry used to hardship. They were ideal for penetrating hostile terrain with little in the way of logistical support.

The initial core recruited in 1830 was drawn from Arab and Berber soldiers who had served the Ottomans. France thus took possession of a reservoir of know-how and behavior it sorely lacked. In doing so, it also inaugurated what would become a tradition of raising native troops within the first days of invasion.

The incorporation of Algerians into the French Army was to prove such a success that their trace may be found in all of its overseas operations of the nineteenth century: Crimea, Mexico, Tunisia, Indochina, Madagascar . . . Later, in 1912, Algerian troops under the French flag would enter Morocco to establish the protectorate (a century on, can you imagine today's Moroccans scolding Algerians for this, citing the duty of remembrance?).

The lack of any clear policy from Paris put all responsibility on the shoulders of the military. Initially, they were satisfied with securing the regions surrounding the coastal cities: Algiers, Oran, Annaba. This changed in 1832 when Abdelkader, a West Algerian worthy, for the first time assembled a large-scale tribal coalition. He forced the French to plunge deeper into the country's interior, ultimately convincing them that its conquest would be long and painful. Abdelkader fought the war that he had to fight: razzia, ambush, the constant movement of troops and supplies. He was a depressing target for a European army accustomed to demolishing enemy barracks, bridges, and

---

10. The word *zouave* originally referred to *zwawi*, the name given to the Kabyle tribes who had for ages specialized in supplying soldiers to the Ottomans. Over time, Arabs from every region in Algeria were recruited, as well as Frenchmen.

cities. Abdelkader had none of those things, he had no infrastructure nor any bases to bombard; he was pure mobility.

With time, the military became convinced that Abdelkader would make a better partner than enemy. He received western Algeria (excepting Oran), while the French got the rest of the territory, where much work still needed to be done to establish their authority. This compromise provided the basis for the treaty of Tafna, which was signed on May 20th, 1837. In December of the same year, the French took Constantine.

With peace restored, Abdelkader settled scores with the tribes who had collaborated with France, massacring and deporting them. France was indifferent to their suffering (a tendency that would resurface 130 years later with the *harkis*). But Abdelkader did not just wish to punish; he also dreamed of building. He founded an embryonic state with a capital city and its own currency, administrative services, tax system, army, and diplomatic corps. He relied heavily on the Sultan of Morocco, seeing himself as a kind of vassal of the latter. In return, he received weapons and horses as well as a promise of military support.

When war resumed in 1839, Abdelkader was the sole master of western Algeria and the forces at his disposal had grown tenfold. Paradoxically, it was at this time that Algeria's fate was sealed, since France was now completely focused on unifying the territory. The time of limited occupation had come to an end. Algeria as it would later come to be known was born of France's decision to rid itself of Abdelkader.

The war would be long (eight years) and cruel, and would witness collective punishment, massacres, *enfumades*,[11] to say nothing of the ravages of such diseases as malaria and dysentery, which would decimate French and Algerians alike.

An Explosive but Mainly Divided Resistance

Faced with the invader, Algerians reacted as their mores dictated: they were ferocious, even heroic, but also disorganized and inconsistent. They inflicted significant losses on the French, but never formed a united front against the

---

11. Trans. a specific technique used during the colonization of Algeria, involving the use of smoke to flush out or suffocate resistance in fortified locations or caves where natives sought refuge.

enemy. Resistance was never as intense as the divisions between the Algerians themselves, which might lead one to believe that there was no national sentiment but rather xenophobia and abhorrence of the Christian; that there was as yet no Algerian identity but rather a fierce love of autonomy.

The only possible response was unity, and this was embodied by an exceptional man ahead of his time: Abdelkader. Where his compatriots saw only Arabs and Berbers, elite tribes and ordinary tribes, masters and slaves, country people and city dwellers, nomads and settled people, mountain dwellers and farmers of the plain, he saw a country. Abdelkader was the man of Algerian nationhood, not a feudal lord of the Arab Middle Ages (which only came to an end in the mid-twentieth century, and even then . . .).

He called for holy war, jihad. Did he have any other choice to transcend tribal divisions? He had to set in motion a body torn apart by 300 years of Ottoman domination in which centrifugal forces had been nurtured and amplified to prevent Algeria from putting up a "united front." To stitch Algeria back together, it was necessary to unite it around a higher principle, the only one that made sense at the time: jihad and its corollary, hatred of the foreigner.

Tribal Dislocation

"We are at peace with the outside world for a good reason: I instigated war among the Arabs themselves"

Thus said General Boyer, governor of Oran in 1831.

Without Abdelkader, Algerian resistance would have been nothing more than a long succession of ambushes, surprise attacks, and last stands—a bit like the pacification of Morocco, which took 20 years, patiently advancing to the southeast along the ridge of the Atlas Mountains. A succession of heroic calvary charges against the backdrop of one long, unbroken retreat faced with the European war machine. Thanks to Abdelkader, Algeria not only slowed the French advance but also discovered a collective future.

Like Bolivar, constantly hindered by the short-term thinking of his associates, Abdelkader was stymied by the cancer of Algeria: disunity, a disease that postponed his achievement and was among the reasons for France's victory.

It is disunity that explains the early and enduring support of several tribes for the French cause.

Among the first to change sides were the *makhzen* tribes of Oran, the Smela and Douair. In 1832, they courted the French without any great conviction, more to sound them out than out of any desire to draw up a treaty committing the two parties. Indeed, at that very moment, "cadres" from these tribes were fighting alongside Abdelkader, while others were in talks with the Sultan of Morocco, who had dispatched his own troops to Mascara, deep within Algerian territory.

Three years later, with the Moroccans gone and the French having won numerous battles against Abdelkader, the Smela and Douair once and for all joined the French.

It would be easy to accuse them of collaborating with the enemy, but it is more important to understand their motives. These men had no concept of nation or sovereignty. They knew only freedom and honor, and freedom meant keeping the hungry lion at bay: first Turkey, then France. Honor meant carrying a saber and mounting a horse to defend one's women and property. It meant convincing the lion to hire you as an auxiliary instead of humiliating you and stripping you of your privileges.

It is not our place to judge this value system, simply to understand it.

Reflections of this kind are foreign to the postcolonialists and other Manichaeans. Confronted with nuance, they despair; presented with unalloyed guilt, they become radiant.

Put yourself in the shoes of an ordinary tribe like the Beni Moussa from the backcountry of Algiers, who from time immemorial had literally kissed the hands of the Hadjout horsemen to avoid being raided. One fine day in 1830, you see the French soldiers arrive. Initially, your abhorrence of Christianity leads you to fight them. You find yourself waging war alongside the Hadjouts, your hateful and revolting oppressors. Yet the more you get to know the enemy—how he eradicates banditry and delivers impartial justice—the more you start hoping for his victory so as to finally free yourself from the "wolf who has been eating you for generations."

Racial Disunity

The country's racial divisions profoundly affected the history of Algerian resistance. Kabyles and Arabs conducted two different wars against the occupation: first the Arabs between 1830 and 1848, and then later the Kabyles.

There were of course occasionally instances of collaboration, but never anything like a joint uprising against France.

Religious Disunity

By sheer "luck," the French never had to confront a united religious league, much less an alliance between religious brotherhoods and tribes.

The brotherhoods' failure to coordinate was the result of mutual jealousy. Emir Abdelkader (a member of the Qadiriyya brotherhood) could thus not count on the Taibiyya which, with around 80,000 members, could have been a great help to him. It would not be until 1845 that the Taibiyya leadership raised the alarm and joined the insurrection—several weeks after the Emir had been defeated at the battle of Isly in Morocco, where Bugeaud wiped out the Moroccan-Algerian forces.

Similarly, Abdelkader was never able to count on the powerful Rahmaniyya order, its great hostility towards Christian incursion into Africa notwithstanding. This does not mean that the members of this order put up no resistance, but they fought in their own corner, never coordinating with Abdelkader. Indeed, the great moment of Rahmaniyya resistance took place in 1871, when this powerful order joined forces with the Mokrani of Kabylia. By then, however, Abdelkader was in exile in Syria, awaiting death.

The brotherhoods resisted the French in the same way they had entered the world and prospered: chaotically.

Even within the same brotherhood, dissension was so great that one faction might declare jihad while another chose inaction. In 1871, the Sidi Ali Bou Azouz faction never joined the rest of the Rahmaniyya brotherhood, its members perhaps recalling the insurrection of 1865 in which their brothers left them to fend for themselves against the French.[12]

Little surprise, then, that the Algerians lost the war. Their disunity counted for as much as the cruelty of French forces, their superior organization, and their weaponry.

Abdelkader surrendered in 1847. The most difficult and most important phase of the conquest was over: with the exception of Kabylia, a few mountain ranges, and some areas such as Zibans bordering the desert, northern Algeria was by and large in the hands of the French.

In 1847, the French may have had a colony, but they still had no plan for

---

12. For an accessible account of the rivalries between religious brotherhoods in North Africa, see: "Les sociétés secrètes chez les Arabes et la conquête de l'Afrique du Nord", *Revue des Deux Mondes*, 1884.

it. They had fought blindly, more in reaction to Algerian resistance than with open eyes in knowledge of the facts. Indeed, what was the French cause in 1847?

No Project for Algeria

After twenty years on the ground, France was not at all convinced of the colonial project's viability. Once the initial illusions had evaporated, the prospect of easy money or the fusion of peoples was no longer on the table. Rapidly, Algeria went from being an opportunity to being a bottomless pit. There were two opposing visions of the path forward: leave after having spent a fortune on conquering the country or make the best of a bad situation and rise to the challenge in the hope of eventually "breaking even." The second option won out, almost by inertia, with France gradually becoming mired in a quagmire of its own making: too much had already been sacrificed to simply pack it all in or withdraw to the coast. France had not gone to the trouble of defeating and exiling Abdelkader to just pull out!

The decision to remain in Algeria was also a matter of not losing face with other European powers, especially England. It was a question of pride and self-esteem. Even as clear-sighted a mind as Tocqueville's subscribed to the idea that retreat meant decadence and a loss of standing for France among its peers.

"I do not think France can seriously consider leaving Algeria. To give up in such a way would be in the eyes of the world a clear sign of its decadence . . . Any people that easily gives up what it has taken and on its own initiative retires peacefully to its original borders proclaims that its age of greatness is over . . . Those who say we are buying at the price of too great sacrifice what advantages Algeria may offer are right."

These remarks come from 1841, when there was still time to leave. The conquest was not yet complete, and colonization (in the sense of settlement) had hardly begun. At that time, the colonists had yet to move beyond the southern suburbs of Algiers.

Algeria was a burden. Any development necessarily raised hopes for a return on investment as uncertain as it was distant. Bugeaud, one of the figureheads of the conquest, let it be known that the lack of security meant that colonists would never be able to move beyond the coastal area. Worse, the climate was so harsh and the soil so poor that the state itself would have to single-handedly finance any new farms in the first years after they had been established.

The reports sent by soldiers revealed the alarm felt by officers when they realized that there was no question of farming Algeria without spending enormous sums and inventing unconventional methods.

Bugeaud argued that converting soldiers into armed agricultural colonists was the only way to deeply penetrate the territory without having to mobilize an army of 100,000 men. Ismaïl Urbain[13] suggested entrusting farming of the country's interior to Muslim fighters who had joined the French cause. In doing so, he was proposing an updated version of the Turkish practice whereby loyal Arabs, along with their wives and children, were settled in the midst of unruly populations. The mission of the newcomers was to secure the surroundings while taking care of their land, in return for which they were exempted from all taxation.

No sooner had Algeria been born than it was at risk of collapsing. The country was bogged down in a frustrating and costly status quo in which the state single-handedly financed pauperized colonists while the army kept the superficially subdued Arabs in check.

The more time passed, the more tightly bound the metropole became to its colony. There was no turning back. The trap had snapped shut. The settlements of colonists en masse starting in 1848 complicated the political equation, for henceforth heed would need to be taken of French public opinion in Algeria. The latter had little use for balancing the public purse, it wanted to survive and prosper. It would force the hand of the Second Empire (1852–1870) and take the Third Republic (1871–1940) hostage.

In private correspondence with his ambassador in London, Napoleon III stated that "despite its advantages for the future, Algeria is a source of weakness for France, which for thirty years now has given it the best of its blood and its gold . . ."[14]

Despite his pessimism, however, Napoleon III would propose what was

---

13. Ismail Urbain (1813–1884) is an unusual figure. A journalist, interpreter, and great friend of the Algerian people, he had a ringside seat for the conquest. Having converted to Islam long before his experience in Algeria, he attempted to propose a political and administrative formula capable of guaranteeing Algerian identity and the modernization of Algerian society. He genuinely loved the Algerians as they were and would have liked France to be their benefactor and not their persecutor. Like all original minds with a talent for nuance, he was sidelined by the hawks and radicals.
14. Letter from Napoleon III to Persigny, French Ambassador to London, July 29th, 1860.

certainly the most decent and promising model for the future of Algeria. In fact, the Second Empire tried to offer Algerians a mode of government that might prove tolerable to them and preserve most of their interests, starting with their way of life.

For Napoleon III, Algeria should have constituted a trinity: a French settler colony that occupied the plains and preferred coastal regions to the interior; an Arab kingdom in which Islam and the tribal way of life were preserved; and a military base, since a large army would be needed to ensure the peaceful coexistence of Arabs and French.

When Napoleon III referred to an Arab kingdom, he of course included Kabylia, even though it is Berber. He above all demonstrated an innovative vision that, had it been implemented, might have been a little less traumatic for the Algerian people.

He wanted to "confine" the French to the country's coastal fringe and push the Arabs towards the inland plateaus (the Kabyles being invulnerable in their mountain redoubt, which jutted into the sea). These two worlds, these two "Algerias," would have been separated by a ring of forts and watchtowers protected by spahis, who were predominantly native troops.

Napoleon III genuinely admired the Algerian Muslim way of life, their skill as warriors, their nomadism, their attachment to tradition. He wanted to benevolently protect them and, who knows, perhaps one day make them part of an Arab empire that would extend beyond the frontiers of Algeria. The French sovereign had his sights on the inevitable collapse of the Ottoman Empire, which, from Tunis to Damascus, by way of Jerusalem, would free the Arab peoples living under its yoke. In this connection, he had long seen Abdelkader, exiled in Damascus since 1852, as a potential candidate for embodying the Arab "renaissance" in the Middle East when the time came. Napoleon III was a "pan-Arabist" before the fact.

Who among the postcolonialists knows that Algeria almost became an Arab kingdom under French leadership?

This genuinely revolutionary vision was bitterly opposed by the colonists, who had absolutely no interest in protecting Algerian interests. In their view, the idea of an Arab kingdom meant the end of colonization since the Arabs still held a large portion of the land.

Worse, the administration dragged its feet when it came to implementing Napoleon III's directives. History would take note of a letter from the Emperor to Governor-General MacMahon in which he reproached MacMahon for not informing him that a terrible famine had descended upon the Arabs, urging him to come to their aid.

Judge for yourself:

"I was sorry that, in your letter, you did not speak to me about the famine and wretchedness of the Arabs (attendant upon drought and typhus), for I would like to know where to stand on this subject, either for the purpose of increasing aid if necessary or for refuting the exaggerations spread by correspondence and newspapers. The day before yesterday, Marshall Randon reported to me that, according to letters he had received from various parts of Algeria, it was clear that 500,000 Arabs would die of hunger this year. I cannot fathom such a catastrophe, and, in any case, I find that the government of Algeria is not making enough of an effort, either to remedy the problem if it is so serious, or to dispel such harmful misconceptions."

(Napoleon III to MacMahon, January 1868)

We are here far removed from the image of a fascist and genocidal France . . .

The fall of the Second Empire shattered this original, humanistic ambition. Algeria was then transformed into two open-air prisons: one for the French, who reproduced the institutions of the metropole there, and another for the Algerians, pushed ever further away from the best land and pockets of prosperity. French Algeria, that of the *communes de plein exercice* (⅓ of the territory), turned its back on Algerian Algeria, that of the *communes mixtes*[15] (⅔ of the territory). The former partook of modernity; the latter lived in a Middle Age that refused to give up the ghost.

Demoralized and humiliated, Muslims suffered another shock when they saw the French administration gradually replace their traditional leaders, the offspring of noble lineages, with commoners whose only quality was loyalty to the occupier.

Defeat was accompanied by plunder. The Third Republic effectively turned a blind eye to the theft of more than 500,000 hectares by colonists

---

15. Trans.: *Communes de plein exercice* were municipalities governed by elected mayors and councils; *communes mixtes* were governed by a mix of appointed French administrators and elected officials.

in the context of various land registry and land ownership reforms between 1871 and 1890.

By the end of the nineteenth century, Muslims presented the hideous face of a drowned man left adrift, a zombie floating in the pool to which he has been confined by army and administration.

Algeria was disfigured.

CONQUEST ON THE CHEAP

"In the colonies, one must spare the country and its inhabitants . . ."

GALLIENI

Having witnessed the vital interests of France being sacrificed for the benefit of the colonists, soldiers retained a painful memory of Algeria. What were the vital interests of France? (a) Making the conquest profitable by seeing to it that the colonization of Algeria proceeded in an efficient and sober manner (economically sober, that is), an objective that the transposition of French-style administration to Algeria and its concomitant operating costs rendered stillborn. (b) Giving as many Algerians as possible a stake in the new regime by leaving them a piece of the pie, even if it meant seeing to it that they specialized in tasks shunned by the French (such as raising livestock). This implied a minimum of respect be shown for their way of life and property. But this was anathema to the colonists, who had not come to Algeria to accommodate Muslims. Their mentality was that of conquerors (or upstarts), and they looked upon the Algerians like the Americans looked upon the Sioux of the Wild West, a negligible mass to be eradicated or confined to a reservation.

This manner of seeing the situation was on the minds of the senior officers and administrators who would be tasked with establishing colonies starting in the 1880s. They would of course commit errors and abuses, but they nevertheless all tried to distance themselves from the Algerian counter-model.

The Doctrine of Constructive Conquest

French soldiers gradually developed specialized know-how for carrying out conquest without devastating the territory or unduly traumatizing the population. It was a philosophy unique to France, a mix of brutality and humanism, and might be summed up in the expression *constructive conquest*.

Lyautey wonderfully defined it as follows:

"Conquest without unnecessary violence, without bitterness, which aims to win hearts even more than territory; conquest with a view to immediate organization, to building confidence and developing the land: in a word, constructive conquest."

To which he added:

"The very basis of my entire doctrine of colonial war is the negation of preliminary, violent force; it involves sending local troops and intelligence officers trained in Muslim customs as scouts. It is this way of proceeding that minimizes effort, risk, and the loss of human life, and that leaves the least damage in its wake, as soon as the concern is to build, which is the goal, the ultimate goal, of every colonial war."[1]

This methodology was first developed in the final phase of the pacification of Tonkin (1892–1896) and the conquest of Madagascar (1895–1896), where these techniques were consolidated and documented as such.

I have quoted Lyautey, but he is "just" the most famous disciple of his predecessor and leader, Gallieni.

Gallieni described what he expected from his troops as follows: "Colonial war is compared to war of Europe, where the goal is to destroy the main forces of the enemy. In the colonies, one must spare the country and its inhabitants, since the former is destined to host our future colonial ventures,

1. This quotation, as well as the information relating to the history of the *goums* in Morocco, comes from an article by Colonel Arnaud de la Grand'Rive, published at the website of the *Centre du Doctrine et d'Enseignement du Commandement de l'Armée de Terre*: https://www.penseemiliterre.fr/le-recrutement-la-formation-et-l-emploi-des-troupes-locales-comme-vecteur-strategique-de-succes-chez-lyau-tey-2-4_114113_1013077.html

and the latter will be our principal agents and collaborators in the success of these ventures."[2]

In practice, the French philosophy would result in a kind of ripple effect, the ultimate goal of which was control of the population. Its originators wagered that, to control a territory, it was enough to control the civilians (individuals, families, tribes) who lived there. Instead of spending a fortune and wasting lives to hold the high ground and roads, it was better to ensure that villagers accept the French presence and perhaps even see it as to their benefit. They would in this way become propagandists for France's action and monitor the territory themselves, since it was above all their home.

This way of doing things was slower than a classic military campaign. For, at each step, all had to be redone. At the outset, force was used (combat, ambushes, sweeps), surrender was obtained, and basic services were provided by way of compensation. To prove that France kept its word, troops were raised from among the freshly subdued rebels to keep the peace locally and subsequently advance on neighboring zones still under rebel control. Hence the idea of a ripple effect.

Recruited from the ranks of yesterday's defeated rebels, these native soldiers were themselves an excellent propaganda weapon: they were well fed, well led, their religion was respected, and they were allowed to keep their wives and property. They embodied the new order and the promise of a bright future under French supervision.

The pacification of Morocco more or less followed the same system. With every conquest, a *goum* was raised, a company consisting of native cavalry and infantry commanded by French officers. The *goumiers* prevented defections among their own tribe and kept an eye on neighbors who were still in revolt. Indeed—and it was no accident—the *goums* were long commanded by intelligence officers.

By the time pacification reached its end in 1934, Morocco counted 51 *goums* employing 10,000 men, both Arab and Berber.

The conquerors of Morocco relied on a precious resource that was unknown at the time of the conquest of Algeria: colonial troops. These foreign troops had a formidable psychological impact on populations tempted by resistance. They demoralized them when they looked the same, spoke the same

---

2. *Rapport d'ensemble sur la pacification, l'organisation et la colonisation de Madagascar* (full citation in bibliography).

language, and practiced the same religion. This was the case of the Algerian and Tunisian infantrymen deployed in Morocco. And they intimidated them when they were of another race. Imagine the fear and astonishment that gripped Moroccans when 4000 Senegalese infantrymen landed at the port of Casablanca in 1912: tall men dressed in red burnooses who had come from Saint-Louis in Senegal and were preceded by a reputation for being merciless warriors devoted to their French officers.

To spare metropolitan troops, the military "internationalized" conquest and pacification by relying on soldiers from other colonies. While Morocco was exemplary in this respect, it was just one example among many others. In Madagascar in the 1880s, one already finds Algerian soldiers serving France. Apart from Algeria, almost no colony was conquered without the decisive contribution of native soldiers, crossing the world to "give a kicking" to peoples they had never met and who had done them no harm. The conquest of the colonies was in its way a sort of world war pitting the Third World against itself.

Bargain-Hunting

The lessons of the Algerian fiasco were taken to heart. The new methods of pacification clearly indicate as much, as did the adoption of the protectorate model. First implemented in Tunisia in 1881, the latter was an implicit *mea culpa* for the Algerian experience. It consisted of a system of safeguards meant to ensure that the interests of natives were (to some degree) taken into account. No one wanted to turn them into "lost souls" forced to adapt to a world they had not chosen. The protectorate model was understood to entail a sort of partnership—an unequal one, to be sure, but a real one all the same.

From a financial point of view, the protectorate was committed to practicing greater sobriety than was possible under (Algerian-style) direct administration, in which a cohort of civil servants was transferred overseas together with their wives and children, paid vacations, and hardship allowances. On paper, the protectorate was a "light" administration to the degree that precolonial-era institutions were partly retained to perform certain tasks, such as urban management and settling disputes among natives.

Jules Ferry himself sang the praises of the protectorate in these terms:

"For the metropole, the protectorate is much more economical. It does not require that horde of civil servants [. . .] ill-suited to properly managing the native population."[3]

This was in 1884. As an administrative and political project, Algeria had already become fossilized, an extension of everything that was most burdensome and hopeless about French bureaucracy. It had been disfigured by the attempt to make it fit the mold of France rather than being attentive to its needs and helping it advance towards progress.

However crazy French colonization may have been, there was at least an attempt to change tack after the Algerian catastrophe.

That said, the scope of reform was far from adequate. There was not enough "innovation" on the part of civil servants, and this was particularly true of civilians, since the military had at least thoroughly revised its doctrine of conquest and pacification. Civilians, for their part, barely succeeded in producing the protectorate concept, which was promising but lacked real depth: to do otherwise would have required clarifying its procedures and training personnel to embody them and carry them out. Were the protectorate to be anything other than a scale model, in other words, an experimental object produced in a lab and likely to collapse upon contact with real life, the whole thing would have had to be built with reinforced concrete. The concept was contrary to the natural instincts of the conquerors: who would want to share power with a sultan or prince whom one had just subjugated? Who was going to consult with the leader of a tribe whose race and customs sometimes disgusted him? Leaving these questions unanswered or with no clear response risked dooming the doctrine of the protectorate to failure. For arrogance and racism are found more abundantly in nature than humility and political intelligence.

The protectorate lacked "flesh and bones." For it had always been a cold monster, a disembodied machine that *managed* rather than *governed*. But while a department could be *managed*, a colony had to be *governed*. It was a real country that pined for its lost sovereignty. Its inhabitants needed to be consoled and convinced they still had rights. More than exercising power themselves, the masses wanted to see it in the hands of minorities with the time, determination, and desire to see to it. These were the native elites: traditional

---

3. Speech delivered in the Chamber of Deputies, October 20th, 1884.

chiefs, worthies, religious leaders, and so on. And yet the native elites, whether old or new, were rarely at the forefront. They should have been included in economic planning and actively involved in decision-making. Instead, they were relegated to the more comfortable role of an opposition figure that criticizes and makes promises. This was the flesh with which the exposed nerves of the protectorate should have been covered. In short, the politico-administrative apparatus needed to be "adorned" were it to appear legitimate in the eyes of the native population. Such adornment might have consisted of mere theatrical costumes, little matter: the essential thing was to pretend that power was being exercised collaboratively.

In Morocco under Lyautey, this administrative symbiosis was taken as far as it could go. It was never perfect, far from it, but it was pursued with enthusiasm and selflessness. But how many Lyautey's did France have at its disposal? Such men were not built on the assembly line, alas. And even the protectorate of Morocco ultimately collapsed after Lyautey's departure. As we shall see, though his disciples stayed on and preserved his heritage as best they could, bureaucracy eventually prevailed over initiative and power-sharing with the Moroccans.

Elsewhere, including Senegal and Madagascar, where direct administration was the rule, the civilians were left to their own devices. In administering the territory assigned them, they had to make do with scant resources and little in the way of doctrine. As soon as one stepped out of capitals and large cities like Dakar and Brazzaville, their isolation was palpable. Far from the eyes of Paris and its over-zealous bureaucrats, they were viceroys without court or treasure, tossed into a sea of humanity that lived off of hunting, gathering, and non-intensive agriculture. The best among them, the noblest souls, moved heaven and earth to serve the natives. The budding dictators, by contrast, became bigheaded, spitting on them and liberally dispensing blows. This is what happens in a system of governance pieced together from scratch to steer an empire born from a feeding frenzy.

NATIVES CONQUERING NATIVES

"He knows how to deliberately sacrifice his property, his family, and even more easily his life. No tribe came to us spontaneously. None submitted without a fight, some having exhausted their last means of resistance".

GENERAL GUILLAUME

"The French and the Annamites certainly fought one another with their weapons and men, but the game was drawn up and decided by a few hundred individuals, perhaps just a few dozen: naval officers, administrators, and missionaries on one side; high mandarins on the other, with 'traitors' and interpreters among them, for very few spoke the other's language."

PHILIPPE DEVILLERS[1]

There was never any unanimity among those who were to be colonized. Some took up arms, others merely pretended to resist the invasion, and yet others, more numerous than is generally acknowledged, were delighted by the arrival of French troops. They had their reasons: weary of their masters' arbitrary rule, French colonization was a deliverance for millions of Arabs, Africans, and Indochinese.

For every shot fired by France, those who had something to gain from regime change twice planted their knifes in the back of the future colonies.

---

1. Philippe Devillers (1920–2016) was a French journalist and historian. This quotation is taken from *"Français et annamites, Partenaires ou ennemis ? 1856–1902* (Denoël, 1998).

Yet this complexity does not disarm the postcolonialists and merchants of outrage, for whom history is to be read in black and white or not at all.

Those who resisted, for their part, rarely presented a united front against France. At every turn, the path of the freedom fighters was undermined by discord, unruliness, and disorganization.

Between Boos and Bravos

When someone wants to invade your country, you may behave in one of three ways: resist, take refuge in apathy, or rally behind the new order.

Let us not judge; let us simply try to understand the motives of each party. If we can succeed in penetrating this mystery, our efforts will have been useful.

Those Who Resisted from the Outset

Warlike populations mounted immediate and uncompromising resistance to French conquest. It was a matter of tradition, mentality, and environment. Between a Tuareg and a gentleman from Fez there existed a difference of civilization resulting from centuries of separate evolution, each adapting as best he could to his ecosystem. The Tuareg was nothing if not fearless and aggressive; the Fassi was nothing if not soft and sophisticated. It was the difference between the plunderer of caravans and the shipowner who financed the caravans, the abyss between short and long term, the irreconcilable gap between ambush and embrace. The Tuareg lived on the edge of destitution and seized what was not his; the Fassi accumulated assets and paid those stronger than him to protect them. One created danger, the other bought security. Two humanities, two *arts de vivre* that dictated different conduct when faced with foreign invasion. Both hated the invaders but, where one resisted them with the saber, the other countered with a dignified hostility combining indifference and snobbery.

One does not become hard and courageous overnight. It is always the result of a story that began centuries ago. Among the human groups that fired the first shots against the French are to be found a few common traits:

- **The capacity to rapidly mobilize,** that is, to shift from a state of peace to one of war in the blink of an eye. This meant then and there dropping everything (fields, harvests, workshops) and taking up position. Whence the decisive advantage of tribal organization, in which everyone already knows his rank and is accustomed to obeying his elders.

- **Mobility,** in the sense that fighting a Western army required drawing it into terrain where it would struggle to make the most of its arsenal. This presupposed that one was able to flee deep into the deserts, mountains, caves, and swamps. This was not for everyone, especially as one very often had to bring one's women and children along to prevent them from being taken hostage by the French or their allies. Nomadic populations obviously had an advantage in this regard, but sedentary Annamite peasants were also known to abandon their crops and fall back—sometimes to the lands of other tribes—for as long as the business of making war demanded.

- **Hatred of the foreigner** because he is a foreigner and thus a potential spy and invader in embryonic form. This xenophobia often went hand in hand with religious fanaticism. One thinks immediately of Muslims here, but one might also mention the Vietnamese, whose fondness for Confucianism made them loathe Christianity. And even among the most devout Muslims, attitudes towards the French were not uniform: in Algeria, the Tijaniyyah brotherhood was in favor of coming to an understanding with the newcomers whereas their rivals, the Senusiyya brotherhood, demanded all-out war.

- **Having everything to lose should the new order be established.** This was especially true of tribes accustomed to pillage and plunder. For them, France was an existential threat, for it brought internal order and security to the roads.

The tribes were not the only ones to oppose French penetration. In some circumstances, the state or intransigent factions thereof attempted to stand in the way of colonization.

In Madagascar, the monarchy long put up intense resistance to colonization. Between 1883 and 1895, it used both diplomatic and military means to resist France's embrace. It simultaneously defended Malagasy sovereignty and its own political and civilizational project, which consisted of uniting the people of the Big Island under the hegemony of the Merina people. France's entry upon the scene in the late nineteenth century disrupted this historic process and the homogenization of culture, language, and mores to which it tended. The Merina, the main protagonists in this process, thus had every reason in the world to reject colonization and support their state to that end.

At the same time on the other side of the world, mandarins led popular resistance in Vietnam. This was triggered by France's July 1885 siege of the Court of Hue, the seat of Vietnamese royal power. Disgusted by this insult, several went underground to "save the king." Their call was heard by the peasants, who in a blink of an eye became partisans, quickly accustoming themselves to clandestine warfare. In Vietnam and Madagascar alike, France came up against a bureaucratic backbone with a lofty conception of its mission and a great sway over the population.[2]

The Soft and Defenseless

Resistance is a skill not possessed by soft and peaceful populations who, for reasons of status or tradition, have no experience of force or violence. Once again, there is no value judgment here, just a genuine desire to understand and account for these phenomena. Populations incapable of resistance included:

The Jews of Morocco, Algeria, and Tunisia, who were defenseless and forever ostracized by their Muslim brothers. Over time, they gravitated towards the only domains where they could be safe: trade, finance, and craftwork. Occupations for meticulous, peaceable, prudent people.

The urban bourgeoisie of the Maghreb, guardians of an intense cultural and religious life. Tétouan, Salé, Fez, Meknes, Tlemcen, Constantine, Kairouan, and Tunis were all islands of refined civilization in the midst of a hostile ocean infested with peasants and rough horsemen: the Shilha of Morocco, the Kabyle of Algeria, the Fraichiches of the High Steppes of western Tunisia.

Tribes that had long been the vassals of the central authority, such as the Angad of the Oujda region of Morocco. Their "DNA" was legalistic, and they were naturally inclined to align with the party most likely to establish a just and stable order. They did not commit themselves from the outset to France, preferring instead to engage in skirmishes and create problems, but they were ultimately open to the prospect of falling in line behind it. After a campaign of conquest designed more to impress the enemy than destroy him, Lyautey and such lieutenants as Poeymirau were able to skillfully win them over to the cause of colonization.

---

2. It is common knowledge that the mandarins were above all a technocracy, recruited on the basis of academic merit rather than martial prowess.

Those who had nothing to lose. Many towns and villages fed up with insecurity merely shook their heads when news reached them that a French expeditionary had arrived. There may even have been a glimmer of hope in some eyes. What a relief news of the Treaty of Fez (1912) must have been for the inhabitants of Taza in Morocco, whose town had been invaded by the Riata, a mountain people skilled in plunder. Its unfortunate inhabitants had been reduced to paying a toll every time they wanted to fetch water from the fountain, located outside the town walls . . . How would you have reacted in their place? For my part, I would not have lifted a finger to defend the freedom of those who shook me down and held me hostage in my own home. Put yourself in the shoes of a peaceful peasant of Upper Tonkin, whose only sin was preferring to grow rice rather than bear arms, and who shook with fear every time he sighted on the horizon the black flag of Chinese pirates, once again come to terrorize the population. This was the soil from which support for France grew, filled with the terrified cries of an industrious and defenseless humanity.

Those Who Immediately Rallied Behind France

Those for whom colonization was literally liberation. Did the Dogon and Bambara of West Africa, peoples reduced to slavery by their neighbors, really have any choice but to collaborate with their liberators? Or were they supposed to find common cause with the monsters who had reduced them to objects? From Senegal to Congo, the desire to avenge oneself against the enslavers was without doubt the French army's best recruitment tool. The *tirailleur* was a product of the intra-African slave trade: he threw in his lot with France to give those who had deported and tormented his ancestors a taste of their own medicine.

Those for whom colonization was the last resort before collapse. These were the elites and regimes circling the abyss and who risked being swallowed up should France not stand between them and chaos. This was clearly the case in Tunisia, where the Dey was bankrupt, and his administration was hanging by a thread (Bardo Treaty, 1881). A similar atmosphere reigned in Fez in 1912, where the regime hated France but rejoiced upon learning that a French contingent had been stationed in Bab Mahrez (a southern suburb) to act as a buffer against the troublesome tribes of the Middle Atlas.

Morocco Conquered Morocco with the Help of France

In this regard, it is worth dwelling on the case of Morocco, which is in many respects exceptional. Indeed, France conquered Morocco on behalf of the Moroccan state and in collaboration with it. Colonization was synonymous with *restoration* and *reunification*. It restored the authority of the sultan, which had been violently challenged by regional powers, and it reunified the national territory under the aegis of a strict and inflexible central adminis- tration. At the top of this administration, one of course found the representa- tives of France, but one also found Moroccan Makhzen who, at least in theory, signed off on the decrees of the Resident-General and approved the policy being conducted in the country.

From 1912 to 1934, the French and Moroccans jointly pacified Morocco. Military operations simultaneously employed four groups of combatants: (ethnic) French troops, Moroccan troops from the army of the Sultan, *goumi- ers* under the leadership of (ethnic) French officers or Algerian and Tunisian NCOs, and tribal forces under the command of the great caids who had rallied to the cause.

In many places, Moroccans conquered and subjugated other Moroccans under the watchful eye of a handful of French "consultants." During the First World War, Sharifian troops (army of the Sultan) thus took it upon them- selves to pacify the Agadir region and raise the tricolor flag! At the same time and continuing through the late 1920s, the men of Caïd Glaoui saw to the pacification of a large part of the High Atlas on behalf of France and the Sultan.

In addition to being a genuine Franco-Moroccan partnership, pacification was also a civil war between Moroccans. The tribes fought each other for a variety of more or less acceptable reasons: vendettas, a taste for razzia, sup- port for or rejection of colonization, defense of the Sultan or a desire to be freed of his yoke. Moroccans threw themselves upon other Moroccans, giv- ing the French an extraordinary opportunity to conquer the country without undue sacrifice of metropolitan soldiers. An extraordinary phenomenon: no sooner had they been defeated than many tribes rallied heart and soul behind France. This attitude is difficult to explain without delving into the Maghrebin mentality, where fear and respect often precede passionate love. Repeatedly defeated by an adversary who was valiant without being cruel, tribesmen con- ceded that France had a title to govern them. The facts proved them right, for as pacification advanced (recall the *ripple effect*), security was established, trade found its feet, and life became at least a little sweeter.

Under these circumstances, the account of the Moroccan civil war offered by the sociologist, historian, and soldier Robert Montagne makes perfect sense:

> "From a common Franco-Moroccan desire for peace and development, a holy war initially conducted against the infidel is thus succeeded by a war to pacify rebellion in which an ever more powerful bloc of tribes are won over and successively bring pressure to bear on the rebels in the Middle Atlas, the Rif, the Central Atlas, the Jbel Saghro, and the 'Mauritanian borderlands.'"

Alongside the romantic and emotional aspects of this tremendous adventure may be discerned the logic of self-interest rightly understood. For at this juncture the monarchy and many traditional elites had an interest in seeing to it that anarchy end and Moroccans learn to obey. Until then, obedience and submission were contingent on circumstances. The chief had to be strong, visible, and capable of punishing the recalcitrant. As soon as he moved away or wavered, love of autonomy and the taste for insubordination meant that chaos would resume. The long-term stakes were thus as much political as they were civilizational, since it was a matter of establishing a new concept of authority in people's minds.

The Makhzen were the great beneficiaries of this earthquake. For the first time in many years, they had a say in the daily lives of peasants in the High Atlas and Sahara. In a country fractured by separatism, in which feudalism only gave way under force and compulsion, it was quite an achievement.

Another fundamental challenge was to unify the population under a common identity, that is, to see to it that Moroccans felt like Moroccans and not just Riffians, Soussis[3] or Fassis.[4] This was a prerequisite for cultivating a feeling of belonging distinct from religion, race, and tribe. Without a strong central authority capable of exerting a powerful influence on society, it would also have been impossible.

---

3. Inhabitants of Sous, a region located between Agadir and Taroudant.
4. Inhabitants of the town of Fez.

In 1916, with the pacification campaign having just begun, Lyautey brought together Moroccan notables, urban and rural alike, to deliver this message, which left no room for doubt:

" . . . And you all know the care with which I and all those who collaborate with me will always seek to ensure that rank and hierarchy are preserved and respected, that people and property remain where they have long been, that those who are natural leaders command, and that the others obey. And now, return to your provinces, filled with trust in the future and joy in your hearts, carry the good news wherever you go. I am counting on you to help Sidna[5] and me deal with the last agitators, who every day are fewer in number. Many among them are simply blind, unaware that here reigns good and order, and when the day comes that they open their eyes and know that nothing threatens their customs and interests, they will come to us, and I will receive them with open arms, and they will feel only regret that they had not understood earlier. Should there remain any who persist in sowing disorder, they will be quelled by the force that we will always be prepared to use when we see that no other means remain available to us."[6]

Amid the sobs of widows and orphans, the conquest of Morocco saw the shock of two competing visions for the country: centrality versus autonomy, order versus rebellion, unity versus diversity. The outcome of this battle was surely much more significant than the temporary loss of sovereignty. It caused Morocco to take a probably irreversible turn.

Postcolonialists and the professionally aggrieved reduce the history of a people to colonization. Yet this is hardly the only factor in the life of a people. Colonization or no colonization, Morocco had an appointment with modernity. Sooner or later, its society would be transformed and give birth to the phenomena briefly described above. And it is no secret that giving birth in this way is painful, even traumatic. How many heads had to roll in France to kill feudalism? How many villages had to burn to impose Jacobinism? How

---

5. Sidna (our lord), i.e., Sultan Moulay Youssef.
6. Taken from *Paroles d'Action*, a collection of speeches and public pronouncements given by Lyautey between 1900 to 1926.

many workers and miners had to lose their fingers to make the industrial revolution possible?

The alliance between Lyautey and a segment of the Moroccan population was as much a wise investment as a blatant "betrayal" of national sovereignty.

Being neither a judge nor prosecutor, I prefer to preserve this ambivalence.

PART III:

A RAW DEAL
(1905–1954)

COLONIAL DISAPPOINTMENT

"Of all the state's enterprises, colonization is the one that costs the most and brings in the least"

GUSTAVE DE MOLINARI[1]

The repentant and the hate-filled love to repeat in unison that France became rich at the expense of the colonies, that it became an industrial power after seizing the resources of its empire.

But this is not borne out by the facts. Colonization was a huge drain on public monies and human resources. From a strictly financial point of view, France would have been better off investing its capital and talent in the metropole or, for that matter, in Europe or the Americas. The success of a few companies that can be counted on one hand must not obfuscate the fact that the French colonies were a financial black hole.

During the two world wars, by contrast, and particularly the Second, the contributions of France's empire were invaluable, with the colonized peoples taking an active role in a struggle that was not their own. Without its empire, France would probably have figured among the war's losers rather than a party to the new world order. If France holds a veto in the UN today, it is at least partly thanks to the Africans and Arabs who fought by its side against Nazism.

---

1. Quoted by Charles Robert Ageron in *L'Anticolonialisme en France de 1871 à 1914* (PUF, 1973). Gustave Molinari (1819–1912) was a liberal Belgian economist.

An Economic Black Hole

Once the conquest was complete, France discovered it had been dealt a bad hand. The colonies had to be taught capitalism, a monetary economy and labor market had to be established, and infrastructure needed to be installed—all without access to local financial resources that might partly or fully cover this colossal effort. Unlike Great Britain and Belgium, France never had any pleasant mineral "surprises" that might have lightened its burden. Neither gold, diamond, or gems: French Africa lacked the blessed subsoil of Botswana or Belgian Congo. Nor did France ever have access to demographic "giants" like India, capable of wolfing down boundless quantities of manufactured goods.

France had to advance money from its own funds and wait for colonial economies to take off. This never happened: the black hole continued to expand all the way up to independence. With the exception of Indochina, which we shall consider shortly, the empire was a fiasco from the point of view of added value, growth, and profitability.

There is no data allowing us to summarize the economic performance of the colonies. Where they exist at all, the statistics are fragmentary for the early days of colonization. The historian Daniel Lefeuvre, a specialist on the subject, provides some keys for unlocking the mystery. The following paragraphs are inspired by his work.[2]

From 1900 to 1962, the foreign trade balance of the colonies was constantly negative.[3] Vis-à-vis the metropole, the trade balance was in deficit two out of every three years. These structural deficits were systematically covered by subsidies and loans from the French Treasury. Altogether, these trade deficits (foreign and metropolitan) amounted to 44 billion gold francs, or three times the aid given France by the United States after World War Two. Had it been invested in metropolitan France instead, this money would perhaps have accelerated reconstruction and boosted the country's economic performance during the "Trente Glorieuses."

Of course, some individuals and companies prospered in the empire. Fortunes were made, but France gained nothing in collective terms. France did not enrich itself; rather, France made it possible (by the provision of secu-

---

2. It cannot be overstated how strongly I recommend *Pour en finir avec la repentance coloniale*.
3. Except in 1926.

rity and infrastructure) for a few French and native entrepreneurs to enrich themselves. Among these happy few were foreigners, including Europeans (German, Belgian, and Dutch trading companies), Chinese merchants, Japanese industrialists, and so on. Their respective governments had not paid in blood to colonize, secure, and implement capitalism where formerly there had just been a subsistence economy or indeed slavery. They did not spend their wealth establishing an administration, guarding the borders, and installing sanitation networks. In Indochina, German merchants merely had to set up shop to start selling their wares, France having built Hanoi and Saigon for them in keeping with European standards. France had laid telegraph lines and built opera houses. In West Africa and Equatorial Africa, the Lebanese, Syrians, and Portuguese skillfully grafted themselves onto the French "war" effort. They certainly contributed to the region's well-being, but never paid the price of sovereignty. That was left to French taxpayers from the Vosges.

In the 1920s, Japan became the second-largest supplier to Morocco, which bought babouche slippers from it. Japanese business flourished even as French troops continued to grapple with resistance from the Atlas tribes. No matter, it was France that covered Morocco's trade deficit with Japan . . .

One might retort that France made up for this by plundering the empire's raw materials. But this is not true. It is just another received idea in need of deconstruction.

Throughout the colonial era, France sought these raw materials on the global market, just like countries with the wisdom to avoid engaging in colonization, such as Sweden, Switzerland, and Denmark. Its coal thus came from Germany, Great Britain, Belgium, and even the United States. Its cotton from the United States. Its wool came from Argentina and New Zealand. Its silk from Japan and China.

Coal was discovered and mined in Tonkin, but nowhere else. Fortunes were spent in vain trying to grow cotton in Algeria and the Niger Delta.

With the exception of phosphates from North Africa, the empire was a source of agricultural products like coffee, rice, cane sugar, cocoa, bananas, peanuts, and wine. These goods were to be had in abundance on the global market and at much lower prices. Colonial bananas were imported with a 20 percent markup over global market prices, as was palm oil from Benin and Cameroon. These prices were only possible due to a kind of "colonial preference," which consisted in barricading the empire behind discriminatory customs tariffs and requiring the businesses of the metropole to buy products *made in the*

Empire. The only advantage of paying more was that this allowed the purchase to be made in francs rather than foreign currencies.

Instead of working for the prosperity of France, the colonial system concerned itself with keeping colonial capitalists and producers on life support. The very definition of a bad deal.

In the case of Algeria, anticapitalism attained new heights. On the eve of independence, the Ministry of Finance estimated that France could reduce its expenditures by 68 percent if it stopped purchasing supplies in Algeria and instead relied on less costly partners like Spain or Italy.

The case of Algerian wine exemplified this "colonial delusion." The metropole was obliged to purchase its total output because, due to its inferior quality and excessive price tag, no one wanted it on the global market. Having little use for this product, it met a properly dreadful fate: one third was used as blending wine, and the rest was distilled . . . In a free economy, Algerian wine would have been wiped off the map.

Discovered by France at the end of the 1950s, Algerian oil was also a bad deal since it was not of the type sought by French industry. Instead, it had to be sold on the international market in order to purchase heavier fuel. In point of price and quality, it would have been more advantageous for the country to take its supplies from Libya. Once again and despite all common sense, the state forced oil distributors doing business in France to buy Algerian oil. This "Algerian preference" survived independence, with France continuing to prioritize Algerian oil in the 1960s, even though this ran counter to its interests.

As an outlet for the country's goods, the Empire was more of a hindrance than a help to the French economy. Lagging in point of competitivity, several metropolitan manufacturers found a captive market there. Protected by prohibitive customs tariffs, they sold their goods there without unduly fearing Japanese[4] or German competition. This comfortable situation could only delay the necessary modernization of the French production system.

---

4. Except in Morocco, where countries from the Far East had access to the market under the same conditions as France. This customs equality dates back to the Act of Algeciras, introduced in 1907, five years before the establishment of the Protectorate. It applied to all of Morocco's trade partners at the time, including the United States and Germany, but it was the Chinese (tea) and Japanese (manufactured products) who benefited the most. Their trade surpluses with Morocco heavily weighed on the accounts of the Protectorate, which had no choice but to honor the commitments made at Algeciras.

Indeed, by a curious coincidence, the growth rate of the French economy only resumed its place among the OECD's top three after 1962, the year Algeria gained its independence.

The Reasons for the Fiasco

What are the reasons for this failure? Five major factors explain the economic underperformance of the empire.

First, the relative poverty of mineral resources. France was never able to count on a mining "miracle" that could guarantee the liquidity necessary for developing the territory. As we have seen, the extraordinary resources of South African and Australian subsoils had no counterpart in the French colonies.

Second, the lack of skilled labor and properly acclimated capitalists. Once again, comparison with the British case is instructive. The latter had transported a corner of England to Southern Africa and Oceania, millions of workers who brought their capitalist values with them (the Protestant work ethic and a desire to get rich). The climate in these lands was not hostile to European man. It neither decimated his numbers nor prevented him from working. Nor was the agriculture there so different from that prevailing in Europe: corn, cotton, wine, wheat, wool, and so on. In these circumstances, it was easier to create an economy from scratch, for the most important thing, the human substrate, was present. France, by contrast, had no demographic surplus to export. And even if this had not been the case, it could not have put it to work, for its colonies were more the white man's grave than his garden of Eden: Saharan deserts, tropical bushland, and forests swarming with mosquitos.[5]

Third, the absence of large consumer markets. At the time of the conquest and the first decades of colonization, Sub-Saharan Africa was virtually empty. North Africa was also underpopulated. Great Britain, by contrast, could count on India and its extraordinary demography (already more than 150 million inhabitants in 1880). Moreover, it exported goods to its nationals, large numbers of whom had settled in Southern Africa and Oceania. In addition to their relatively large numbers (considerably more than those for the overseas

---

5. Algeria is an exception to this rule because its climate is similar enough to the climate in the south of France. Lacking French settlers, contingents from Europe (Malta, Italy, Spain, etc.) were introduced. However, the economic potential of this colony was always limited due to the scarcity of fertile soil and the absence of significant mineral wealth. Oil would only be extracted towards the end of the colonial period.

French), they were solvent, for these colonies were profitable in the nineteenth and twentieth centuries.

Fourth, the poverty of the economic model chosen by the empire. The trade economy set the tone almost everywhere, excluding any attempt to locally produce the products consumed by inhabitants, whether European or native. We shall discuss this aspect a bit later, but it is worth noting at this stage that the trade economy did away with the domestic market, which by definition held no interest for it. Whence a total indifference for the natives' purchasing power and, ultimately, their productivity. This was reflected in the very low savings capacity of these populations and thus their inability to contribute to investment. The trade economy was a poverty trap.

Finally, France ran out of time. Economic miracles do not happen in thirty or fifty years, that is, in the span of time allotted France to create value outside periods of pacification and global conflict (1914–18 and 1939–45). The United States was not built overnight: it took the British more than two hundred years to lay the human substrate that produced development. And once it had won its independence, it took another hundred years for the American people to truly emerge.

Generally speaking, the course of development is more plant-like (cumulative) than animal (explosive). It requires an "eternity" to teach capitalism, establish a monetary economy, set up a labor market, and install infrastructure. France did not have the time.

Those who have tried to force march development have inflicted great violence on their peoples. The Soviets and Chinese under Mao are instructive examples: one cannot take short-cuts in the process without brutalizing the peasants, confiscating their crops to feed urban workers, slashing wages to make production more competitive, keeping a lid on the labor movement, and so on. Had France pursued such a policy, one can only imagine the severity with which it would have been criticized after the fact. In fact, it might have lost control of its colonies had it put too much pressure on individuals and families. It is one thing to be governed by a foreigner, quite another to be forcibly deported to a distant construction site to build a port or a dam.

The Black Box

The financial balance sheet of colonization is a source of controversy. Two visions collide. On one hand, some historians, like Jacques Marseille and

Daniel Lefeuvre, assert that the empire was a financial black hole that impoverished France. On the other hand, Élise Huillery, an economist at Paris-Dauphine University, underscore that the colonization of French West Africa cost France virtually nothing. She demonstrates that this colonial territory was itself forced to pay for the salaries of the colonial administration as well as its public investments in keeping with the principle of colonial self-financing (established by law on April 13th, 1900).[6] In fact, this self-financing principle was applied everywhere (even in Guyana and the Antilles). Only Algeria was exempt, because it was a French department and as such eligible for national support. The protectorates of Morocco, Tunisia, and Indochina were also affected by this principle. Elise Huillery goes even further, seriously challenging on methodological grounds the conclusions of Marseille and Lefeuvre.

What to think? Whom to believe?

The statistics required for a proper accounting of the colonies' economic performance are lacking. In itself, this lacuna in our knowledge suggests that France's colonial possessions were not good business, as if one had to break the thermometer so as not to read the temperature. If the news had been good, if El Dorado had lived up to its promise, the colonial lobby would have crowed from the rooftops, with statistics in hand for proof.

For the moment and until proven otherwise, the academic consensus underscores the extremely poor economic record of the Empire. Élise Huillery's approach challenges this consensus, but she limits her discussion to French West Africa and does not consider, it seems to me, the totality of costs borne by France during the colonization of this region. She thus neglects the transfers that were necessary to readjust French West Africa's payment balance, which was in serious deficit most of the time. She also works on the assumption that the colonies continued to repay the loans granted them by Paris well after they became independent. This is not at all likely given the mindset of the new authorities who had been installed to lead the former colonies of Africa. Finally, her analysis does not consider the write-off involved in abandoning private and public capital at the moment of independence: businesses that went bust, the expropriation of the pied-noirs, hasty departures caused by political unrest, brand-new infrastructure left in place without any hope of collecting tolls or taxes on their future use, and so on.

---

6. Élise Huillery, *The Black Man's Burden: The Cost of Colonization of French West Africa for French Taxpayers*, 2009.

For the moment and given the present state of knowledge, it is impossible to draw up the true "bill" for colonization. It was undoubtedly very steep. Nor is there any doubt that it had its ups and downs. Until 1900, conquest was expensive (weapons, soldiers' pay, installation of fortifications, etc.). At the same time, there was little to no revenue as capital and colonists were afraid of risk. Mineral resources, when there were any, were not immediately available due to the lack of extraction and transportation infrastructure. Between 1900 and 1945, France attempted to "disengage" from its colonies by making them finance a portion of their own expenses. This was a waste of time and effort, in my opinion, since this policy did not concern Algeria—a major burden with its sizable French community demanding schools, roads, and jobs. What's more, those territories that were subject to the self-finance policy were not always able to find the resources necessary to support themselves locally: French Equatorial Africa, for example, regularly required help covering its operating costs. After 1945, France took a U-turn and decided to properly equip its empire so as to foster economic development and social well-being. Huge amounts of capital were swallowed up without obtaining the hoped-for return on investment. In this instance, the financial black hole was deep and undeniable. With the wars of liberation, it would become quite a lot deeper still.

Indochina is an exception, since it had been generally profitable since the 1900s. Everything was lost, however, in the war of liberation that broke out in 1945–46. When the capitalists withdrew, they were unable to move their physical investments to Singapore, Hong Kong, or elsewhere in the Empire: factories and plantations were burned, sabotaged, or simply shut down. Public investments were either destroyed in hostilities or freely bequeathed to the North and South Vietnamese authorities. The unprecedented military expenditures involved in fighting the insurgency only added to the catastrophe. It was a sad end for the only French colony that had a real chance of taking off and bringing real wealth to France and the native people.

Indochina, A Wasted Opportunity

More than Laos and Cambodia, Vietnam might have had an economic "future" under French colonization. It had many cards up its sleeve but was hindered by poor political decisions.

Among Vietnam's assets: a large and industrious population capable of shouldering difficult labor conditions; an abundance of anthracite and iron ore; a suitable climate for tropical export crops; enormous hydro-electric potential; neighboring China, a formidable market; and the dynamism of the Chinese diaspora, which operated as a network in Vietnam and neighboring countries, strongly favoring the establishment of commercial and financial ties.

France brought technology, significant public and private capital, and of course security, which is an accelerator of economic activity. It invested heavily in the creation and improvement of infrastructure: more than 4000 kilometers of navigable canals, more than 2100 kilometers of north-south railroads connecting China to Saigon and Cambodia (including the famous Trans-Indochina, opened in 1937).

Over the long term, Indochina's GDP grew by 50 percent between 1890 and 1940. Rice exports multiplied sevenfold between 1880 and 1930. Indochina also enjoyed a continuous trade surplus,[7] an exception in the empire. In the 1920s, Vietnamese rubber was directly exported to the American West Coast at the behest of Goodyear.

Local authorities would later be so rich that they could pay the cost of occupation demanded by Japan from 1941 onwards, without seeking help from Paris.

That said, the stakes were minimal, for the local economy was minuscule in absolute terms: in 1938, it represented only 2.5 percent of the French economy.[8] It was not with the colony's budget and balance of payment surpluses that France was going to offer itself a second Château de Versailles!

Had its potential been unleashed, the economy of Indochina might have been a good deal more profitable and genuinely enriched France and the natives. Yet the colonial authorities constantly refused to give Indochina what it needed to develop: a domestic market and an industrial sector. Indeed, due to the low wages paid native workers, the Indochinese market was always meager. This low level of remuneration may be explained as an effect of the mass

---

7. Except in 1931 due to the collapse in raw material prices that followed the 1929 crisis.

8. 10 billion francs (or one billion piastres, the local currency), for a total national production of 394 billion francs.

   See: Vincent L-A. Évolution de la production intérieure brute en France de 1896 à 1938 : Méthode et premiers résultats. Études et conjoncture—Institut national de la statistique et des études économiques, n° 11, 1962.

   See also: *Aperçus sur la situation économique des États associés d'Indochine*, Revue d'économie Politique, vol. 64, n° 2 (Éditions Dalloz, 1954): http://www.jstor .org/stable/24690175 (page accessed December 2021).

unemployment that resulted from overpopulation (23 million inhabitants in 1938). To remedy this, it would have been necessary to provide the economy with an industry capable of generating a large number of jobs. Yet France always rejected this option under pressure from lobbies such as the cotton industry group, which would not hear of textile factories in Indochina. The opponents of Indochinese industrialization cleverly disguised their corporate interests behind the fear that the region's economy might become autonomous, an eventuality that could over time lead to the territory's secession.

Among French capitalists were figures capable of breaking with the status quo and demanding a new economic policy for Indochina. These included Paul Bernard, a businessman and graduate of the École Polytechnique.[9] In the 1930s, he campaigned for France to finally provide Indochina with what it required to become wealthy and enrich France in return. The Third Republic, Popular Front included, would hear none of it. It was Vichy that would lend him an attentive ear, in 1941 requesting that he plan the industrialization of Indochina. However, with one foot in Vichy and another in the Resistance as a member of the Alliance network (specializing in intelligence), this fascinating figure was playing a double game. Bernard would be unmasked and arrested by the Gestapo in 1943. He survived detention and returned to the fray after Liberation, but it was too late: the war of liberation had already begun.[10] It would decimate France's public and private investments in Indochina, but that is another story.

International Prestige Fizzles Out

Until 1945, the Empire was a source of influence, or *soft power*, to use a fashionable term. The colonies were a showcase for French genius as this was expressed in the planning, transformation, and embellishment of the landscape. The

---

9. Trans. The École Polytechnique is part of France's prestigious *"grande école"* system of institutions of higher learning. Since its founding in the French Revolution, it has educated successive generations of French mathematicians and engineers.

10. For Paul Bernard (1892–1960), there were above all two priorities in Indochina: (a) to diversify the economy via industrialization (chemicals, textiles, metallurgy, etc.); and (b) to promote fertilizer use in order to maximize rice production, thereby allowing the population to be fed while reliably assuring that a surplus be available for export. Since fertilizers are expensive, Paul Bernard encouraged the colonial authorities to subsidize their prices as a way of accelerating their adoption by farmers.

prestige that resulted from this had more to do with aesthetics than with the economic or military aspects of the French presence. The Hanoi Opera House, the Hermitage district in Marrakech, the wooded promenades of Tananarive, the gleaming cranes in the port of Abidjan: all this new life, meant to convey health and vigor, was France's "calling card," which it happily presented to diplomats and foreign visitors. The goal was to dazzle and astonish at once: dazzle with the harmony of forms and astonish with the contrast between France's achievements and the *non-achievements* of the colonized peoples. The more chaotic and dilapidated the native cities were, the more beautiful and healthier the quickly constructed European quarters seemed.

The world of that time was essentially a conversation between Europeans about topics dear to Europeans. Life, the only one worth living, took place in Europe, and the colonies were only one more backdrop for displaying the genius of France vis-à-vis its British and German competitors.

The native was merely an extra, an eternal child who had to remain silent while the grownups were speaking or seated at the table. The nonexistence of the native made the overrepresentation of the European possible: only the thoughts of the European mattered, only his concerns were meaningful. Europe was everywhere the European was, everywhere he carried out his civilizing mission.

This disregard for the native was almost comical. In 1917, the French, British, and Germans clashed on Lake Tanganyika as if it were merely an extension of the Somme or Verdun, and as if the black men watching the conflict (or catching stray bullets) were mere features of the landscape rather than the legitimate masters of the land. Similarly, in November 1942, the French and Americans ripped into one another in Casablanca, Safi, and Port-Lyautey under the gaze of bewildered Moroccans, who found themselves totally sidelined by History.

The spirit of the times completely changed after World War II. Overnight, the empire became a moral burden, apologizing for its continued existence. The colonial powers drew the criticism of the entire world in the name of human rights and the right of peoples to self-determination. Pride had given way to opprobrium.

In the context of the Cold War, colonialism was a blemish on the past that had to be swiftly erased, in the same way that the odious transatlantic slave trade had been abolished before it. From Moscow, the Soviets called with all their might for decolonization (while at the same time extending under the banner of communism *their* colonial empire from East Berlin to Samarkand). From Washington, the Americans "communicated" admirably about notions of liberty and dignity. In 1957, Senator John Fitzgerald Kennedy declared, "The time has come when our Government must recognize that this is no longer a French problem alone; and that the time has passed, where a series of piecemeal adjustments, or even a last attempt to incorporate Algeria fully within France, can succeed."[11]

In the blink of an eye, the empire had gone from a symbol of power to a sign of weakness. In the 1950s, France was constantly on the defensive at the UN, endlessly explaining and justifying itself.

The Empire Supports France during the Occupation

Contributing to the Liberation of France and participating in the war against Nazism: two objectives that the Colonial Party would never have imagined in its wildest dreams. Who could have imagined the decisive role that the colonies would play in the Second World War?

500,000 men answered the call of Liberation. Muslims, colonists, and pied-noirs, French overseas civil servants, French people from the metropole who had taken refuge in the colonies after the defeat of 1940: one and the same mobilization for the French cause. As this epic tale is (or should be) already known to all, there is no reason to linger over it other than to underscore the selflessness displayed by the *goumiers* and *tirailleurs* during the Provence landings, the capture of Marseille, and the grueling reconquest of Italy. These fighters, Arabs, Berbers, Africans, and Asians, demonstrated their willingness to die for France side by side with men who might have despised them in civilian life

War, blood, and horror had awakened the unthinkable: brotherhood between oppressor and oppressed. At the lowest point in French history, men of all races and confessions spontaneously and voluntarily decided to join their efforts. Was it patriotism, love of liberty, a taste for adventure? Perhaps they were simply answering a call that few generations have the opportunity to experience: devoting oneself body and soul to a cause greater than the individual.

---

11. Trans. Remarks of Senator John F. Kennedy in the Senate, Washington, D.C., July 2, 1957, https://www.jfklibrary.org/archives/other-resources/john-f-kennedy-speeches/united-states-senate-imperialism-19570702, accessed 5 September 2024

Eighty years later, it is difficult for us to appreciate the degree of harmony achieved by the Frenchmen and natives who served alongside one another under the French flag. This prayer for the dead recited by the French officers of the *goums* captures the atmosphere of the time:

"We pray to you, our Lord, for the dead of Islam.

. . . they came, Lord, from the Saracen shores of your Christian Mediterranean.

How many among them have died on the roads of France, from the cypresses of Provence to the snows of the Rhine, so far from that land where their heart remained, so far from the black tents and tawny *ksours,*[12] from the blue mountain and twisted olive trees, from the gentle rustling of palm trees in the southerly breeze and the bitter song of the wind in the powerful branches of silvery cedars.

Filled with the memory of a singular light, their eyes closed upon the mists of the West.

Though it is true they never admitted the law that is ours, they offered, oh marvel of Charity, their simple lives to a Christian land.

And when a compassionate fate momentarily freed them for a few hours from the mud and the cold and their immense fatigue, from the roar of tanks and the thunder of cannons and the specter of Death, they accompanied us with a brotherly gaze to the doors of your sanctuaries where we were to plead for ourselves and for them.

Lord, in your infinite goodness, despite our pride and weakness, if you grant us at the end of our trials the grace of your eternal blessing, allow the hardy warriors of Barbary, who liberated our homes and brought the comfort of their smiles to our children, to stand alongside us, shoulder to shoulder, as they stood on the front line, in battle, and, in the ineffable peace of your Paradise, allow them to know—oh! that they should know, Lord—how much we loved them!"

I wish today's youth a life of such moral elevation and fulfillment in action. Our ancestors managed to transcend the colonial order to bring forth

---

12. Ksour (plural of ksar): a fort or a fortified village in the Saharan or pre-Saharan region of Morocco and Algeria.

brotherly love and fight Evil. What a contrast with our own era, in which the excuses and scruples of a false morality are stumbling blocks to our will!

The sacrifice of all its children of colonization (Europeans and natives) allowed France to sit at the victor's table in 1945. Recall the lucid words of Gaston Monnerville, president of the Consultative Assembly, on May 25th, 1945:

> "Without the Empire, France would only be a liberated country today. Thanks to its Empire, France is a victorious nation."

Thumbing the Nose at the Fascists

Nothing we have just described would have been possible had the *goums* not faded into the woodwork between June 1940 and November 1942, an extraordinary operation that allowed the Moroccan *goumiers* to form the first underground resistance force against Nazism. They were the first both in terms of their date of formation (1940) and in that of their size (50,000 fighters). In metropolitan France, the internal resistance would make its appearance much later and never count more than 30,000 combatants.

The story is extraordinary, incredible even, both in point of the audacity of their undertakings and in the nature of the men who undertook it. For it was officers loyal to Vichy rather than Gaullists who came up with the ingenious plan to "camouflage" more than 50,000 Moroccan *goumiers* pending the resumption of hostilities. Stripped of their uniforms, they were transformed into rural laborers and unarmed indigenous police officers. Their pay was deposited into a special fund of the Residence-General expressly created by the Vichy government for that purpose.

Weapons and equipment were meticulously stored in farms, caves, and other hideouts: 50 tanks, 250 trucks, 150 automobiles, 60 cannons, 4000 automatic weapons, 20,000 small arms.

The Germans and the Italians of the Armistice Commission never saw a thing. Stationed in Casablanca and Mohammedia, Axis military observers carried out many inspection patrols without noticing the subterfuge, and no Moroccan gave the game away. To the contrary, *goumiers*, Muslim civilians, and French civil servants seamlessly collaborated to keep the secret and outwit the vigilance of the fascists. Trust between Moroccans and French was such that maneuvers could take place without arousing suspicion, with the largest occurring near Oulmes (Middle Atlas foothills) in 1942. At other times, the *goumiers* conducted firearms and mountain combat training at night.

The ringleaders of this masquerade were officers loyal to Vichy about whom no one today wants to hear for fear of being associated with "the bad guys." This is cruel ingratitude towards the men who gave De Gaulle the nucleus of his liberation army. It is also to show shameful contempt towards those who fooled Hitler and Mussolini when all seemed lost. Among these men were Marshal Weygand, General Noguès, and Colonel Guillaume.[13]

Let the aficionados of purity choke on their facile indignation: I much pre-fer to salute the memory of these great Frenchmen who madly loved their country than align myself with political correctness. Yes, they served Vichy just as they calmly and masterfully prepared for the resumption of hostilities. That is enough for me to tip my hat to them.

After November 1942, the date of the Allied landings in Morocco, the camouflaged *goumiers* were "made visible" and integrated into the *tabors* (in-digenous battalions) that would soon hurl themselves upon Southern Europe.

The attitude of the French Army under Vichy was much more ambivalent than is generally believed. They camouflaged men and weapons, as we have just seen, established an independent spy network to monitor Axis forces, and remained in contact with the British and Americans in North Africa.

We have not moved beyond the immaculate purity of General de Gaulle and the absolute filth of the men of Vichy. The reality is much more complex. Why should we refuse to reconstruct it?

---

13. Trans. Maxime Weygand (1867–1965), Chief of Staff of the French Army at the time of the German invasion in 1940 and Delegate-General to French North Africa under the Vichy Regime. Weygand largely rejected the policy of collaboration and was arrested by the Germans following the Allied Invasion of North Africa in November 1942. Charles Noguès (1876–1971) was a highly decorated veteran of the First World War and Commander in Chief of all French forces in North Africa at the outbreak of the Second World War. Despite dutifully carrying out Vichy-era policies, Noguès ensured that French forces put up little resistance when the Allies invaded in 1942, greatly hastening their conquest of the region. Augustin Guillaume (1895–1983) commanded the Moroccan goumiers in the Italian and southern French campaigns and the 3rd Algerian Infantry Division following the D-Day landings of June 1944.

A RAW DEAL FOR THE COLONIZED, TOO

"Our actions are but drops of water, and in each of them you may see, depending on your mood, the light of the sun or the darkness of the mud."

CAMEROONIAN PROVERB

Hardly had France arrived in the colonies than it turned its back on the colonized. Promises and statements of intent were forgotten, giving way to the harsh reality of pacification and the mediocrity of an ill-prepared and under-equipped administration.

Territories were conquered and princes subdued by bayonet and cannon. Tractors, schools, and free clinics ought to have picked up where they left off, putting the philanthropic side of colonization into practice. Yet most natives saw only the negative and galling aspects of the French presence.

What really happened on the ground for France to betray its promises? How had destitution become so widespread in the colonies by the time they achieved independence?

Answering these questions requires keeping a cool head and examining the facts without excessive severity or a surfeit of indulgence. Let us know our place: that of a comfortably ensconced observer, safe from mosquito bites, rebel ambushes, and the humiliations inherent to the colonial order. We are neither colonists persuaded of our superiority nor overworked coolies, but simply people of good will who wish to understand.

Good will and good faith: two raw materials on the verge of extinction in our era.

The Impossibility of Development

"On the whole, the labor markets of pre-colonial Africa boiled down to slave trading."

Professor Gareth Austin[1]

The Empire of Scarcity

One needn't have a PhD. in economics to realize that economic development did not take place. Nowhere did France leave behind a flourishing economy supported by a prosperous society.

Just after independence, there was just one public toilet for every 7000 inhabitants in the Treichville neighborhood of Abidjan. In the Adjamé neighborhood, there was just one for every 15,000![2]

According to Daniel Lefeuvre, 93 percent of Algerian Muslims belonged to the poorest strata of society in 1955. Between 1 and 1.5 million Algerian Muslims were unemployed or only intermittently employed (or one quarter of the working-age population, men and women combined).

As the years went by, Muslim Algeria sank ever deeper into *pauperization*.[3]

In the 1950s, most Algerians lived in the countryside, in a *gourbi*[4] or tent. In the city, they endured the humiliation of shantytown life, a scourge that encircled Oran, Algiers, and Constantine. They ate poorly and dressed poorly. Winter brought cold and humidity, summer, heat and sweat. There was no insulation, wood for heating was expensive, hygiene was makeshift and running water a luxury. Men's skin was weathered by the sun, their teeth hurt and, as the years passed, they had no alternative but to have them pulled out. Women feared giving birth and knew nothing of obstetrics. Neither had time to complain, children complained enough as it was, beset as they were by flies and

---

1. Taken from "African Economic Development and Colonial Legacies", *International Development Policy*, 1, 2010.
2. Taken from a study by Jean-Pierre Besancenot. See: *La santé en Côte d'Ivoire, d'hier et d'aujourd'hui. Cahiers d'outre-mer.* No. 162—Year 41, April-June 1988.
3. Such is the diagnosis formulated by Germaine Tillon (1907–2008), an ethnologist well-versed in North African realities. She studied Algeria, and specifically the Aurès region, over the course of two separate years: 1940 and 1955.
4. *Gourbi* is the generic name given to the (fixed) dwellings of the lower classes, consisting of a low, poorly ventilated, rectangular room made of packed earth or stones and mortar.

ticks. At first light, they would have to get up to seek work at the construction site or farm. Ever since he lost his land in the great despoilment of property orchestrated by the Third Republic, the Algerian had been a day laborer. He had no choice but to sell his labor to the Europeans. A pity that it was of such low quality, no one having taken the trouble to teach him the right skills, much less how to read and write.[5]

The same deprivation characterized the condition of native populations in Senegal, Indochina, and Madagascar.

France should have done more, but was it able to?

Colonization Was Not Adequately Funded

The colonial lobby promised commercial opportunities as well as abundant and easily accessible natural resources. Men were sent to bring about this utopia but reaped nothing but disappointment and contempt. Far from laying hands on the fountain of youth, France had conquered a cumbersome and sickly body.

Underground, the ore dreamt of by geologists vanished before their eyes. Above ground, jungles, swamps, and fever placed an obstacle between the engineer's technical ambitions and the territory's potential. It was one thing to collect high-quality wood here and there, quite another to make profitable use of a forest without succumbing to malaria.

Poverty-stricken and insolvent, local populations were unable to finance the least economic development by means of (free and spontaneous) investment or taxation.

From a moral point of view, France should have financed the implementation of material and human progress in its colonies. From a practical point of view, it was incapable of doing so. Indeed, this would have required the transfer of colossal fortunes overseas. Given the real needs of the people, colonial spending could easily have grown beyond measure. Yet the colonies, even deprived of any development policy worthy of the name, were already costly for France. Between 1850 and 1930, they consumed almost 10 percent of public spending,[6] a considerable sum.

---

5. Regarding the productivity deficit of the Algerian and North African workforce in general, see Daniel Lefeuvre's essay, *Pour en finir avec la repentance coloniale.*
6. Clément, Alain. "*L'analyse économique de la question coloniale en France (1870–1914)*", *Revue d'économie politique* (online): https://www.cairn.info/revue-d-economie-politique-2013-1-page-51.htm.

The flight of human resources only compounded this lack of money.

From the very beginning of colonization to its final day, French citizens were never seduced by the colonial adventure. There was no jostling of candidates to open roads in Gabon or treat the sick in Tonkin: too many diseases, too much bureaucracy, and not enough money to be made. Thirty years after it had been conquered, only 45,000 of Tunisia's 148,000 European inhabitants were French (compared with one million natives, both Muslim and Jewish alike) in 1911—and this in a colony reputed to be "easy" in terms of its climate and the mildness of its inhabitants.

Could France have fallen back on indigenous human resources? The answer is no. Skilled labor in the sense understood in a capitalist, mechanized economy was practically non-existent.

This observation was blindingly obvious throughout the empire, and indeed found its way into newspapers and journals. There was nothing secret or counter-intuitive about it. Unfortunately, the "shot had already been fired," and no one dared acknowledge that they had been sold "a bill of goods."

The solution that was found was to sweep the problem under the rug.

The finance law of April 13th, 1900, mentioned earlier, had introduced the principle of the colonies' financial autonomy. Until 1945, the territories had to self-finance, that is, pay out of their own pocket for local expenses. For this to work, it "sufficed" to simply tax the inhabitants under colonial supervision. But this was wishful thinking, for the fiscal potential of the natives was very limited: even bled dry, they were incapable of furnishing the sums necessary to finance the titanic costs required by development. Self-financing consisted in asking for help from those one had come to help.

Everyone knew this but pretended otherwise. Pygmies were thus taxed with one hand while the other borrowed from the fisc to finance public works projects. The remainder had to come from private capital. With only a few exceptions, however, French capital snubbed the colonies in favor of the New World, Europe, and Russia. In 1913, barely 10 percent of capital outflows went to the Empire.

The Ghetto Economy

From impotence, France chose the cheapest economic model: a ghetto economy. It was the most useful from a political point of view; also, the most cynical. Economic development was reserved for the little white world it had established and for which it was able to provide with basic infrastructure (ports, roads, etc.), security, and the French way of life.

France never looked upon the colonies as future emancipated countries that would have to stand on their own two feet. To the contrary, the economic transformation carried out by colonization contented itself with turning Morocco, Senegal, and Guinea into satellites, automatons responding to the impulses of a distant brain as these were communicated to it by the administration and large companies. From this perspective, it was not necessary to provide them with an industry, a robust and competitive energy sector, or agriculture capable of feeding the population and generating an exportable surplus. As long as the metropole sent them machines and consumer goods, no one saw any problem with making Ivory Coast specialize in cocoa or Senegal in peanuts.

The first few decades of each colony thus resulted in a micro-GDP that, relative to the total population (foreign and native), was ridiculously low. If one only considers the European-origin population, however, it was perfectly respectable. This limited ambition had the advantage of catering to the interests of the pied-noirs, who were tempted to run off with the winnings for themselves without sharing the fruits of economic growth with the colonized. As we pointed out earlier, the colonists took French colonial policy hostage thanks to their influence in Paris and their deputies, chambers of commerce, and newspapers. In the case of Algeria, this downward spiral reached scandalous proportions, with the state subsidizing and repeatedly bailing out the colony's economy in the sole interests of its colonists from 1870 (the fall of Napoleon III) to World War II (or even later). Whatever considerations of economic rationality might have said and despite the legitimate interests of Algerian Muslims, it was the interests of the electoral base that took precedence.

Elsewhere, in Sub-Saharan Africa and Indochina, veritable fortunes were amassed by entrepreneurs holding a legal monopoly or oligopoly. River transport in Gabon, Congo, Ubangi-Chari, and the Mekong Delta; import-export companies that bought tropical goods at low prices and sold them in France at a favorable price set in advance;[7] maritime transport companies and courier

---

7. Like the French West Africa Company (CFAO), whose origins date back to the trading houses opened in 1852 by Charles-Auguste Verminck in Ivory Coast, Sierra Leone, and Senegal.

services linking the colony with France; and, of course, banks. All of these cartels and trusts certainly worked hard, but they also benefited from the highly advantageous rents of their situation. The natives, devastated by hunger and scabies, could only look on.

Private capital had it very easy, in general. It captured the advantageous positions described above and sought to maximize profitability while minimizing risk. This meant occupying areas with sufficiently strong demography to make for commercial opportunities—Indochina, for instance, which was inundated with French textile products. This also meant seizing the most easily accessible mineral deposits, such as tin in New Caledonia and phosphates in Tunisia.

Over time, the colonies developed a dual economy. On the one hand, a modern, mechanized economy, well-versed in the most advanced management methods, organized around the concept of productivity, and open to international trade. On the other, an archaic but no less active and bustling economy, on bad terms with science and technology and beyond the reach of the banking system, which would have happily taken its savings but was reluctant to extend credit for lack of collateral. Two economies lived side by side, sizing each other up: the European economy and the indigenous one, the formal and the informal, the modern and the traditional. Two ghettos, each facing the other.

In Morocco, two forms of agriculture cohabited like two distant planets orbiting the same sun. On one side, modern, irrigated export agriculture, at the cutting edge of genetic optimization techniques, such as grafting plants and cross-breeding animals. This was the agriculture of model farms in the Guerrouane region near Meknes (vineyards, almond trees, apple trees), the Moulouya River valley (citrus trees), and the Gharb plain (sugar beet, sugar cane, rice). On the other side of the wadi,[8] there was subsistence agriculture, depressed and depressing, for it depended on the generosity of the sky, which varied from year to year, the rains having always been sporadic in Morocco. It knew nothing about fertilizers other than manure; it did without veterinary care and resigned itself to dairy cows that produced little and died quickly.

Traditional agriculture repeated ancestral behaviors and mistakes. Its outlook was one of fatalism: the eternal return of the cycle of scarcity. It sold its meager surplus at the weekly souk, always in a race against time as high temperatures and the absence of proper storage facilities reduced the shelf life

---

8. Trans. A "wadi" is a stream or riverbed in Asia or North Africa that remains dry for much of the year, only filling with water in rainy seasons.

of harvests. The Moroccan fellah,[9] who always feared that his olives would be infested by earthworms or that his tomatoes would rot in their crates before his eyes, got rid of them as quickly as he could at a price dictated by the buyer.

My own family experienced this dichotomy. My eldest uncle managed an ultra-modern agricultural estate in the highly fertile Sous plain (near Taroudant), an operation in which the family of former French President Giscard d'Estaing had invested. At the same time, my grandfather fattened poultry and sheep in a cave carved out of the rock. Two universes within a single colony and, between them, little to no ripple or trickle-down effect.

As always in life, clever, lucky, or particularly skilled individuals were able to create a "situation" for themselves, despite the de facto apartheid separating the European and indigenous worlds. Between the world wars, some Algerian Muslims bought up land let go by pied noirs who had given up on colonial agriculture for good in favor of the easy living of the cities. In Morocco, the Laghzaoui family prospered in the interurban transport sector despite the privileged position occupied by the CTM (*Compagnie de Transports au Maroc*). In Cochinchina and Cambodia, Vietnamese entrepreneurs rode the rubber tree boom and created their own plantations, where they too exploited the poverty-stricken coolies from Tonkin. Among them (and by way of example), the plantation of a certain Ly-Ba-Dung, who owned eighty-seven hectares 112 kilometers from Saigon and employed twenty-five workers, including native coolies. In West Africa, black entrepreneurs also took advantage of peace and the customs union of French West Africa and French Equatorial Africa to extend trade networks over long distances. The young M'ba, for example, an Ivorian from the Mandinka ethnic group, became a wholesaler of food products enjoyed by the black people of the region of Bouaké. He brought in fish from Mopti (present-day Mali), rice from Sikasso (Mali), and early yam, corn, and millet from every corner of French West Africa. In the 1950s, he received up to sixty tons of goods per day! M'ba deftly occupied a "juicy" niche neglected by colonial capitalism. Was he, too, a victim of colonialism?

Last but also Least: The Human Element

Natives witnessed the advent of the *miracle* of progress. Within the first years of colonization, they saw their landscape transformed. Despite chronic

---

9. Trans. North African term for a peasant or agricultural laborer.

under-investment, bridges were built where once there had been only fords, and roads were laid where once there had been only mule tracks. Natives of course worked on the construction sites as laborers, workmen, and peddlers, but their lives did not improve for all that. Colonization can be thought of as a sumptuous feast from which the natives were always barred.

No, France never carried out the Marshall Plan that would have been required to raise the human and material standards of its colonies. Indeed, to make Morocco an emerging agricultural power or Senegal an intermediate industrial hub at the gateway separating the Sahara from Africa's savannas would have required more than a single Marshall Plan; it would have required an entire battery of ambitious (and thus costly) plans.

To get an idea of the lag that had accumulated, let us consider the objectives of the Constantine Plan, made public in September 1958. In surprisingly frank terms, it laid out the real needs of Algeria after 130 years of French colonization. Among the most pressing of these:

- Building housing for one million of Algeria's nine million Muslims;
- Enrolling two-thirds of all children in schools within the next three years;
- Distributing 250,000 hectares of land;
- Developing the irrigation system.

The Constantine Plan was an admission of failure.[10] Its lofty ambitions implicitly reflected deep disappointment with the colonial project in Algeria. It was a project that never gave serious consideration to the human element. If Algeria, a settler colony, lagged so far behind, what was one to say about Madagascar, Congo, or Indochina?

Everywhere, the human element was neglected for lack of financial resources, but also because the emphasis was almost exclusively placed on the material aspect of development.

In 1913, the loan granted for capitalizing the colonies allocated only a paltry sum to social and cultural spending: 2.5 percent in French West Africa, 5 percent in French Equatorial Africa, and 1.4 percent in Indochina.

---

10. A twist of fate would have it that the Constantine Plan was dead on arrival for, barely a year after its launch, De Gaulle announced the principle of self-determination, that is, the possibility of Algerian independence. From that time on, entrepreneurs stopped believing in the Algerian economy . . .

Between 1922 and 1932, barely 10 percent of the credit extended to Morocco's Sharifian Empire was committed to projects with a social or cultural dimension.[11]

The fact that repayment of these loans was partly covered by taxes levied on the natives only makes these figures so much more intolerable. These poverty-stricken natives would surely have preferred to finance hospitals or vaccination campaigns than railways for moving phosphates and cocoa. The sacrosanct civilizing mission had upended their world, bringing them new risks and unusual diseases. Wherever man was rooted in soil or tribe, colonial capitalism demanded he be relocated to the city, close to communication hubs and closer still to Europeans' places of residence. In the New World that the Frenchman had brought with him, mobility was an end in itself; it was also synonymous with new illnesses. There were labor accidents on the construction sites of great infrastructural projects and fingers lost by Tonkinese coolies while clearing brushwork for rubber tree plantations. There were also venereal diseases—syphilis, gonorrhea, and so on—a scourge wherever the working class was concentrated. And, of course, alcoholism, an evil associated with wage labor, with some in West Africa receiving half their pay in alcohol. And so many other diseases "awoken" by the opening of roads where once there had only been flooded forests or deserts, allowing viruses and pathogens to spread farther and faster, causing carnage at both ends of transportation routes.

Colonization also brought its share of mental illnesses. Stress, anxiety, the malaise of the man who feels out of place in his own country, forced to accept a foreign civilization that looks down on him and runs counter to what he believes to be good, just, and desirable. The shock of colonization was a clash of values. Muslim men were thus confronted with unveiled women and obliged to show them what was, in Islamic lands, unaccustomed consideration. They saw Jews overtake them and achieve the status of first-class citizen.[12] By the will of the French, yesterday's commoners became *caids* and *pashas*, noble offices that were traditionally reserved for prestigious lineages. Their world was thrown into disarray, enough to drive anyone mad. Perhaps the mental patients Franz Fanon cared for in his psychiatric hospital in Algeria were also victims of the

---

11. These figures are supplied by Adam Barbe, *Public Debt and European Expansionism in Morocco from 1860 to 1856.*
12. True equality in Algeria thanks to the Crémieux Decree, which mandated gradual alignment with the status of French citizens in Morocco and Tunisia. In these two countries, Jews were thus admitted to French schools well before the Muslims.

shock of modernity: patients suffering from the "*diversity*" imposed on society that aspired to uniformity and conformity under the banner of Islam.

Educational Apartheid

Without human resources, there is no human development. Once again, the colonial promise here gave way to disillusion, and this time definitively, it seems to me.

While one might find attenuating circumstances for French charitable efforts in the health sector (diseases unfamiliar in France, massive dispersion of populations, etc.), it is very difficult to understand the refusal to educate the natives. France educated neither the masses nor the elites. In general, it allowed the precolonial educational systems to wither without offering an alternative to the peoples under its supervision.[13] By the time of independence, illiteracy rates had thus reached unbelievable levels: 87 percent in Morocco, 85 percent in Algeria, 90 percent in Indochina.

The engine of literacy was never fired in the colonies. The number of natives enrolled in schools constantly stagnated at an indecent level. In 1942, the school attendance rate in Vietnam did not exceed 3.15 percent of the population (Annam, Tonkin, Cochinchina). Barely 100,000 Muslims were enrolled in primary schools in Algeria between 1940 and 1942, and only one thousand attended secondary schools. A poor showing for a heavily financed colony so close to the metropole and endowed with a significant number of civil servants.

That Europeans were offered an excellent education in the colonies—in many cases, better than that available in the metropole—only made this state of affairs all the more repugnant.[14]

---

13. In Vietnam, the traditional Confucian system was actively and relentlessly combatted by the colonial authorities, who ended up "getting its hide" in the 1910s. In its place, nothing had been planned apart from a hybrid system covering only a tiny fraction of the school-age population.

14. Philippe Séguin (1943–2010), former president of the French National Assembly, lived in Tunis until the mid-1950s. As independence approached, he had to leave the French high school in Tunis to prepare for his baccalaureate at the public high school in Draguignan. Upon arriving in France, he was surprised to find himself "at ease" among his metropolitan classmates, the level expected of students in Tunisia being much higher. In Algeria in the 1920s, a certain Fernand Braudel taught history in high school ...

Everywhere, one encounters an unspoken, never theorized policy of educational apartheid. For Europeans, progress and Enlightenment; for natives, the shadows of ignorance, with here and there a few islands of knowledge where an effort was made to sparingly train skilled workers and *enlightened* individuals for subaltern and even mid-level tasks. These little islands were schools for natives (called Franco-Vietnamese in Vietnam and Franco-Muslim in Algeria) where individualized instruction was offered to a select few. For a long time, the resulting diploma was not intended to open the door to French universities, where the student would have found himself on an equal footing with his French counterparts. Rather, these schools were rightly seen as offering a third-rate education in point of the insalubrity of their facilities (the schools were referred to as *dump*-schools[15] in Algeria) and their lack of prestige.

The history of education in the colonies varied from one country to the next and depended upon the relative progressivism of its French governor and the quality of his relationship with native elites. It seems to me that Indochina was an outlier in this respect, having a relative advance on other colonial territories. Beginning in 1902, its doctors could receive training on site in Hanoi and, starting in the 1920s, the same academic qualifications dispensed in the metropole could be received there.[16] A high school education was available to the children of the indigenous bourgeoisie of Hanoi, Saigon, and Phnom Penh (1935). This should perhaps be seen as reflecting the traditional attachment of Indochinese elites to education in general, whether Confucian or Western.

Elsewhere in the Empire, it would not be until the Second World War that educational apartheid began to crumble, and past neglect repaired.

Beginning in 1945, France put its foot on the accelerator, creating classrooms, schools, and university programs in the colonies. Considerable budgets were set aside for this, particularly in Algeria, where the French provisional government's plan for 1944 sought to construct 400 classrooms per year. In addition, the distinction between French and Muslim instruction in that country officially came to an end. Times were changing and, for the first time, France was pulling its weight. Racing against the clock, it set itself the task of ensuring that, within the next twenty years, the entire Muslim population complete or nearly complete school. It was a genuine and necessary effort at catching up, but nearly impossible given the substantial growth of the Algerian population.

---

15. Trans. "*écoles-gourbis*"
16. The degrees awarded by the University of Dakar were valid only in Africa.

Despite the best intentions, the results were thus disappointing: in Algeria, only 15 percent of natives were enrolled in school in 1957.[17] In the same country, barely 40 percent of Muslim boys attended school in 1962, the year it gained its independence. For girls, this figure was 22 percent. This means that, out of a population of two million school-aged children, only 750,000 attended school.

Moreover, these rates only reflect the number of children enrolled in primary school, only a tiny minority of whom would go on to receive secondary education, while those lucky enough to attend university could be counted on one hand. In Algeria, the Muslim contingent at the university was negligible: in 1954, out of a total student population of 5096, only 481 were Muslim men and 22 Muslim women, or roughly 1 out of every 10 students.

The situation was hardly any better in Sub-Saharan Africa. In 1957, the school enrollment rate for natives in French West Africa was 10 percent.

In Morocco, my father completed the "certificate of Muslim studies," a kind of undergraduate degree for natives. His teacher was an aviator who, in his free time, would come up to the village of Bhalil to teach courses to the sons of prominent villagers, handling all the subjects on his own. This French aviator (a *vile and despicable* expression of the colonial order) gave my father a taste for learning and above all self-confidence. He would play a fundamental role in my father's life, guiding him towards the BEPC[18] against the wishes of his family, who initially rejected any involvement with France, which they saw the school as embodying.

Later, in Marrakech, my father was admitted to a high school where only two Muslims were allowed to study for their baccalaureate: my father and the son of an important Moroccan notable who was dropped off in a Bentley every morning and had his schoolbag carried by a black *chaouch*.[19] Once my father had obtained his baccalaureate, he headed to France for military studies, the only way to obtain a free education with an elementary mathematics baccalaureate. In 1957, he arrived at the air force telecommunications school in Auxerre. My father was a walking miracle.

The educational failure of colonization neatly embodied the conceptual

---

17. These figures come from a study by Pascale Barthélemy of the École Normale Supérieure in Lyon. See: "*L'enseignement dans l'Empire colonial français: une vieille histoire?*", *Histoire de l'éducation*, 128 | 2010, (online): http://journals.openedition.org/histoire-education/2252 (page viewed March 2021)

18. Trans. *Brevet d'Etudes du Premier Cycle*: a school certificate that was obtained after passing exams at the end of the fourth year of secondary education.

19. Trans. Servant

contradictions of the *civilizing mission*. Above all, it deprived French colonization of a "good deed" that it might legitimately have laid before History.

But was France capable of this? Did it have the money and method needed to educate the peoples under its supervision in their masses?

~

It would have cost a fortune to educate millions of children. France had a foretaste of this after the Second World War when it began to take education in the colonies seriously.

In Sub-Saharan Africa, it was necessary to increase the education budget by 63 percent between 1953 and 1957 to raise the rate of enrollment by 3.8 percent. A back-of-the-envelope calculation suggests that, in order to enroll all school-age children, it would have been necessary to spend at least forty-seven billion CFA francs[20]—a nearly fivefold budget increase. When converted to French francs, the additional sum needed to educate the indigenous people of Sub-Saharan Africa approaches the 100 billion mark. A bank-breaking sum!

Year	Credits in millions of CFA francs	Number of students	School-age population	Enrollment rate
1953	6,230.5	625,000	5,245,960	11.6%
1957	10,148	902,000	5,645,000	15.4%

Budgets and students: primary, secondary, and higher education—Sub-Saharan Africa (French West Africa and French Equatorial Africa)[21] 1 CFA franc = 2 French francs according to the exchange rate of 17 October 1948, subsequently revised in 1960.

The challenge was not just financial, but also human (where was one to find the teachers needed to carry out such an undertaking?) and logistical (how to

---

20. Trans. The CFA franc, named after the Communauté Financière Africaine (African Financial Community), is a currency used in fourteen African countries. It was created in 1945 to compensate for the weakness of the French franc, which had been devalued as part of the Bretton Woods Agreement, and thereby allow the colonies to continue importing goods from France.
21. This data comes from the excellent study by Abdou Moumouni Dioffo, *L'Éducation en Afrique* (online): https://scienceetbiencommun.pressbooks.pub /educationmoumouni/ (page viewed March 2021)

reach students in the bush or the middle of the Sahara, places where the life expectancy of Europeans was limited, at best?). In 1945, e-learning was still unheard of . . .

And politically, the expansion of indigenous schooling was a long, hard battle. For colonist circles took a dim view of making education compulsory for the colonized. In Algeria, this hostility was total and goes a long way toward explaining the extreme delay in teaching Muslims to read and write. Since the end of the nineteenth century, Paris had set aside a budget for the construction and maintenance of Muslim-only schools. But all of the municipal councils were in the hands of the pied noirs and they were extremely reluctant to allocate these monies.[22] Very few schools were built, and those that already stood were in poor condition.

Everywhere else, Europeans rejected placing native students in the same schools as their own children, making exceptions only sparingly and under pressure from the French authorities, who wished to find places for the sons of good families as a way of ensuring the loyalty of native elites. In general, the governors were not convinced of the need to educate the people under their supervision. This was for a simple, indeed self-evident reason: what positions could be offered to "intellectual" and "literate" natives if, as non-citizens, they were by definition denied access to the civil service? And how was one to explain to a Senegalese alumnus of the *École normale supérieure* like Léopold Sédar Senghor or a young Ivorian doctor like Félix Houphouët-Boigny that they would forever earn less than a Frenchman with the same degree? How was one to make them accept that they could never reside in the European quarter or travel wherever they pleased without a pass?

Among the first to complain were Vietnamese doctors who had graduated from Hanoi Medical School. As early as the 1920s, they were outraged that they could not have private medical practices like their European counterparts who had received roughly the same education. They would swell the ranks of the nationalists and add a corporatist demand to their love of country. Some, like the surgeon Ton That Tung, would opt for an original critique that nonetheless constituted a danger for French domination. Upon returning from Europe in 1939, Tung campaigned for a purely Vietnamese "national medicine" that

---

22. It must not be forgotten that, prior to the municipal reform of 1956, only the pied noirs were authorized to elect mayors and city councilmen in Algeria.

aimed to be something other than a mere iteration of Western medicine adapted to tropical conditions.[23]

That said, it would be inaccurate and unfair to lay the entire blame for the fiasco that was colonial education at the feet of France. The natives often resisted French educational efforts as a way of rejecting colonialism. This phenomenon diminished after the First World War[24] but remained pronounced among some segments of the population, returning with a vengeance during the wars of liberation.

The refusal to send children to school was not just a nationalist reflex, but also an economic necessity, child labor being widespread in both town and country. It was also a conservative reaction to the prospect of seeing younger generations influenced by new ideas and values. Cultures seek to perpetuate themselves, and no one wants to disappear. Whether native or European, all parents know, even if they do not always admit it to themselves, that the classroom is the site of tremendous brainwashing.

This brings us to the crucial notion of the *curriculum*. What was to be taught young Malagasy, Moroccans, and Senegalese? That they descended from the Gauls or rather from Merinas, Arabs, and Fulas?

In other words, *assimilation* or *association*? The decision was never really taken, much less assumed. Some wanted to Gallicize indigenous children to make them French or an "evolved"—that is, improved—version thereof. Others considered it impossible and even dangerous to bring the natives into alignment with Europeans, preferring an education that prepared one for life in the colonies as a colonized person.

George Hardy, rector of the Academy of Algiers in the 1950s, put his finger on the problem when he tried to formulate a goal for colonial education:

> *"France does not ask that it be supplied masses of counterfeit Europeans [. . .] Make it so every child born under your flag, while remaining a*

---

23. Monnais-Rousselot, Laurence. *"Paradoxes d'une médicalisation coloniale"*. *Actes de la recherche en sciences sociales.* Vol. 143, June 2002 (online): www.persee.fr/doc /arss_0335-5322_2002_num_143_1_2853.

24. It was at this time that natives became convinced of the usefulness of medicine, and thus gave more credit to European ideas. Moreover, there is no doubt that the war brought communities closer together, with natives providing a significant contingent of soldiers on the European front.

man of his continent, his island, his nature, shall be a true Frenchman
in language, mind, and calling!"

What a mission! What a demand for subtlety, balance, and good measure! The question was nothing less than to manufacture human beings bearing two civilizations, their own and that of France, while hoping that these two private universes did not crush them under their respective weights or compete with one another in their innermost being. In fact, only a small minority, selected for its ability to inhabit two different worlds without giving in to schizophrenia, can aspire to such an education. The others, the masses, the normal people, will choose one world and pretend, if necessary, to inhabit the other.

How was one to be at once African and French? Sédar Senghor had the courage to put his finger on this impossibility. The African side demanded spontaneous fidelity to the world of spirits and magical beliefs, whereas the French side mobilized the human spirit around Reason and Technology. It was like drinking a poison and its antidote at the same time, day after day.

How was one to be at once Muslim and French? What is given to one is taken from the other. Islam is less Liberty, Equality, and Fraternity. France is less attachment to eternal life, less family solidarity, and less patriarchy. And yet colonial France was much "closer" to Islam than is the France of today, where materialism, individualism, and hatred of the male are cardinal values.

Far be it for me to reject the idea of cultural duality or openness to the world. I simply wish to underscore the risk of making *counterfeits* who lack the mental efficiency and moral quality of *purebloods*. By dint of promoting hybridity, one may end up sacrificing performance.

In their youth, Descartes, Pascal, and Chateaubriand received a bicultural education, at once steeped in French civilization and the Greco-Latin heritage. This is true, but they were never led to believe that they were Greeks or Romans. They were French and only French, Antiquity serving to cast a welcome light upon their moral and intellectual origins.

This question is very much of the moment. Faced with Diversity, the teachers of today respond with the same equivocation as their predecessors assigned to the colonies: they do not really know whether to assimilate young people (i.e., Gallicize them) or to associate them (i.e., teach them skills and knowledge without touching their souls). The problem has not changed: should we "manufacture French people" or simply level up the foreigners (in mathematics, physics, general knowledge, etc.)? I fear that the answer is still not forthcoming, and that every teacher and every student is trying to invent his own path, in keeping with his own sensibilities and the conditions in which he works and learns.

Personally speaking, I have the impression that the National Education system has become a counterfeit mill, putting hundreds of thousands of counterfeit French people on the market every year.

One Cannot Say Nothing Was Done

While the French did not usher the natives into Paradise, they did extricate millions of them from Hell. It was an incomplete and oh-so-questionable project, but a tremendous achievement all the same. The simple fact of having put an end to the slave trade and intra-African slavery was a feat in itself. The post-colonialists will never admit it, and the French themselves refuse to believe it, but the truth must be told.

The foremost service rendered by the French was undoubtedly to ban the abhorrent trade in human beings. These two scourges bled Africa dry for centuries and were only eradicated by the decisive action of European powers, whether it be France, Britain, or Belgium. The advent of colonization was a shock for some, but also a joy for others: the captives, slaves, and hostages. This is called progress and, like it or not, it does honor to the civilizing mission. Little matter that, in doing so, France hoped to free up for the capitalist economy millions of mobile workers (because no longer tied to a master) ready to put themselves to work for a wage. Little matter, indeed, because the qualitative leap from servitude to freedom, however artificial, was immeasurable.

Wherever Europeans had not set foot, slavery persisted: it was not until 1960 that Saudi Arabia outlawed it. And wherever the colonial presence was feeble (such as the deserts of the Sahara), abolition proceeded with much equivocation—in Mauritania, for instance, the practice would not be abolished until 1920. Ethiopia only put an end to slavery and voluntary servitude in 1942, and then in response to pressure from the Italians, who had some years earlier invaded the country and freed more than 400,000 of the poor wretches.[25]

---

25. The fact that the Italian troops who invaded Ethiopia in 1935 were fascists does not excuse us from historical accuracy. The armies of Mussolini liberated captives even as they devastated Ethiopia.

The *mean* French put an end to corporal punishment, not just of slaves, but also of free men and women. Tongues were no longer cut out nor flesh branded with red-hot irons. They also ended degrading practices such as the use of human beings as security for commercial and private debts. Before colonization, whether in Indochina or West Africa, an uncle could offer his nephew as collateral against a loan, with the person thus offered forced to work without pay for the creditor until the day the debt was settled in full.

When it came to freeing the Jews of North Africa from their millennial servitude, France was a liberator. For the first time, Jews were able to leave the *mellah* where they had lived one on top of another for fear of harassment and pogroms. For the first time, their physical integrity was assured and their faith respected. They knew dignity. Before France arrived, Jews could neither mount a horse nor wear whatever clothes they liked. As *dhimmis*, they were obliged to walk, sometimes even barefoot, and dress in a way that distinguished them from Muslims (by means of a red *belgha*[26] for example).

For all natives, the return of security constituted liberation. The end of banditry gave new life to regions formerly ravaged by razzia and crimes of all kinds. The peace imposed by France allowed for a revival of local trade. Caravans were once again able to move freely, and insurance costs dropped once the pirates had disappeared.

Consider this snapshot of Morocco in the 1880s as experienced by Charles de Foucauld. In your view, how was trade supposed to flourish in such chaos?

> "If, in the qçars[27] and wandering tribes, custom offers each individual some protection from his fellow citizens, there is nothing that anywhere safeguards the foreigner: all is permitted against him. He can be robbed, plundered, killed: no one will defend him; if he resists, all will set upon him."

The Fight against the Major Scourges

After having eradicated such "moral" scourges as slavery and the slave trade, the French strove to eliminate the viral and bacteriological scourges afflicting

---

26. A type of slipper.
27. Trans. I here adopt the author's spelling (in *Reconnaissance au Maroc*), even if today it is customary to write Ksar in the singular and Ksour in the plural.

the peoples under their supervision. For the first time in history, smallpox, plague, cholera, yellow fever, jaundice, malaria, syphilis, and so many other diseases came up against a force capable of combating them.

It was thanks to French doctors and nurses that, when Madagascar gained independence in 1960, it was free from plague, cholera, smallpox, and typhoid fever. Among these medical professionals were true heroes like doctors Girard and Robic, who developed the first vaccine against plague at Madagascar's Pasteur Institute and injected themselves with it to convince the Malagasy of its harmlessness (1931).

Little matter that the French did this for selfish reasons (safeguarding the indigenous labor force) or purely philanthropic reasons. The numbers speak for themselves and indicate significant population growth in the immediate aftermath of the First World War, the result of progress in hygiene and the battle against endemic diseases. They also reflect the end of razzias and civil wars.

Between 1907 and 1956, the Senegalese population doubled, reaching 2.2 million inhabitants. Between 1935 and 1960, Morocco gained 4.6 million inhabitants. It was much the same in Algeria, where net population growth in the 1950s was 250,000 souls per year. Impressive, to say the least!

In what regards health and hygiene, French colonization "invented" everything. It brought free clinics, surgical units, laboratories, medical schools, and research institutes to places where there had once been nothing to diminish sorrow and suffering. Like it or not, France helped to significantly improve the human condition in the colonies.

The statistical record is always worth recalling, even if it fails to fully capture the human reality of the care given and knowledge accumulated. In 1960, a pivotal year in the process of decolonization, France was preparing to transfer 2500 clinics, 600 maternity wards, 216 hospitals, and 41 major hospitals to its former colonies.

Inside these facilities was written the heroic story of tropical medicine, with its innovative health protocols and revolutionary molecules, like quinine (for malaria) and pentamidine (for leishmaniasis). It was a militant medicine that waged silent war against insidious enemies: mosquitos, tsetse flies, germs and bacilli unknown in Europe. A medicine of scarcity, always on the verge of collapse. Above all, a forgotten medicine, scattered across the sad tropical expanses, single-handedly practiced by isolated doctors with no one, or almost no one, upon whom they could count. In Ivory Coast in 1916, there were four doctors for the entire territory! Hospital capacity was limited to 28 "European" and 46 "native" beds.

Far be it from me to dream of writing a history of colonial medicine (a history that in fact remains to be written). It is enough for me to merely point out that it was born in Madagascar, at the very end of the nineteenth century, thanks to that "villainous" man Gallieni, whose statue a famous French footballer wanted to topple in 2020.[28] It is to him that we owe the creation of the Tananarive School of Medicine (1896), the Pasteur Institute (1899), and the Indigenous Medical Assistance system (*l'Assistance médicale indigène*, or AMI), in which French doctors and nurses (civilian and military) offered free care. The AMI doctor was a *bush doctor* who spent the better part of the year in his clinic, the only European among the natives. He was often the kindest side of France ever encountered by colonized populations.

AMI was gradually deployed beyond Madagascar, be it in Africa or Indochina. To make up for staffing shortfalls, a medical school was opened in Hanoi (1902) specifically for the purpose of training Vietnamese doctors. In 1918, a medical school also opened its doors in Dakar. These two schools, together with a third in Tananarive, were mere drops of water in an ever-deepening ocean of suffering. For endemic diseases made great inroads during the First World War. Cameroon was hit particularly hard, losing a quarter of its population to sleeping sickness, which is transmitted to man by the tsetse fly.

The first major turning point came in 1924, when Édouard Daladier, Minister of the Colonies, secured a threefold increase in the health budget. Hospitals (in the administrative capitals of each colony), clinics (in local district administrative seats), and medical posts (in villages) began to be built. While too slow to meet the needs of the people, this process proceeded at a steady pace.

Something had to be done. Courageous men responded to the call and threw themselves into battle against the most appalling diseases, with Jamot and Muraz taking on sleeping sickness, and Marchoux, leprosy.

---

28. Trans. This (former) footballer is Vikash Dhorasoo, who played for Paris Saint-Germain (1999–2006) and was on the French international squad. Dhorasso was sacked from Paris Saint-Germain in 2006 for "disloyalty," "disobedience," and "insubordination". In 2020, along with other anti-racist activists, he covered the statue of Gallieni in Place Vauban with a tarpaulin, claiming it was necessary to remove "statues that represent colonialism." He suggested that the statue of Gallieni be replaced with a statue of Zinédine Zidane or Kylian Mbappé.]

Doctor Jamot in this way sacrificed his career to develop a mobile health unit that was constantly on the move. Instead of waiting for exhausted victims to present themselves at one of the handful of fixed AMI posts, he tracked down and treated sleeping sickness deep in the bush. Relieved of his duties around 1934, he watched as the flame was passed to Doctor Muraz, who pursued the same policy and would in his turn be "punished" and sidelined by the bureaucracy after 1942.

The ideas of these two doctors would nevertheless be central to the SGHMP (*Service général d'hygiène mobile et de prophylaxie*), founded in the wake of the 1944 African Conference at Brazzaville. The service operated as a "task force" sheltered from bureaucratic considerations, its headquarters in Bobo Dioulasso, at a remove from large administrative centers like Dakar and Abidjan. The SGHMP was at once a sort of French-style Centers for Disease Control and a hub for tropical disease research.

Everything changed after the Second World War: there was more money, more personnel (the colonial medical schools were running on all cylinders), and more attention paid to natives' health. A new chapter had begun. Indeed, one no longer spoke of the *indigenous*,[29] but of *natives* instead.[30] The AMI became the AMA.[31] The methods were the same as under Jamot and Muraz, but they were better and more intensively applied: permanent structures were built for doctors, the range of care was expanded (including the generalization of tropical ophthalmology), and the territory was divvied up for the purpose of maintaining close contact with the population, especially given that patients were known to hide for fear of being stigmatized, especially in cases of leprosy. Most importantly, wonderful new molecules like sulfones were made available in the 1950s, allowing leprosy to be effectively treated for the first time ever.

The record is thus bittersweet. To the degree that it denied blacks, Arabs, and Asians access to quality medical care, postcolonialists will find ample reason to vilify France as racist. And they will be right to point out the constant preference given infrastructural investment over health sector investment. They will also be right if they claim that, despite their doctors' best efforts, the AMI and AMA were spread far too thin to effectively treat a population

29. Trans. "*indigène*"
30. Trans. "*autochtone*"
31. Trans. "*Assistance médicale indigène*" thus became "*Assistance médicale autochtone*".

scattered across bush and desert. They will be right, in short, to underscore the fact that Europeans were entitled to better healthcare than the colonized. All of this is true. But it is also true that there was absolutely nothing before this. France did everything; it might have done it poorly, but at least it took the initiative.

Given the scarcity of human and material resources, there is indeed much to admire. The achievement is all the greater in that many of the diseases in question (e.g., sleeping sickness) were unknown in Europe and treatments had to be developed "on the fly." French doctors innovated in a context of crisis, for the mortality rate among whites, including that of the doctors themselves, was extremely high.

The fundamental problem was demographic in nature. Caring for people is expensive, exploiting them not so much. Philanthropy has its limits, both financial and political. What French president could have convinced his fellow citizens to remove the food from their mouths and give it to the colonized?

DICTATORSHIP AND APARTHEID

"Colonization is theft," it was said. To which we add: "rape and murder, too."

HO CHI MINH

"I was in Bamako, the capital of Sudan, sitting among natives on the market steps, much to the astonishment of the European folk. The passing whites looked at me like I might have been a train! They made no attempt to hide the fact that I was losing face by mixing my good self in this way with the Sudanese people."

ALBERT LONDRES

In the colonies, there was no room for love. The rape that was colonialism could not result in consuming passion or sincere affection. Nor was there any question of a marriage of convenience, in which one keeps up appearances for the sake of a higher good while waiting for the children to grow up. No, colonization was, from beginning to end, a series of misunderstandings, dirty looks, and ulterior motives. A long stream of recriminations and grievances, each side seeing the other as the barbarian, the foreigner, the danger. There may have been some sincere friendships and perfect symbioses, but these were but a silk thread hoisted over the border, a border made of barbed-wire, travel passes, and prejudice. A border that only held by dint of violence.

This violence reflected a stillborn political system that lost its way as soon as it came into the world. After the initial excitement of pioneers and adventurers, the harsh reality of the tropics reminded the French of the extent of their *colonial folly*. Instead of the Promised Land, they found only the white man's grave. They thus turned inward, relegating the native to the status of a "problem," at once "lazy," "thieving," and "fanatical."

Colonization Is Dictatorship

We are all a little schizophrenic. The French republic is no exception. The regime of the rights of man installed and maintained ferocious dictatorships across the world. Right, left, and center all pursued roughly the same policy in the colonies: that of the truncheon. Even the Popular Front kept quiet about the bullying and harassment inflicted upon colonized peoples. Even as Léon Blum gave all of Europe a lesson in democracy, torture continued in Rabat, Dakar, and Saigon.

For the sake of intellectual honesty, it is worth recalling that French colonization nowhere took place at the expense of a democratic regime. Annamites, Kabyles, and Bambaras lived under inequitable laws enforced by brutal elites. The Sultan of Morocco was never a democrat, to say nothing of Emir Abdelkader or King Behanzin of Benin. It is nevertheless easier to put up with arbitrary rule when it is enforced by people who resemble you than when it is the work of foreigners. Such is human nature.

In the colonies, special legislation allowed for the suspension or significant curtailment of the rights and freedoms guaranteed by the French constitution.

Freedom of opinion and expression. Natives were of course forbidden to criticize the principle of colonization or campaign for independence. One of the surest ways to get locked up was to assert that a people had the right to self-governance or to denounce this or that crime committed by a French civil servant.[1]

That said, provided they respected certain rules of precedence and did not cross the red lines established by colonial authorities, native elites had the right to speak. These lines changed with the political context and the mood of French leaders. An article that was acceptable one day might thus land you in prison the next.

In Morocco, a half-dozen newspapers and weeklies in French (*L'Action du Peuple*, *L'Action Populaire*, etc.) and Arabic (*Al Atlas*, *Al Houria*, etc.) circu-

---

1. "All harmful criticism of the acts of the Cambodian or French administration will be punished by imprisonment for three months to three years, and a fine of 10 to 100 piastres." Quoted in *Indochine SOS*, by Andrée Viollis.

lated without major hindrance in the 1930s. The articles went through preliminary censorship, but an authentically Moroccan message managed to get through: the writers openly demanded that the dignity of Moroccans be respected by putting an end to the "double standards" that excluded Muslims from economic, political, and cultural life.[2]

After 1937, the climate grew more tense. Several Moroccan cities saw nationalist riots. And the Moroccan press, despite its moderation and courtesy towards the colonial authorities, was persecuted, with several of its "pens" being forced into silence or exile.

The Indochinese press also got a taste of the truncheon. In 1925, major repression rained down on the Annamite-language newspapers of Saigon. Journalists were imprisoned, and popular protests supporting freedom of the press were violently broken up.

Freedom of assembly and association. Natives did not have the right to organize politically or form clubs or secret societies. Those who did so anyhow risked prison and aggressive interrogation. Whence the reliance in North Africa on mosques or even *zawiyas*, refuges that were to some degree respected by the colonial authorities, especially in times of peace.

Freedom of movement. A luxury rarely enjoyed by the natives. In general, they needed a laissez passer or other such document to travel beyond the confines of their village or province. Changes of address also had to be reported to colonial authorities.

In Saigon, for example, the Vietnamese had to justify their presence in European neighborhoods by means of a booklet containing their photo, name and surname, and occupation.

Freedom of religion. Highly variable. Islam was for the most part respected, as were Christianity and Judaism of course. Asian religions such as Buddhism were also treated with necessary respect. The same cannot be said of sects and marginal religious movements like the Cao Dai in Indochina, who were persecuted despite their pacifism and legalism. The Cao Dai religion was born of the encounter between France and Indochina, grafting European spiritual lodestars like Victor Hugo, Louis Pasteur, William Shakespeare, and

2. The historian Amina Ihrai-Aouchar offers a fascinating study of the Moroccan press between 1918 and 1939. See : *La presse nationaliste et le régime de Protectorat au Maroc dans l'entre-deux-guerres. Revue de l'Occident musulman et de la Méditerrannée*, no. 34, 1982.

even Joan of Arc onto a Buddhist foundation . . . In the early 1930s, it counted more than five million followers, quite an achievement for a religion born only twenty years earlier.

These restrictions on basic freedoms were part of the more general justice of exception. The native was targeted by a set of rules and punishments that only concerned him and had no counterpart in the legislation in force in the metropole. He could find himself in hot water for reasons as absurd as refusing to use French currency, failure to comply with the dress code, or refusing to obey the orders of the administration (night watch duties, participation in compulsory labor details, requisition of livestock and goods). These infractions and the punishments that accompanied them were adjudicated and carried out by colonial administrators, who were both judge and jury. Any district leader or traditional chief turned civil servant by the French had the power to condemn a native to prison or impose a fine on the spot and without awaiting the results of a police investigation or court verdict. As he had no right to a defense or basic legal protections, the risk for the native was enormous should he happen upon of a sadist or psychopath.

Every colony was different but all were to one degree or another familiar with this special and unequal form of justice, which was only abolished in 1946. In the colonies properly so-called, it was practiced in the name of the *code* or *régime de l'indigénat*,[3] which was in force in Algeria, Indochina, and Sub-Saharan Africa. Elsewhere, as in the protectorates of Morocco and Tunisia, the code was not applied, with the surveillance and punishment of natives theoretically incumbent upon the precolonial authorities left in place by the occupier. In practice, however, it was never wise to get on the wrong side of the local administrator, unless you liked having a boot on your neck . . .

Still, it is important to not overestimate the omnipotence of the colonial administration. It was itself under pressure from the big colonist lobby, which influenced state action via masonic lodges, political parties, and newspapers. This influence tended to further disadvantage natives to the degree that judges, police officers, and colonial officials were encouraged to speak on behalf of colonists rather than the French Republic.

One must put oneself in the shoes of a magistrate obliged to spend two or three years in a Saint-Louis or Abidjan courtroom. What was his priority?

---

3. Trans. Indigenat Code or Regime, that is, a set of laws and regulations specifically governing the lives and legal status of native populations before 1945.

Defending the natives or looking after his career? For many, the answer was obvious: keep your mouth shut and don't rock the boat. In any case, the barriers of language, race, and religion provided an additional alibi for these *autists* who, in the course of their overseas assignment, neither saw nor heard. There were exceptions, of course, and there is no question of denying them; to the contrary, they were all the more noble.

While France indisputably brought internal peace and security to its colonies, it failed to establish justice, the foundation of any self-respecting civilization. Overwhelmed by the task at hand, it withdrew into a haughty and readily aggressive attitude. To the natives who reminded France of her duties, it responded with censorship and repression. To Europeans who did the same, it replied by glorifying a civilizing mission measured in kilometers of paved roads.

Republican Apartheid

There is nothing excessive about describing the colonial regime as a form of *apartheid*. Of course, the French in the colonies were much less obsessed than the Anglo-Saxons with notions of purity of blood, but the fact remains that they established and enforced spatial, moral, mental, and political separation between the European and native elements.

A double standard: two different systems for two antagonistic peoples. The French and Europeans (Portuguese, Spanish, Italian, etc.) had every freedom and were the objects of every solicitude. The far more numerous natives were neglected and constrained.

These two worlds turned their backs on each other and were encouraged to do so by the colonial administration. As we have seen, the natives could not go just where they wished. But nor could the Europeans: to move into native neighborhoods or associate with native people was frowned upon. Colonial city planning clearly speaks to this obsession with separation and social distancing. In Fez, nearly two kilometers separated the Arab and European cities. And, until the Second World War, bourgeois Moroccans found it extremely difficult to find housing in modern neighborhoods, as real estate companies preferred European residents. In Rabat, the medina was separated from the European city by a large and very wide avenue (present-day Hassan II Avenue). A floral park also formed a buffer between these two worlds. Lyautey demanded that European buildings not open windows giving on to the Arab houses across the avenue.

As a boy in the early 1950s, my father was expelled several times from Rabat's Agdal neighborhood, a French enclave, where he liked to visit the cinema. In general, Moroccan Muslims were nowhere to be seen in the cafes, libraries, and casinos of European neighborhoods.

At the time, segregation was justified for both good and very bad reasons.

(A) Europeans had to be protected from epidemics and thus separated from the real (not imagined) insalubrity of native dwellings, which were in general poorly ventilated and without indoor plumbing.[4] The natives, for their part, also had to be protected from the Western lifestyle, which might have shocked them. Imagine alcohol spreading through Muslim neighborhoods or European women without veils in the medinas. It seemed sensible to keep the European lifestyle as far away from the view of Muslims as possible, so as not to add an obligation to accept "scandalous" morals right outside their front door to the humiliation of defeat. It was also a matter of preserving the architecture of native towns, especially in the Maghreb, to prevent Europeans from taking advantage of their economic hegemony to destroy the Moorish architectural heritage.

(B) Segregation was also based on arguments that today strike us as totally deplorable. The native was seen as a threat to the European race due to his degenerate customs. The list of *threats* was long: opium and games of chance (the infamous fan-tan) in Asia, witchcraft in Sub-Saharan Africa, pederasty in Asia and the Maghreb. At issue was the necessary separation of *savage* and *civilized*. Separation was thus a matter of hygiene: and who but deviant and degenerate minds could oppose hygiene? Each time the European tried to take the native into his arms, in both the literal and figurative senses of the expression, right-thinking voices warned of the risk of contamination: beware of lice, venereal diseases, and such moral diseases as fanaticism (Muslims), laziness (Africans), and hypocrisy and dissimulation (Asians)!

---

4. The high mortality of Europeans subjected to tropical or even North African climates fueled a search for "refuges" at high altitudes or near the sea where people could rest easy far from germs, heat, and humidity. In Asia, France built magnificent hill stations like Da Lat and Bana in Vietnam and Bokor in Cambodia. The latter was connected to Kep, down below, a seaside resort with villas and a club for Europeans. In Morocco, Ifrane was a destination of choice for those wanting to escape the suffocating climate of Fez in the summer.

Among the groups allowed to "mix" were the Christian religious orders that made a calling out of feeding, nursing, and educating the wretched of the earth. And even these good souls were subject to judgement by the guardians of colonial apartheid. Such was the fate of Sister Ignace, a Catholic nun who distributed rice to the Annamites of the Vinh region during the great famine of 1931. In *Indochine S.O.S.*, the journalist Andrée Viollis reports that the Catholic hierarchy left Sister Ignace to manage on her own in feeding the thousands of peasants (men, women, and children) who walked by night up to 40 kilometers to receive a single bowl of rice! Their sin: being heathens.

By design, the colonial system generated repulsion, not attraction. Colonized and colonizer were obliged to keep their distance from one another, with little room left for love or collaboration. For loving one's oppressor was seen as betrayal by the indigenous community, and loving one's subaltern was held as a sign of weakness in European circles. Affection was studiously avoided, for otherwise a process of osmosis might occur leading to the collapse of retrograde notions of racial superiority. Without some being savage and others civilized, there is no longer any justification for colonization.

This repulsion was reciprocal: the native also did all he could to avoid mixing. The idea of their daughters or sisters marrying a Frenchman was the stuff of nightmares for Muslims, while the Indochinese despised converts to Catholicism and blacks clung to their spiritual life (their secret societies and shamans, in particular), even as they accepted conversion to Christianity on a more or less pro forma basis. There were barbarians on both sides of the partition, with the natives considering several aspects of European culture to be intolerable proof of savagery.

A French gynecologist recounted this extraordinary episode that took place in Saint-Louis, Senegal, in the late nineteenth century. I reproduce it here in full:

"For reasons of economy, a European family had just moved into a little brick house at the north point near the Mosque. The family's father, a state civil servant, had voyaged with me on the transport. The young Frenchwoman, curious and good-natured, had struck up an acquaintance with the local blacks from the area, and taken on a little twelve-year old negress as servant. After some time, the negress' sister, a splendidly built girl of sixteen, came to tell her sister's mistress that she was to be married. She married a well-to-do merchant and recounted all the beautiful gifts given her father by way of dowry. The lady reproachfully said to her: 'What? Are you not ashamed to boast of being bought from your father, as if you were an animal?' She drew this rude reply from the negress, who had been cut to the quick: 'Everything my fiancé offers my father so as to possess me proves that he loves me and sets store by me, whereas your men find you and the other Toubab wives so ugly that you are obliged to buy your husbands, for without the money you give them, you would not find any man at all.' This allusion to the dowry of European women was not lacking in bite, and it was a most excellent riposte."[5]

The native feared assimilation. He did not want to lose his identity even if he was attracted by the material and intellectual progress of French civilization. He also ghettoized himself of his own volition, insisting on living among his own kind even if he regretted that his neighborhood was flooded during the rainy season and without drinking water in the dry.

It was a cruel irony of colonization that each of the concerned parties saw the other as the embodiment of barbarism. Barbarism, however, is a threat to civilization, and wisdom dictates that it should be avoided at all costs.

Mixed-race people paid dearly for this mutual aversion. They were the product of a forbidden mixture. They were also the antithesis of the colonial regime since their very existence showed that the encounter between opposites can generate life and thus hope for reconciliation. Everywhere, they were combatted and belittled. In Indochina, they were so often abandoned that societies for the protection of mixed-race orphans were founded in Saigon (1895), Tonkin (1898), Laos (1908), and Cambodia (1909). In Sub-Saharan Africa, they were misunderstood, split between two allegiances that were impossible to reconcile in a world where one always had to choose a side: victor or vanquished.[6]

During his four-month tour of Black Africa in the 1920s, Albert Londres had the last word on the misfortunes of the mixed-race:

---

5. This passage is drawn from *L'Amour aux colonies*, pseudonymously penned by a certain Dr. Jacobus X, a treasure trove for the study of the mores (sexual, in particular) of the French colonies.
6. It seems to me that the fate of mixed-race people was less tragic in the Portuguese-speaking colonies of Africa. The Portuguese were clearly more inclined to mix their blood with that of the local populations.

"They are like those toy boats floating around municipal basins. As soon as they approach the edge, a stick pushes them away; when they reach the center, they are drenched by the fountain. Many sink. The survivors lose their color."

Colonial Crimes

They were numerous from the first day of colonization to its last and are of three types: administrative crimes committed by the state, private crimes attributed to companies and businessmen, and everyday crimes in which the European reminded the native of his inferiority.

Civil Servant Abuses in the Colonies

The offenses and acts of violence to which colonized people were subject observed a continuum. It was the customs official confiscating the books he found in the bag of the native student returning from France. It was the police officer swinging his club to clear a path for himself through the crowd. It was the civil servant insulting the native who had come to ask that a document be stamped.

In early twentieth-century Gabon, the government's Commissioner-General, Émile Gentil, went around with two henchmen ordered to beat up anyone who failed to greet his excellency correctly. It is easy to imagine the hatred that this kind of behavior inspired among the Gabonese.

It can always be argued that this was sporadic, localized abuse, and that may be true, but several incidents recorded in the four corners of the Empire show that arbitrary rule ran in the administration's veins.

On September 13th, 1930, Vietnamese civilians peacefully marched towards the resident-superior (a kind of prefect) of the Vinh region. They were dispersed by aerial bombardment. Several hours later, the survivors came to retrieve the dead for burial: they, too, were bombarded. More than one hundred people died, and many more were seriously wounded.[7] The air force would never be used without written instructions, without accounting for the munitions spent, and without "cover" from high places . . .

In certain detention centers, the worst forms of torture were practiced. It would make one sick to describe them. It should be underscored that

---

7. *Indochine S.O.S*, page 58.

these violations of physical integrity in detention did not take place in a context of insurrection. During travels in Indochina in 1931, Andrée Viollis gathered chilling testimony as to the widespread use of torture in police stations. The station in Cholon, a city adjacent to Saigon, invented highly sophisticated forms of torture, quite different from such "classic" practices as beatings or sleep deprivation. Two examples will illustrate this, and may the reader forgive me in advance for the brutality of these descriptions: "With a razor blade, cut the skin into long furrows, fill the wound with cotton, and burn the cotton." In the Sa Dec police station (South Vietnam), the native administrative delegate, Le Phu Man, inserted ant nests into the private parts of young girls accused of passing information to communists and nationalists.

The destruction of bodies and souls was not the exclusive domain of law enforcement. Torture was not only visited upon activists and militants. Anyone might be carted off to perform compulsory labor, the abuses of which dishonored the French administration.

Generally referred to as *services* (an early example of Newspeak), compulsory labor broke bodies and destroyed France's image among natives. Many lost fingers, hands, or loved ones.

Compulsory labor was not a bad idea at the outset. In Morocco, it was even part of tradition, as in the *touiza*, which consisted in a few days unpaid labor in the fields of the *caïd* or repairing irrigation canals. Morocco did not wait for France to requisition healthy men for collective labor. Nor did Vietnam. Traces of it can also be found in the work performed in the collective fields of Sub-Saharan Africa, labor that could only be shirked at the risk of expulsion from the village.

The French *innovation* consisted in utterly perverting compulsory labor. It was a widespread phenomenon in French Equatorial Africa, where the lack of manpower pushed a number of colonial administrators to commit genuine crimes. Limited to the period between 1900 and 1930, this phenomenon is explained by the specific conditions in this part of the world, which was underpopulated and totally lacking in roads and mechanized transport (cars and trains). Hence the permanent need (365 days a year) for porters able to carry several dozen kilos on their backs or heads. Barefoot, they could travel 50 kilometers or more per day, transporting dismantled machines or engines (sometimes from boats), merchandise, and food products.

The slightest uptick in activity led the authorities to overwork these men, cancelling their rest days, increasing their loads (up to 50 kilograms per porter), and lengthening the distances they had to cover. These excesses were aggravated by a lack of medical care and adequate accommodation: most of the time, the porters slept under the stars.

During the First World War, such needs skyrocketed, among other reasons because it was necessary to supply military forces in the vicinity of Cameroon, a German colony. Caught off-guard and convinced of their impunity, several administrators completely emptied villages located near major roadways of all able-bodied men. Women and children had to fend for themselves, working the fields and warding off prowlers. Tens of thousands of Africans preferred to flee deep into the forest, where the French could not reach them. Ghost villages thus began to appear in Gabon, Congo, Ubangi-Shari, Chad, and elsewhere. In some cases, the natives found refuge in German-dominated Cameroon or British-dominated Ghana.

It would take a catastrophe for mentalities to change. This catastrophe was called Congo-Ocean, after a railway line that cost the lives of thousands of black workers to construct. The most reliable estimates place the death toll between 15,000 and 20,000. The construction project involved laying nearly 600 kilometers of rail from Pointe Noire, on the Atlantic coast, to Brazzaville, on the banks of the Congo River. It traversed a terrain covered by equatorial forest that, for its first 140 kilometers, was nothing less than "infernal": mountains, narrow valleys, slippery soil. Due to lack of funding and resources, it took thirteen years to construct (1921–34), but the mortality rate was most intense between 1925 and 1928. During this period, the colonial administration went mad. Showing utter contempt for human life, it sent all the men it could find within one thousand kilometers to the slaughter with no provision made for housing, food, medical care, or equipment. Besides work accidents, the main causes of death were extreme fatigue, respiratory disease, and stress. Imagine the shock felt by a man from the dry savannah thrown deep into the equatorial forest. He was terrified of this dark and damp botanical prison, home to strange animals and evil spirits. Some of these press-ganged workers panicked at the sight of the mountain, which was seen as a taboo, indeed dangerous, place in their folklore. Others lost their composure upon contact with the ocean, a baleful malevolence in some African cultures. Imagine the man cut off from his environment, separated from his wife and his spiritual leader, forced to eat food that corresponded neither to his metabolism nor to his taste. Imagine also the vulnerability of these bodies, transposed to an environment infested with germs against which they had no immunity.[8]

Things changed drastically in 1929. Several parliamentary missions as well as Albert Londres' reporting[9] caused a great stir in French public opinion. The colonial authorities had no choice but to mend their ways. Within a few months, the number of doctors increased severalfold, barracks worthy of the name were built, and above all workers were allowed to clear sections of the forest where they might grow the leguminous plants that made up their habitual diet. In many cases, women were able to accompany their husbands, giving the worksite what would have been the familiar air of a normal African village were it not constantly on the move.

The Abuses of Businessmen and Concession Holders

The political vulnerability of the colonized was not lost on capitalists. Among them was a corrupt fringe of soulless businessmen who exploited the colonial workforce without any sense of pity or humanity. We should not paint all entrepreneurs with the same brush: several conducted themselves honorably regardless of whether they made a fortune or were ruined. Among them (and there are many such examples) was Jacques Lemaigre-Dubreuil, owner of Lesieur Oils, who established several production facilities in Algeria and Senegal while respecting both human dignity and labor laws.

The same cannot be said of the concession holders who preyed upon the workforce of Sub-Saharan Africa and Indochina, with the complicit silence of the authorities.

Rightly arguing that the colonies were not an El Dorado and that the resources promised at the time of conquest resisted extraction, several capitalists convinced the state to grant them a monopoly over massive regions, where they had exclusive rights to exploit a specific resource (rubber trees, wood, metal, etc.). Along the way, they monopolized for themselves the trade in goods bought and sold by native inhabitants of the territory.

---

8. For a detailed analysis of the causes of excess mortality during construction of the Congo-Ocean, I recommend this short and very well-researched study: Sautter Gilles. *Notes sur la construction du chemin de fer Congo-Océan (1921–1934). Cahiers d'études africaines*, vol. 7, no. 26, 1967.
9. Londres, Albert. *Terre d'Ebène*, Paris, Albin Michel, 1929.

This phenomenon corresponds to the period 1898–1945. Before 1898, insecurity was too great for private enterprises, which were often listed on the stock exchange, to risk investment. In the aftermath of the Second World War, the state heavily committed to promoting the economic and social development of the colonies, conscious as it was that the private sector could not accomplish this mission on its own.

In some places (in particular, Sub-Saharan Africa), the colonial administration asked natives to undertake forced labor for the benefit of concession holders and under their supervision. The inhabitants had to collect a certain quantity of cotton, rubber tree extract, or cocoa and deposit it at a central location—sometimes several days' walk from their village. Should they fail in this, they were immediately punished by agents of the concessionary company, with many crimes committed in the name of profit. In his description of the Congo, André Gide told of the torments inflicted upon Africans who failed to gather the required quantities, some of whom were put to death without further ado. One of them was executed by the detonation of a stick of dynamite placed in his anus.[10]

In Indochina, where economic activity was more intense than in Africa, private companies did not need to ask the authorities to provide them with a servile workforce. Recruitment was open in the sense that recruiters scoured the land, vaunting the advantages of working on the rubber plantation and in carbon and tin mines. They offered reasonable wages and a work contract of three to five years' duration. They neglected to mention the deplorable working conditions (bordering on suicide) and the various wage deductions made with the utmost malice on the pretext of feeding and housing the worker, providing him with medical care and days off, and so on.

Once recruited, workers were transported long distances to reach production sites. A coolie from Tonkin was frequently sent almost a thousand kilometers south to work on a Cochin Chinese farm. Once there, these laborers were kept in total isolation, prevented from leaving or using the telephone. Their mail was censored: only "appropriate" messages, those making no mention of their fate, were allowed to pass through.

The despicable Vietnamese foremen—the dreadful *cais*—submitted recruits to a shameful regime of mistreatment and malnourishment. The workday could last fifteen or sixteen hours. In the event of illness or accident, there

---

10. This story was vehemently denied by the managers of the concessionary company.

was no use expecting treatment. Driven to despair, some coolies committed suicide. Those who got out alive, returned to their villages years later, aged, exhausted, and penniless, only too happy to have survived their "penitentiary" excursion.

Labor inspection was absent: Annam counted only three inspectors in the early 1930s. The sovereign authorities turned a blind eye, all too happy to let French businesses prosper, whatever the cost.

Over time, people grew distrustful, and recruitment became ever more difficult. Recruiters thus turned to the colonial administration, which put mandarins and village chiefs to work encouraging (if not forcing) peasants and the destitute to sell themselves to the tricksters. The French state in this way participated in human trafficking to satisfy the needs of crooked capitalists.

This scandalous traffic was not limited to that between Tonkin and Cochinchina; Vietnamese coolies were also sent to French colonies in the Pacific (Tahiti, New Caledonia, New Hebrides). This was a good deal for French private companies in need of manpower, but a very bad deal for the Vietnamese workers and a catastrophe for France's image in Asia.

These events took place in the 1920s and involved the highest colonial authorities of Indochina, who helped hire more than 20,000 laborers on behalf of French companies that kept plantations in the Pacific Islands. Contracts were for five years and applied to men, women, and children. Entire households were enlisted, with the husband sent to Tahiti and the wife, Nouméa . . . During the boat journey, which lasted several weeks, men and women were mixed together. Women finding themselves alone with twenty men sometimes suffered the worst indignities.

Once there, some Kanak foremen lashed out against the Vietnamese coolies, thereby confirming a major tendency of colonial crime. For most of the abuses committed overseas were co-authored by natives, who were thrilled to oppress other natives. We shall return to this point shortly.

In his eye-witness account, *Les Jauniers*, published in 1928, Paul Monet supplies the most revolting details of this traffic. Out of consideration for the reader's feelings, I will refrain from reproducing the most troubling passages.[11] Here is one of the more bearable ones:

---

11. Paul Monet (1884–1941) was a former captain of the colonial artillery and employee of the geographical service of Indochina who became an anti-colonialist after having witnessed the ordeal of Vietnamese workers.

"It is the return, here in the midst of the twentieth century, of the slave market, but without the variety of tone and opulence of flesh that characterized that famous painting,[12] for the merchandise is already spoiled [. . .]. I spoke of slavery; it is worse than that. The slave owner had an interest in taking good care of his chattel, which had value. He who purchases a Tonkinese for five years, however, sees the value of his purchase diminish by a fifth each year. He thus has an interest in getting all that he can out of this purchase in just five years . . . Little matter if the man is at that point emptied, finished, good for nothing [. . .] Certain acts of barbarism are the result of women's absence. To avenge themselves against a woman who remains faithful to her husband, the brutes slit the throat of her newborn. Venereal diseases wreak appalling havoc. Carefully chosen, healthy individuals come back rotten. Recently, we saw a shipment of twenty-four women land in hideous condition, in the last stages of syphilis."

The Crimes Committed by Mr. and Mrs. Everyman

Man is wolf to man. In the colonies, this maxim acquired the contours of absolute truth, since the colonial order saw to it that some were artificially demoted, and others undeservedly promoted. It was all too easy for European men and women to become wolves to native men and women.

Having seen them in action in the early 1930s, Andrée Viollis is not gentle with the wives of French officials in Indochina:

"Here, placed in a position of superiority to which nothing has accustomed them, they take advantage of it, have themselves served like queens, tyrannizing their houseboys and, what's more, looking upon and treating all Annamites as their servants."

There is no need to recall that this kind of behavior hurt the colonized, not because they were accustomed to equality (Vietnamese culture was anything but egalitarian), but because they preferred to obey people who were genuinely their superiors: mandarins, members of the royal family, warlords, and so on.

---

12. Trans. Very probably an allusion to the 1866 painting of the same name by Jean-Léon Gérôme.

Albert Londres recounts the story of the son of King Behanzin of Benin who, upon boarding an ocean liner with two of his (black) brothers, is refused a drink at the bar.

"Leave!" says the barman. "No negroes here."
"But I am a first-class passenger", says Ouanilo.
"You, alright, I can serve you, you're clean. But not the two monkeys!"

If princes of royal blood could be treated like this, one can only imagine the lot of the average black person.

Londres recounts that, a few days after this incident, Prince Ouanilo, the protagonist in this affair, succumbed to sudden fevers. And one might indeed die of rage and shame faced with such contempt on the part the lowest classes of French society. A barman on a steamer is no marquis or marshal of France! The pioneering figures of conquest and first governors of the colonies were drawn from affluent, even aristocratic circles, where they had learnt the *art de vivre*. They had no need to mistreat the black man, the yellow man, or the Arab to feel superior: their family tree spoke for them, and their trajectory through life raised them above other men. A man like Lyautey venerated Moroccan civilization and did not allow the Moroccan people to be underestimated, even though he was never more Catholic or French than during his time in Morocco.

Unfortunately, there are very few Lyauteys in the world . . .

The list of offenses is long, and includes over-familiarity, derogatory remarks, refusal of service in cafes or prefectures. This list also contains true crimes, like beatings and homicides. These were very rare, but very real. It would be unfair and incorrect to give the impression that the French vented their rage against the natives. No, they were merely "worked up" by the architecture of the colonial system, which placed them on a pedestal. Some let it go to their heads, abusing their privileges, for which nothing had prepared them. The underlying problem is not the supposed malice of the French, but the toxicity of the relationship of domination. Or of any relationship of domination of whatever type. Do you not see see the resemblance between the slaps doled out to natives by petty colonial officials and the vicious beatings that some immigrants dole out to the ethnic French? It is the same thing: an abuse of domination in which the strong strikes the weak instead of collaborating with him. Yesterday, the stronger party was the French policeman or the French postman's wife in Tananarive. Today, it is the unaccompanied minor who has just arrived from Ventimiglia and uses a hammer to crack open the skull of the first French person who refuses him a cigarette.

The Complicity of the Natives

The French who behaved badly in the colonies rarely got their hands dirty. They had their *houseboys*, their *chaouches*, their guards to dole out slaps and canings for them. Such is the hidden face of colonial oppression, practiced by black men, yellow men, and Arabs themselves. Little smartasses, sadists, and those bent on revenge thought colonization would last forever and rushed to become interpreters, clerks, militiamen, and minor civil servants in order to persecute their peers.

The most ardent critics of colonization acknowledge that the French as such were not (with rare exceptions) monsters. It was their native auxiliaries who committed the worst atrocities. Instead of alleviating French guilt, this in fact aggravates it, for it would have been enough to say the word and the abuses would have stopped.

Listen to the suggestions of Paul Monet, author of the anti-colonial polemic, *les Jauniers* (1928):

> "It is the 'cais' who have to be closely monitored and kept in hand by a large body of upstanding French personnel well-acquainted with the Annamites. These 'cais' and their wives are generally oppressors, liars, and downright thieves, as are, in fact, a good number of Annamites who possess a measure of autonomy."

Further on, Monet remarks of the indigenous hospital in Hanoi, where "everything has to be paid for, and not according to fixed prices, but a tax proportional to the fortune of each patient. He who can not or will not pay will die in his corner . . .; in the course of his long night and perhaps even day shift, the solitary subaltern staff member would sooner help him die than go to the trouble of offering a glass of water. I am not in the least exaggerating: the whole Annamite population knows about this, and the French, too, to the extent that they concern themselves with such matters and do not deliberately cover their eyes."

Andrée Viollis, a woman of the left, had much the same to say: "The mandarin system . . . is rotten from top to bottom. The mandarins or *tri-phus* are tasked with administering the districts and collecting taxes by any means necessary. Under the aegis of France, most of them commit the worst abuses, they harass, steal, and rape, unchecked and unashamed."

At this same time, Albert Londres noted of Africa: "As soon as the black man represents authority, he becomes ferocious towards his brothers. He strikes them, ransacks their huts, eats their millet . . .". On the Congo-Ocean construction site, Londres witnesses the torments inflicted upon ethnic Sara workers by sadistic black foremen. Physically exhausted after sever.il weeks of forced labor, the Saras were forced to cut down a tree with their bare hands and no protective clothing. The lash of the whip rained down, striking even their faces, the skin of their backs was in ribbons, fingers crushed. No one came to their aid, especially not the porters charged with transporting the journalist. And for good reason: they came from a different ethnic group than the poor Saras, "foreigners" from Central Africa:

> "The ordeal of the Saras and the Bandas does not affect them. They [the porters] were Loangos. From one race to the next, black people hate each other. For a Loango, a Sara is nothing but a dog."[13]

If France was able to conquer Africa and maintain its presence with so few men, it is because blacks preferred torturing other blacks to repelling the white man.

The Failings of the French Administration

Everything we have just seen, this retrospective litany of crimes and offenses, took place under the gaze and sometimes with the complicity of French officials, great and small.

What had happened such that the "democrats" educated by the French Republic (the Third Republic of Gambetta, Blum, and Clemenceau) behaved so badly overseas?

The answer is simple and boils down to one word: decay.

It all comes down to the slow but definitive decay of the French administration. Like a pristine plank of wood left on the edge of a laguna, it only took a few months before it began to decompose, lose its (democratic) veneer, and be-

---

13. *Terre d'Ebène*, chapter XXIX.

come one with the sand and dead leaves. Well, the colonial system was the la-guna, a fetid swamp where callings were perverted, and noble souls corrupted.

In the beginning, the administrative apparatus was made up of great men who believed at least a little in the civilizing mission. After subduing the na-tives, they still hoped to lead them towards progress. Among these men were superior beings like Lyautey (Morocco), Gallieni (Madagascar), Faidherbe (Senegal), Combes (Tunisia), Varenne (Indochina), and Sarrault (Indochina). They were men of both right and left, but at this level of responsibility such labels matter little: all that matters is the stuff from which these men were made. Not just anyone can be viceroy.

With time, the pioneers departed (Lyautey was relieved in 1925) and were for the most part replaced with bureaucrats who had no desire to "make waves." But a viceroy (for such is the true vocation of the governor-general) makes waves by definition, for he is the vector of change. He rebuilds the house without ejecting its occupants. He creates friction, and forms alliances. He is a man with a mission. He is neither a looter nor a Nazi gauleiter.

Inevitably, the colonies were taken by storm by a cohort of civil servants ob-sessed with advancing their own careers and specializing in conformity. This was the opposite of what the colonies needed: civilian and military command-ers with a passion for solving problems and the ability to take the initiative.

The scourge of bureaucratization was only aggravated by the decision on the part of French officials to irreversibly distance themselves from the natives. In the early days, French officials would set up house with an Indochinese con gái or African mousso;[14] now, they arrived from the metropole with their wives and children in tow.

"Gone is the early enthusiasm, the romance of colonization, the ap-petite for risk, the bush hut, the conquest of the negro soul, the little mousso! One now lands with wife, children, mother-in-law. The colony wears curlers."

Albert Londres had the lucidity of the independent man who simply ob-serves and draws his own conclusions. Andrée Viollis reported much the same from her mission to Indochina in 1930–31.

---

14. Con gái: woman or young woman in Annamite. Mousso: idem in Sub-Saharan Africa.

" . . .before, the young men of the administration married Annamites, grew close to their yellow families, learned the language. Now, they live apart, think of nothing but how to line their pockets, how to save as much as possible so that they might more quickly return to France. The connection has been severed."

Saving as much as possible, that was the problem. For what was needed was to *invest as much as possible*. The mission required sincere commitment in order to create affective, moral, and intellectual bonds with the people under French control. To invest in the human element rather than turning one's back on it in favor of offices and typewriters.

Paul Monet took a strong view of the problem: "One cannot be at once on the scene and in the office, for at the office, it is the paperwork alone that counts, that alone attests to everything being above board."

What was necessary was to be at the office and on the scene at the same time, to construct a powerful administrative apparatus and fully immerse oneself in native life. To do so would have required exceptional men and adequate staffing. France had neither.

The disconnect between France and its colonies was born of under-administration. This phenomenon was aggravated by the introduction of the automobile, which limited the presence of administrators rather than reinforcing it. Indeed, they now only saw places connected to the road network, neglecting remote villages where the administration was represented by native delegates of often very questionable morals.

This disconnect generated mutual incomprehension and reinforced fantasies on both sides. Poorly informed by their native auxiliaries and often incapable of understanding local languages, French civil servants overreacted every time natives expressed their discontent. When faced with nothing more than a peaceful protest, they sometimes lost their heads and began swinging the truncheon. Ill-acclimated at best to local culture, they tended to wall themselves off behind their native guard, to whom they delegated the job of answering grievances. Among native populations, there was growing misunderstanding of the intentions of France, which ultimately had nothing to say to them. No project for their country, no plan for development (not before 1945, anyway), just taxation and abuse.

In this way, under-administration (lack of personnel and inadequate presence across the territory) and bad administration (the autism and incompetence of officials) sowed the seeds of rebellion. The absence of communication and mutual empathy could only ever lead to riot, sabotage, and noncompliance.

The particular colors of this portrait varied from one colony to the next. Where the population was defended by native elites or the remnants of local elites, they were less vulnerable to the abuses of the administration. Morocco belongs in this category: despite their shortcomings, the Makhzen and the great caids acted as *shock absorbers*, capable of reducing, however slightly, the brutality of the colonial order. In that country, France showed some consideration for the prestige of the sultan and the great lords who helped it pacify the country. The experience of Tunisia was similar, with the Arab bourgeoisie of Tunis exerting a moderating influence on French authorities. In Algeria, by contrast, there was no cartilage to protect the bone from friction. Lacking elites, which had been eliminated or discredited over the course of the nineteenth-century wars of pacification, Algeria was at the mercy of the administration, which was free to be as oppressive as it liked.

In this connection, it is worth underscoring that civilians were generally less well-behaved than soldiers. Until 1870–80, soldiers were exclusively responsible for managing relations with Algerian natives and treated them relatively well, taking care to respect their property and way of life. Civilians would later supplant soldiers and applied a resolutely anti-Algerian policy that gave free rein to all variety of arbitrary conduct: despoilment of land, double standards in the legal system, and so on.

In Morocco, the soldiers resisted pressure from the colonist lobby and civilian administration for the entire duration of the protectorate. The Native Affairs office, under the command of officers, thus managed local relations with the Moroccans (at the level of a valley or cluster of douars, for example). Trained in a special school located in Rabat, the Native Affairs officers were exposed to the Lyautey doctrine: no excessive violence, never disparage the Moroccan, be fair but firm, respect Islam, build *with* and not *in spite of* the Moroccan element, and show some deference towards traditional elites. And it worked . . .

The Solidification of the System

In the long run, the putrefaction of the administrative apparatus resulted in a stiffening of mindsets. The colonists' way of thinking (anti-native, sure of itself, and repressive) infected the civil service, which withdrew into its stubborn convictions. Instead of being agile and fluidly adapting to the changing circumstances of the colony and the world (the crisis of 1929, the war of 1939–45), the administration grew fossilized. Where haggling was needed, it instead chose to send in the tanks. Where rubbing people the right way was needed, it instead opted to censure and punish. Where the friends of France needed an attentive ear, they instead felt the tip of a bayonet poking their cheeks.

The alliance between monied power (wealthy colonists, financiers with interests in the colonies), soldiers, and the civil service characterized the final state of the colonial government. In Indochina, this symbiosis was probably established as early as the 1920s. In Morocco, it emerged following the departure of Lyautey and his last lieutenants (in the 1930s). In Algeria, the fossilization of the system may have preceded 1900.

Sufficient unto itself, the deep state that resulted from this alliance no longer feared the metropole and did not hesitate to disobey it. Some directives, such as that ordering additional measures to combat the coolie trade in Indochina, were not applied when they went against the status quo: the administrators acknowledged receipt of these instructions but did not "go out of their way" to put an end to abuses, for that would have meant jeopardizing "business."

The police and security forces took it upon themselves to conduct their own policy. Between 1950 and 1955, nationalist circles and liberal and progressive Frenchmen were targeted for extrajudicial execution in Morocco. That police officers were involved in these homicides is undeniable: they enjoyed carte blanche to act as they pleased despite the protests of the Parisian press and the deputies and ministers of the Fourth Republic.

Autonomy became a sort of rebellion on the part of a system that only did what it liked.

At the origin of this downward spiral was of course the temptation of corruption, but also a sort of colonial embarrassment to the degree that the administrative authorities did not know what to do to "make the colonies work." This embarrassment was the product of impotence vis-à-vis the sheer scale of the task to be accomplished. The mission was extraordinarily difficult, for official France demanded both that order be maintained and that social and economic development proceed apace (for which the native population would have to be stimulated, thus provoking friction and crisis). The bureaucracy chose the easy way out: it fell back on maintaining order.

After all, who am I to judge the conduct of colonial administrators? I am not unaware that it was extremely difficult to reconcile conflicting objectives with so little support and thousands of kilometers from the metropole.

It was the machine itself that was flawed. Colonization could not produce everything it was asked to produce: domination, prosperity for the colonists and for France, moral and material progress for the natives. The problem goes back to the very conception of the system; the idea was contorted at birth.

THE REVENGE OF THE WEAK

"One day, I saw her walking on the road, her breasts uncovered, carrying a basket of fruit on her head: all the splendor of the female body in its tender adolescence, all the beauty of life, of hope, of a smile, and a gait like nothing bad could ever happen. Louison was sixteen and when her chest was pressed against mine, I sometimes felt I had held it all, done it all. I went to see her parents, and we celebrated our union after the fashion of her tribe . . . Louison came to live with me. Never in my life have I felt greater joy in just watching and listening. She did not speak a word of French, and I did not understand a word of what she said, except that life was lovely, happy, unsullied. It was a voice that made you forever indifferent to any other music. I didn't take my eyes off her . . . And then, I noticed that she coughed a little, and, very worried, dreading tuberculosis in this body too beautiful to be sheltered from the enemy, I sent her to be examined by Dr Vignes, our squadron M.O. The cough was nothing, but Louison had a curious mark on her arm which attracted his attention. He came to see me at the bungalow that same evening. He seemed worried. Everyone knew how happy I was. It was so obvious. He told me that my little Louison had leprosy and that I would have to leave her."

ROMAIN GARY

Poor Louison. Poor Romain Gary. Even the purest love succumbed beneath the tropics. One would think that the colonies just could not bear noble sentiments and were repelled by the most beautiful expressions of empathy and

177

affection. Interracial love was the antithesis of the colonial order. A white man could not revere a black woman. At most, he might possess her sexually, but never hold her in high esteem.

If love was impossible, nothing remained but its poor substitutes: mischief, prostitution, and perversion. If cooperation was forbidden, nothing remained but its opposites: trickery, deceit, and dissimulation. The Frenchman did not always come out the winner in this game. His status, money, and pistols did not guarantee him the upper hand in interpersonal relationships. Avoiding direct confrontation, the colonized fell back on the weapons of the weak and—more than one might think—shifted the balance of power in his favor.

Escape

Refusing to live side by side with the colonizer, many natives simply fled all contact with France. Some Africans made for the forests or moved to colonies under German or British control: in the late 1920s, Albert Londres estimated that about one million black people had found refuge in Nigeria. These numbers are impossible to verify, but there is no doubt that the desire to avoid compulsory labor and military service drove population movements.

In North Africa and Indochina, middle-class families fled. Muslims headed to Egypt. Annamites settled in China and Japan. In these countries, quite a few men of letters pursued their studies and sought to understand how an old civilization might reinvent itself without first having to go through the experience of colonization.

Escape sometimes meant relocating beyond colonial city limits to evade the scrutiny of police and municipal authorities. Between 1920 and 1930, the demographic growth of the villages around Hanoi and Saigon was fueled by the exodus of Vietnamese who wanted to escape urban planning and hygiene regulations imposed by the French. In these villages, the street vendors were in their element, beyond the reach of any health inspectors: they could sell whatever they wanted, including spoiled goods.

Sometimes, escape meant settling in France, because the fate of the native was much more pleasant there than in the colonies. Andrée Viollis remarks upon the divergence between the life of an Annamite student in Paris and Hanoi. In the former, he was invited to join his professors and their families for Sunday dinner and could go to nightclubs and dancehalls. In the latter, he was constantly reminded of his inferior status, the police confiscated his books and censored his letters, the lowliest civil servant mistreated him, and he had no right to travel freely or frequent European circles. In Hanoi, there was no question of exchange and cooperation, no question of becoming intimate with France and the French.

Colonization was a mill for turning out enraged peoples.

Secrecy

Deprived of free expression and barred from public life, certain natives created their own parallel world. Behind a screen of submission and despondency, they withdrew into secret societies where their souls might find refuge. Whether spiritual, religious, or political, these organizations offered a sanctuary where the colonized could relax, recuperate, and develop a response to humiliation.

The Gabonese had their Bwiti, an ultra-secret sect open only to initiates. North Africans had their religious brotherhoods. The Indochinese had their syncretic sects like Cao Dai or Hoa Hao, syntheses of Marxism, Buddhism, and Christianity. Both required initiation and were practiced in relative secrecy, both to stave off repression and to put some distance between France and the native. Distance, even if only mental, was needed if one was to breathe again.[1]

There was also secrecy when it came to education, with young Moroccans, Algerians, and Tunisians given clandestine courses in Arabic.

The Flight into Spirituality

In Senegal, there emerged one of the most elegant and perhaps most effective forms of resistance to colonization: the Mouride movement which formed around the figure of Amadou Bamba (1853–1927), a religious leader with a frail body and an iron will. When France sought to exile him to Gabon, he responded by saying his prayers upon the water, floating by divine grace on the waves of the Atlantic a few meters from the boat that was to take him far from his homeland. Or so the Mouride legend would have it.

Amadou Bamba drew the lesson of overwhelming French domination: since it was impossible to defeat the colonizer by force of arms, it was better to

1. Another example is Egypt's Muslim Brotherhood, a clandestine organization formed in the 1920s–30s along the lines of Freemasonry.

escape his grip by cultivating autonomy in the spiritual (Islam) and economic (prioritizing work and commerce) domains. The Mourides (Arabic for "those who want" or "those who desire") therefore pursued the love of God (their sole master) and prosperity, so that they could live alongside the French without depending on them or their self-interested philanthropy. The Mouride aspired to genuine autonomy. He acknowledged the presence of the settler and the tricolor flag, but his heart and mind were elsewhere. He formed a counter-society that peacefully coexisted with France, since it did not deny colonization. Instead, it ignored and transcended it by clearing a path for the freedom and salvation of the black man.

After having fought Amadou Bamba to the point of exiling him to Gabon, then Mauritania, France finally came to terms with him, bringing him back to Senegal in 1907. The Mouride movement had so grown in Senegal that it had become necessary to accommodate it. This was an admission on the part of colonization, which lost touch with the native, who had closed himself off in a spiritual and economic bubble that shielded him from humiliation and assimilation.[2]

Corruption

We have a mistaken idea of the French colonial administration's omnipotence. Its power was diminished by corruption, the baksheesh being a breach through which the native could influence the French official. Bribing a municipal agent to obtain a building permit, for example, amounts to assuming control of the administration. He who gets paid is indebted to him who pays. Of course, each case is different, and the relationship of domination can always change according to circumstances. Sometimes, the baksheesh means the colonized is being extorted by the colonizer. At other times, it means a shift in the balance of power in favor of the colonized.

It is a fascinating question and deserves study in its own right in order to explore the nature and extent of corruption in the colonial administration. It would be especially interesting to establish whether corruption was an issue

---

2. Today, the Mouride movement is a crucial component of the Senegalese political framework. It brings together nearly 30 percent of the Senegalese people, who are told by the Mouride marabouts how to vote. If Senegal has managed to navigate the last sixty years without political upheavals, it is at least partly due to the stabilizing influence of the Mourides and their rivals, the Tijanis.

with French agents or just local agents, as the accounts of travelers would have us believe. A nice starting point for a future book?

Laziness, Theft, and Bad Faith

Private correspondence from the colonies is filled with stories of thieving *houseboys* and impolite housemaids. Household staff lived in close quarters with the French. They were in the vanguard of the clash of civilizations, right on the razor's edge of colonial apartheid. They thus adapted, sometimes in the worst way possible, confirming the stereotypes constructed about them by the French.

Albert Londres, though a humanist, described the highly questionable morals of his *houseboy* Birama, who never did his laundry, stole his soap, and squandered the shopping budget on trinkets and gambling.

The *houseboy* replaced the *valet de chambre* of the Ancien Régime, who ransacked the kitchen while his lord slept. It is the revenge of the weak, of he who cannot kick back.

Pretending to be lazy was a surefire way to avoid being overburdened with work and irritate one's European boss. A kind of small-scale sabotage of colonization. From the *houseboy* who works little or badly to the wood cutter who drags his feet, there was a subtle continuum of refusal and dereliction. Nothing especially extravagant or heroic, but a stubborn dedication to causing harm. If the white man had power, the native had a capacity for harm.

Sometimes, this harm attained a high degree of perversity, leading to the degradation of the white man. He might be tormented by a curse or have his food surreptitiously poisoned with some potion. All it took was to find the right fetish-priest. Who could tell the difference between a malignant fever and poisoning? After all, many colonies did not have a toxicology lab.

Sometimes, the contamination was carnal. The *houseboy* was a sex object in the eyes of certain colonial officials, who were often single or had left their wives behind in France. This was especially the case in the early days of French Indochina, when women were few in the colony.

To read the first-hand accounts of the time, temptation was at its height in Saigon between 1860 and 1880, well before a decent ratio of men and women had been restored:

"Unless he had exceptional strength of character, it was extremely difficult [for the single man] to not slide down the treacherous slope of vice, and in the evening, if he had the energy to take a short walk to help him sleep, a whole swarm of lascivious of boys would surround him, offering their sordid favors."[3]

The *houseboys*, like the *nays*,[4] or porters, offered an alternative to solitary men, whether civilian or military. Of course, there were brothels, but very few were up to "European standards," at least until 1880–90 (see below). The availability of young, servile Vietnamese boys allowed one to indulge in homosexual practices that were deeply frowned upon in France. For the price of a little pocket change, the "problem" was settled, and all in the privacy of one's home. No need to visit any unsanitary, poorly ventilated places. It is not to be forgotten how vulnerable the European was prior to the advent of quinine and the expansion of healthcare: he feared leaving European neighborhoods to venture into the insalubrious huts and shacks of the natives.

The boy who slept with his master was performing a "political" act, perhaps even a subversive one since he degraded the European's body via the transmission of germs and microbes, and by homosexual contact. Two powerful symbols in an era persuaded that the native was dirty and "pederasty" an abomination.

Sex for Money

Of course, one cannot talk about sex without talking about venereal disease, whether it be from homosexual or heterosexual relations.

During the first twenty years of the French occupation of Indochina (1860–1880), syphilis cases accounted for half of all patients in hospitals. A weapon of mass destruction! And a weapon of the weak par excellence, for it was cheap and quiet.

---

3. *L'Amour aux Colonies*, page 54. Read today, this book can seem scandalous, because it is permeated by overt racism and a frank aversion for all that is not white and French. That said, if the reader can set aside their preconceptions, they will discover in this text a window into the colonial unconscious, blending fascination with interracial sex, repulsion towards the native, and the venereal peril. These three ingredients blend and separate according to circumstances and emotions. In the end, there is no room for love; such is undoubtedly the book's true lesson.

4. In the Annamite language, *nay* means basket. These were children of between seven and twelve years old, equipped with a basket, who crowded around the shops to offer their services as porters.

It was thus no surprise that the army gave itself the task of establishing Military Field Brothels near the barracks. The famous BMCs[5] were meant to keep the men away from women (and men) of questionable health and were subject to the strictest health inspections. A waste of time in many cases, for the allure of the forbidden was always more eloquent than the admonitions of generals. And in any case, a "state" brothel would never have the perks of a private establishment, which was subject to competition and free from bureaucratic regulation.

In order to satisfy the steady demand for European and yellow women, prostitution took on considerable proportions in Indochina. European "desire" encountered a nimble local supply that knew how to organize itself while staying a step ahead of the colonial administration. This supply drew upon a long tradition of Chinese and Japanese brothels that predated colonization and was accustomed to serving foreign clientèle. Prostitution had long been practiced in precolonial Vietnam, but the practice caught fire upon contact with colonization (due to the influx of single men).

In 1931, there were seventeen regulated brothels in Saigon (offering Indochinese, Asian, and European women), and dozens of clandestine establishments. One could also find girls in certain opium dens and Chinese theaters, not to mention furnished hotels, which were ideal for discrete and furtive encounters. So many places that were difficult to monitor, inhabiting as they did the fringes of art, entertainment, and hospitality. As the city government tightened its grip, prostitution relocated to the suburbs and the country, beyond the purview of the vice squad. This was the case in Hanoi, where the madams and girls took up residence in the suburbs, which, due to administrative boundaries, fell under the authority of the Tonkin Protectorate, while the city itself was a French colony in its own right.[6]

In the end, who controlled whom? Some will say that the white man dominated the body of the Indochinese woman. Others will emphasize the fact that

---

5. Trans. "Bordel militaire de campagne"
6. At the time, the colonial authorities in Indochina took Casablanca as their model. That city (God bless Lyautey) had taken the initiative as early as 1924 by establishing a prostitution district that was walled, self-contained, accessible through a single door, and equipped with a clinic, a police station and gendarmerie, and a prison, not to mention cafes and shops. This was Bousbir (a corruption of Prosper, the name of the landowner on whose empty land the district was built). However, in Indochina, the transplant did not take. Its prostitution "scene" was stronger and more agile than anticipated and refused to be confined to a restricted area.

the madam and certain high-class prostitutes played their cards right, taking advantage of men who were slaves to their passions to make money. Whatever the case may be, venereal disease wreaked havoc in both camps. Let us call it a draw.

Self-Interested Love

In 1928, a certain Douchet (likely a pseudonym) published *Métis et Congaïes d'Indochine*, a thirty-page polemic that served as a warning to whomever might consider forming a couple with or (worse yet) marrying an Indochinese woman. The tone is spirited and uncompromising. The work is also typical of the atmosphere of the time, in which one freely inveighed against native morality. To avoid anachronism, it must thus be read with some indulgence, all the more so as its author decided to write it after the death of his daughter, Jeanette, carried off by an unknown illness at age 13. A father's suffering argues for dropping one's guard when reading this piquant description of mixed marriage:

> "The con gái does not love the Frenchman, with whom she has only agreed to live out of self-interest, not friendship or love.
>
> She even comes to harbor more or less concealed hatred for him, for once she has obtained sufficient financial advantages from him, she can never forgive this Frenchman for having prevented her from living with a man of her race.
>
> The early days of the relationship are always full of charm. The con gái is sweet, attentive, and even loyal . . . In general, however, that does not last long. After a time of variable length, the con gái becomes overbearing, insulting, shrewish, only too happy to enact, on the part of the conquered race, revenge against a man of the conquering race."

The colonial question thus plays out within the intimacy of the couple, and reparation for the harm wrought by France on the colony is obtained. To ruin the life of an official, soldier, or employee of a French company was just one more way to redress the balance of power.

As someone who has observed several examples of mixed marriages between cultures sharing a colonial past (Franco-Moroccan, Franco-Algerian,

Franco-Cameroonian), I do not find myself particularly surprised by Douchet's testimony.

The fate of children born of such marriages is *almost* a political matter since the two camps (father and mother) fight one another for their allegiance: France *or* Morocco, Algeria *or* Cameroon.

In *Mémoire du Fleuve*, Christian Dedet relates the tragic fate of a mixed-race baby named Daniel, the child of a Gabonese mother (Meli) and a French father (Jean Michonnet). As soon as he was born, Daniel's mother took him to the forest and placed him in the care of a fetish-priest. The latter laid him on a dunghill to "cure" him, turning this "ill-fated little creature, covered in excrement and flies, wrapped in filthy rags" into a theater of colonial war. Daniel would not survive the experience.

The weak had other weapons as well, and these deserve to be studied in their own right if one is to get a full picture. Among them were the vice of gambling, which ruined so many families in the colonies, particularly in Asia, where Chinese and Annamite games soon won followers among the colonials. Another vice was provided by local drugs, and opium in particular, which created quite a stir among European communities in Indochina. A fascinating subject. For a later book, perhaps?

PART IV

A FORMALITY CALLED DECOLONIZATION (1954–1962)

THE ILLUSION OF DOMINATION

"Between the submission of princes and the assimilation of subjects, however, there is a long way to go."

SIMON AYACHE

"Administrators live too far from the villagers, the peasants, they are ignorant of their merits and their pride. They judge the whole race on the basis of pilfering boys and groveling, corrupt officials, the dregs of the population."

ANDRÉE VIOLLIS

Contrary to what is generally believed, French colonization only brushed the surface of colonial societies. It was more like a skin condition than a systemic infection of vital organs.

Customs and mentalities did not change, dominated peoples relinquished nothing of their identity and were in no rush to merge with French civilization or take on its qualities. It was enough to cross a bridge in Saigon or turn a corner in Rabat to once again find yourself in the native world as it was when the French first encountered it: immobile, compact, elusive.

Anyone taking a walk in the Medina of Fez in the 1930s would have felt completely free from France: the mosques were full at prayer time; the muezzin could be heard from afar; marriages were arranged and celebrated in keeping with tradition; the diet had not changed from precolonial times, though soft wheat, tea, and sugar were more often to be found; Jews continued to be hemmed in by a complex of prejudices; visiting peasants were regarded as ignorant bumpkins, just waiting to be taken for a ride by the first swindler. Nothing had changed . . .

Bodies were of course subjugated, territories segregated, but had the individual consciousness been annexed? Not at all. France exerted its domination firmly—but superficially—from afar.

The native never stopped being himself and was always aware of his difference as well as of the reversibility of the colonial order. He had only to wait for the right moment to demand France's departure. That moment arrived after 1945, much to the surprise of the colonial power, which believed the colonial subject to have been thoroughly subdued. In fact, he had merely been put on ice.

The Perennial Neglect of Public Opinion

Pacification did not result in peace but rather forced submission. The rebel returned to being a peasant, but his war was not over. He would pursue it by other means, the only ones available to the weak. He tolerated the new authority, but he did not consent to it. Like a false convert, he pretended to profess a faith that was not his so as to save his skin and live in peace. It was a fool's game. Clear-sighted men like Bugeaud understood this and warned of it: domination may only be maintained by force; it is not desired, only tolerated, for lack of other options.[1] In other words, it is not legitimate and will never be legitimate until it is accepted as a natural and self-evident fact against which nothing can be done without knocking the world off kilter.

To transform the relationship of domination into partnership, in short to bridge the divide, would have required extraordinary individuals on both sides of the barrier, men capable of overcoming racial prejudice and quelling painful memory: men like Auguste Pavie, the diplomat and explorer who singlehandedly won over the hearts and minds of Cambodians to the French cause.[2]

Such high-value men would have had to be served by a dynamic administration, sufficiently staffed to oversee, understand, "love," and respect native populations. Just the opposite of the official who travels to the *douar* once a year to collect taxes and then immediately disappears whence he came.

---

1. "Our empire rests on force alone; we have no other—and can have no other—power over the Arabs; we can only remain in Africa by force."
2. Auguste Pavie (1847–1925).

Men and institutions should have put forward a project: a shared destiny with the natives (not in opposition to them, or at their expense), a convergent vision of the future, where both peoples came out on top. In short, a promise based on harmony and justice.

Men, institutions, a project: as we have already seen, none of these three preconditions were met. Rare pearls like Lyautey, Poeymirau, Cambon, and Van Vollenhoven[3] could be counted on one hand. Civilian and military bureaucracies were for their part all too ready to blunt the "Swiss army knives" required for colonization. And this is to say nothing of the vacuity of the colonial idea, lacking as it did any long-term vision. It was as dissatisfying as a novel that ends with its preface, for lack of any thoughts or feelings to share with the reader.

And yet, on the surface, all seemed normal and under control. There may have been sporadic protests or even riots here and there, but these were rare enough to not threaten the colonial order. Before 1945, the natives were not particularly restless.

In fact, the population was divided between three main groups: a very small minority of die-hards who openly rejected colonization, a majority that obeyed the authorities but among whom a number of silent grievances towards France accumulated, and finally a stratum of society favorable to the status quo. These three categories encompassed as many gradations as there were individuals, with their specific characters, situations, and interests.

The relative size of each group varied by time and place. In one colony, public opinion might change from one region to the next, depending on the personality of its administrators, or whether certain projects had been carried out. A road or an irrigation project could cement pro-French sympathies in one valley and arouse simmering hostility in the "forgotten" and "disregarded" valley next to it. In Morocco, France was probably never more popular than in the late 1920s, with security restored on major routes and completion

---

3. Joseph François Poeymirau (1869–1924). A close collaborator of Lyautey in Morocco, he implemented the policy of ripple-effect pacification. As an officer, he was known for his political prowess in native environments (or what we would today call his "intercultural" talents). Paul Cambon (1843–1924), first Resident-General of Tunisia, "inventor" of the protectorate formula. Joost Van Vollenhoven (1877–1918), the young governor of French West Africa in 1917. He managed to convince the French government of the moral and physical exhaustion of the natives under his supervision.

of the first development projects, such as the Marrakesh-Fez railway line. The situation was quite the contrary in the 1930s following the Berber Dahir, a legal reform regarded as an effort to separate Arabs and Berbers. In truth, it was nothing but a simple (albeit very clumsy) effort to bring existing texts into line with reality: the Berbers of the mountainous regions followed customary laws distinct from the Islamic laws enforced in Arab areas. Daughters inherited nothing, for instance, and a man could marry his wife's sister if he so pleased.[4]

Between 1920 and 1930, genuine public opinion began to come into its own as something more than just a series of tribal, regional, or communitarian opinions. As a form of national identity first began to emerge, a shared way of seeing things developed across what were sometimes ancient internal borders. It found expression on the radio waves, blending regional accents and putting individuals in touch with a national culture: Senegalese, Ivorian, Algerian, and so on. As it could be accessed by the illiterate majority, radio participated in the massification of information. For the restoration of security had allowed regular communication between regions to be established, facilitating the spread of rumors, scandals, and aspirations. Travelers recounted what they had seen and heard. They spread the good news about what France had done in the big cities, as well as the bad news about its neglect of the burgeoning urban proletariat. The peasant of Tonkin thus discovered a common destiny (or at least condition) with the coal miner and the "boy" assigned to a European family. The shepherds of the Atlas Mountains for the first time realized that they were in the same boat as the Casablanca shoe shiner. Distrust between town and country persisted, of course, as did ethnic rivalries, but such internal divisions were no longer absolute.

Between the world wars, the challenge was thus to organize this nascent public opinion, orient it in a direction favorable to France, and distance it, as far as possible, from nationalism.

Contrary to what is commonly believed, the die was not already cast. The French cause could still muster arguments in its favor in the 1920 and 30s. The first and most important of these were security and internal peace. Fear was

---

4. Some surprising aspects of Berber customary law are highlighted by Gilles Lafuente in his comprehensive and readable study, *Dossier marocain sur le dahir berbère de 1930. Revue de l'Occident musulman et de la Méditerranée*, no. 38, 1984.

gone, one could travel freely, take the train or coach without a second thought, and make the pilgrimage to Mecca or some other holy place without running the risk of being kidnapped or extorted (at least in the French zone).

The Jews of North Africa gained much from France's arrival and were grateful for it. In Algeria, they became full French citizens in 1871. In Morocco and Tunisia, the majority remained what they were, but were given the right to leave the ghetto and study at French middle schools— a true revolution in their condition. Yet, regardless of their individual or collective successes, these Jews were in no position to defend the French cause in Muslim eyes, since the latter still looked down on them. In contrast to the Andalusian of Fez or Tlemcen, the North African Jew never enjoyed elite prestige. He was never listened to, for he was always seen as an outsider.

In addition to the Jews, many natives also sympathized with the French cause, but they did not necessarily give voice to it. One might cite, in this connection, the populations liberated from slavery by the arrival of France in West Africa and the Indochinese rubber tree planters who profited from the rubber boom of the 1920s. Such favorable attitudes often remained confined to the private sphere. And for good reason: why would they risk sticking their neck out when France was so far away, when it was rare to see a single French uniform outside the European districts? A more robust administrative presence would have been required for ordinary people to openly say that colonization had improved their lot in life. Failing that, it was fear (fear of social stigma) that won out. To compensate for this under-administration, it would have been necessary to reassure the friends of France, letting them know that they were not the only ones who thought as they did. In general, this is the job of political parties and mass movements: uniting isolated individuals, motivating and disinhibiting them. A "Party of France" could have helped people drop their masks. But such a party never existed, as the colonial authorities never bothered to create one. Thus, with very few exceptions, the friends of France never came out of the woodwork.

One of the paradoxes of colonization is that, while many natives benefited from it, very few risked standing up for it. France was never able to rely on a local elite aligned with its interests, an elite that would have had everything to lose were France to leave, and that would have been capable of exerting some degree of influence over the rest of the population, whether by persuasion or the use of force. The fault lies entirely with France, for it never managed or sought to organize the social landscape to its advantage.

It was not a question of winning over 100 percent of the population to the cause of colonization. That would have been impossible. What needed to be done, what it was France's responsibility to do, was to see to it that hegemony was conferred on those fringes of the population who had an interest in maintaining the colonial status quo. Such groups certainly existed and revealed themselves in the 1950s when the independence struggles burst upon the scene. As we shall see shortly, hundreds of thousands of natives joined the French forces in Algeria and Vietnam, to just mention these two cases. But it was already too late: to prevent nationalist circles from taking control of public opinion—that is, the silent majority—these men and their families would have had to be mobilized twenty or thirty years earlier.

From the outset, France lost the battle for public opinion. To tell the truth, she forfeited it. France's inaction is among other things to be explained by the absence of any direction or doctrine from Paris, the colonial idea being vague and ill-defined. At one moment, one dreamed of assimilating the natives; the next, they were driven back into their prehistory and their customs. Left to fend for themselves, the administrators did what they could: they bought time by maintaining the equilibria inherited from pacification. In many cases, they also had been captured by European communities who demanded ever more rights, infrastructure, and subsidies.

While France was neglecting to engage in politics, two unstoppable phenomena unfolded before its eyes and would have the last word as regards the fate of colonization. On the one hand, the appearance, discourse, and methods of resistance all changed. On the other, the friends of France grew weaker.

The Resistance Passes the Baton

In 1934, when the last rebel Berbers in the Atlas Mountains were laying down their arms, a group of educated Moroccans submitted the Plan of Moroccan Reforms to the Resident-General. This was an audacious attempt to recalibrate relations between Muslims and French within the framework of the Protectorate. Written in Arabic and published in Cairo before being translated into French, this text was the first act of Moroccan nationalism: with absolute sincerity, it identified the aporias of the colonial system, the dead ends which could not be resolved without bringing an end to colonization. Among its demands were freedom of expression and access to economic opportunity for Moroccans.

The coincidence of these two events had nothing to do with chance. In the mid-1930s, the same thing was witnessed nearly everywhere in the empire, as the old guard (more or less discreetly) passed the baton to the new.

Like the worm-eaten trunk of an ancient tree, the old world was withering away and wished to hear nothing more about resistance or armed struggle. Soundly beaten by France, it had nothing more to offer. Its recipe, which had consisted in disorganized resistance to the invader, marked by guerrilla warfare in the countryside and the abandonment of the cities, had failed. Often based on a sense of belonging to a given land (the Sous, this or that oasis, this or that ethnicity or tribal confederation, etc.), this resistance had proven itself ineffective against the French steamroller. Something more was needed if France was to be repelled: the possibility of a united front made inroads as one of the principal lessons of pacification, and the concept of nationhood gained ground as a space where the common good might be defined. Similarly, the idea of total struggle began to emerge: a war that would mix propaganda, politics, and armed resistance—so many repudiations of the first resistance fighters.

Their prestige had been damaged, not just by defeat, but also by the fact that several of them subsequently rallied to the colonial order. The decision to ally with France on the part of some of yesterday's resistance fighters, including some of the fiercest among them, marked the pacification of Morocco, Algeria, and many countries in Sub-Saharan Africa. Weary of war, many Indochinese mandarins, also rallied to the French side.

The comfortable habit of obedience had in a sense "softened" these new supporters. They had their income and status, and no desire to risk it all again. Having become worthies, they tended to act like it. Many of them wished to give France a chance to get their country onto its feet and carry out necessary reforms so that, when the time came, it would be prepared for emancipation. They let themselves be persuaded that France was there for good, and that Franco-Annamite or Franco-Sudanese friendship would overcome all obstacles, beginning with the sensitivities of all parties and the glaring lack of resources allocated to development.

Those who wanted to continue the struggle were weakened. Indeed, the crème de la crème of the resistance had been killed or forced into exile by pacification. Those who wanted to carry on the fight had their property seized, depriving them of the capacity to mobilize their essentially rural clientèle, who followed their chief because he guaranteed material survival and victory. They were doomed to go underground, roaming the margins as highway bandits.

As a whole, the traditional world was aging and faltering under the weight of indolence. Disarmed and forced to keep quiet, tribesmen gradually lost the habit of fighting. Condemned to a life with nothing at stake, the bravest among them sunk into a life of tedium; like an eagle whose claws have been pared, he may fly high, but he no longer catches any prey. He no longer frightened anyone, not even the rabbits who used to tremble at the mere mention of his name.

"We are going to be very bored, and our sons, who will never have known war, will become like those men of the plains, who only know how to count their sheep and pay taxes."

Thus confided a warrior of the Ait Sedrate[5] tribe to a French colonial officer in the early 1930s. The peace and relative prosperity brought by the French, in other words, was the kiss of death for tribal forces. Their blood had cooled from lack of adrenaline and strong sensations.

Prevented from pillaging his neighbors and discouraged from taking the law into his own hands, the traditional man lost his taste for life. His innate qualities were useless in a world where the police (meaning France) put strong and weak on an equal footing. He thus proudly withdrew into his folklore and traditions, becoming a kind of living exhibit in some identitarian museum. From a distance, tribal life seemed magnificent, full of dynamism and fervor. Close up, it was merely a last stand.

The heirs of the generation that went underground to resist the French invasion took refuge in a mental bubble. Traditional chiefs in Africa looked after the spiritual lives of their peoples and did not deal in politics. The same held for North Africa, where the zawiyas and tribes steered clear of all forms of agitation. The mandarins in Indochina mentally *expatriated* themselves by preserving their traditional way of life and teachings. There was no longer any question of resuming hostilities or organizing resistance by other means.

One world was on its way out, silently bidding farewell with all the panache of the aristocrat, but on its way out, nevertheless. Conquest and pacification had, in many cases, led to the collapse of one society without giving rise to another in its place.

Such developments deprived France of an adversary it had learned to fight. Without support in French civil society and international public opinion,

---

5. Residing in the area of Tafilalet, in southeast Morocco.

Lyautey and Gallieni, to only mention them, developed a suitable doctrine for dealing with insurrections led by flamboyant but often isolated chiefs. The Abdelkaders of yesteryear were an endangered species; they would be replaced by ideologues and terrorists.

In the 1930s, the latter were still finding their calling and putting the finishing touches on their education.

Influenced by new and newish ideas—socialism, communism, pan-Arabism, Salafism—new avant-gardes were coming to the fore. Long the exclusive monopoly of warlords, the rejection of the colonial order was now the prerogative of merchants, students, teachers, and members of the liberal professions.

Allah al-Fassi (Morocco) was a religious scholar. Ferhet Abbas (Algeria) was a pharmacist, Bourguiba (Tunisia) was a lawyer, Ho Chi Minh was a photo retoucher, Moumié (Cameroon) was a doctor, Sékou Touré (Guinea) was a PTT trade unionist.[6]

All were young in the 1930s and still had the courage needed to confront oppression, the courage to set off on the long march towards national liberation. They had been exposed to new ideas at school, in literary and philosophical circles, and of course in the colonial cities where books and journals circulated despite censorship. Most had left their country at least once and had direct experience of the West. This was the case of the Moroccan Balafrej, who visited Berlin in 1936 to understand Nazism and observe Germany, France's great rival.

The new nationalist cadres had accumulated immaterial goods—rhetoric and networks—that the first resistance fighters had cruelly lacked. The art of discourse suited the new language of the masses, who could now be reached by radio broadcast. Networks, in turn, allowed awareness of the "national cause" to be raised in international public opinion and among the public intellectuals of the time. Some of these networks were of course communist, but others were socialist, Asian, or pan-Arab.

Soon, these young upstarts would add an essential string to their bow: an apprenticeship in violence. They would then be transformed into a fearsome

---

6. Sékou Touré (1922–84) played a prominent role organizing postal, telegraph, and telephone service (PTT) workers in Guinea and was among the founders of French West Africa's *Confédération générale des travailleurs africains* (General Confederation of African Workers, or CGTA). He would later become the first president of Guinea.

war machine combining the power of the word with that of arms. Beginning in 1945, a new chapter of history would be written.

The Friends of France Fall Behind

As nationalist circles professionalized, the friends of France ossified. They failed to see that a new era was coming, one in which ideology and internationalism would seize hold of nascent public opinion. Rigid, white-hot ideology would radicalize attitudes, as internationalism spread revolutionary doctrine to the four corners of the empire.

Thami El Glaoui, France's number one ally in southern Morocco, had no "ambassador" overseas. No one spoke on his behalf in Paris, London, or New York. Nor did he have any connections in the international press. No newspaper was in his corner. In the world of ideas, he simply did not exist, even though his views were of interest to many Moroccans. He had "nothing to say," even though he embodied a story that could so easily be sold the Western public: a son of the mountains, intrepid warrior, guardian of millennia-old traditions, sherif of a territory worthy of the Thousand and One Nights. El Glaoui had chosen France to reform and modernize Morocco, though he kept this to himself.

The same mediocrity was to be found everywhere. In Indochina, palace intrigues undermined the standing of the royal house. The royal family, the Nguyen, had nothing to say to the Vietnamese to get them to put their trust in France. They succeeded only in irritating them with their scandalous luxury and their eccentricities.

Wherever one turned, the situation was the same. The friends of France were losing status, at best they were on the defensive. In Algeria, the colonial authority's auxiliaries, the Agha and the Bachaga, were no more than a shadow of what they had once been, reduced to the rank of tax collectors and impotent spectators of the pauperization of their tribes. No one was fooled: these traditional chiefs no longer had anything but a decorative role, like an old piece of furniture covered in dust. The FLN would deal them the final blow in the 1950s, with terror attacks and targeted assassinations.

The gravest fault of the pro-French elites—and by extension the colonial authority—was their failure to prepare for the future. They refused to see the grievances of militant nationalists as expressing a desire for a piece of the pie. It was still perhaps possible in the 1930s to give moderate nationalists (not all of whom were communists or radicals) a role in the exercise of power. This would have been a clever way to co-opt worthy factions and offer a third way between separation and submission. Unfortunately, and despite a few ephemeral overtures, the choice was made to imprison, torture, and exile them. In doing so, the pro-independence side assumed the mantle of the Promised Land, while the pro-French elite had to bear the stigma of the inevitably unsatisfying and frustrating present.

In defense of the chiefs who I am criticizing here, the sheer depth of certain ethnic and regional prejudices is worth noting. In Morocco, the nationalists of the 1930s were often bourgeois urbanites, many of whom were from Fez. They were the product of Andalusian-Arab families, far removed from the Berber clans to which pro-French caids like El Glaoui and El Ayadi belonged. It was difficult for Berbers to put themselves in the shoes of bourgeois Arabs, who had always looked upon them as savages. This enmity was mutual, something members of the Istiqlal Party would prove in the 1950s by organizing targeted attacks against a number of Berber chiefs.

Ultimately, the true problem for the friends of France was their premature aging. Old age is not just a question of years, but also of mentality. They were still living in the nineteenth century, falling back on their lands, preferring the invigorating country air to the suffocating atmosphere of the cities. Under the pressure of the rural exodus, however, the colonies were turning ever more towards the cities and ports. The native discovered the shantytown,[7] he was a déclassé in the sense that he had lost his ancestral moorings: he no longer had a fixed place in the village and suffered profound anguish as a result. He was in dire need of answers to his new questions, and the pro-independence side would give him these after 1945.

South of the Sahara, a Pleasant Surprise

During this process, and by what seems to me a stroke of luck, Sub-Saharan Africa was a case apart. Petty kings and traditional chiefs allowed themselves to become obsolete, of course, but in many cases managed to avoid being supplanted by the enemies of France. In Senegal, Gabon, Ivory Coast, and Congo, the fresh faces, educated in France or by contact with France, thus

---

7. It was in the Morocco of this era that the term *bidonville*, here rendered by "shantytown," made its first appearance [trans. a "bidon" is a container or jerrycan].

did not demand independence, and when they envisioned it, they did not do so while hammering their fists on the table. Even in Belgian Congo, the great Lumumba did not dare dream of total emancipation but rather insisted on the need for a frank and sincere partnership between Belgians and Congolese. One has the impression that an authentically African and Francophone elite, one committed to carrying on for some time with France, was in the process of emerging. It would therefore be rash to classify Senghor (Senegal), Houphouët Boigny (Ivory Coast), or M'ba (Gabon) as independentists. As we shall see, they would have preferred that colonization continue in modified form. Unable to fulfill this desire, they became, with De Gaulle, the founding fathers of Françafrique.

South of the Sahara, France was able, without any real effort on its part, to count on a modern elite that saw some merit in colonization.

PEACEFUL DECOLONIZATION

"Holding on to one's conquests is much more difficult than making them thanks to a fortunate and short-lived arrangement of circumstances . . ."

HEINRICH BART (1821–1865), GERMAN EXPLORER

Taking place between the mid-1950s and the early 1960s, decolonization was less a break than the rectification of an anomaly. Independence aligned institutions with mentalities. The Algerians, Congolese, and Malagasy were already emancipated and autonomous in their heart of hearts. Decolonization simply brought their public lives into line with their private ones.

Did Hitler Help Liberate the Colonies?

The war awakened the masses, leading them to discover, ten or fifteen years after the nationalist avant-garde had done so, the notions of self-determination and democracy. All of a sudden, colonial oppression became intolerable. In times past, it had been relatively well-concealed by resignation and the still painful memory of the disorder that preceded colonization. Following World War II, it was no longer possible to ignore it. Change was necessary, but in what form?

The conflict had touched everyone, rich and poor, apathetic and engaged, indifferent bystanders and long-standing militants. No matter their rank or place of residence, all suffered privation and even bombing. Almost everywhere, food became scarce, and prices skyrocketed. The disorganization of logistics and transport played a major part in this, as did requisitions (wheat, rice, coffee, etc.).

The war had revealed in broad daylight the absurdity of the empire's economic model. The colonies understood that they were totally dependent on the metropole, which produced everything, while they only extracted wealth (when there was any to extract) from the soil or subsoil. Hence the hardship when boats were requisitioned for the war effort or when they were sunk by German submarines. The absurdity reached its apogee once it became clear that supplies would not be forthcoming from neighboring countries because the colonial authorities did not allow this. Madagascar thus could not turn to South Africa, which possessed all the goods it lacked, since the Vichy authorities opposed doing so on principle. The colonial economic model, in other words, proved a threat to the very survival of the people under French tutelage.

Compounding this hardship, there was a hardening of the colonial order. Freedom of expression, little more than an idle fancy before the war, was put even further out of reach for colonized populations, since war entailed suspicion and paranoia. Restrictions were placed on the circulation of newspapers and books, and nationalist agitators were placed under surveillance for fear they would engage in sabotage or enter into contact with German or Italian secret agents.

Peasants were forced to work more and eat less. On the one hand, they increased the area of cultivation; on the other, they neglected subsistence crops (those that fed them) in favor of rice, wheat, and sugar cane for export.

How to convince them of the benefits of colonization or ask them to be patient in anticipation of some hypothetical progress?

The nightmare did not end with the surrender of Germany in May 1945 or the defeat of Japan in September 1945. Hardship continued until the late 1940s, the time needed for reconstruction and economic reorganization, and to reopen trade routes with the metropole, the source of cotton, clothing, shoes, medicine, and most consumer goods.

The war had obliterated the main foundation of the colonial order: the moral and almost anthropological superiority of the Frenchman over the native. Gone was the notion of a "superior race": the Frenchman had suddenly become a man like any other, capable of crying, fleeing, hiding, and obeying the stronger party. Gone was the extraterrestrial, who was right about everything and always had the last word.

Certain scenes had a profound impact on the collective imagination of the colonized populations. In North Africa, for example, Muslims understood that the French had come down a peg in the world when they saw American troops passing under their windows, following their landing in the region in November 1942. Loaded with equipment, well fed, and confident that their luck would hold out, the American forces clearly had the upper hand over their French counterparts. But it was in Indochina that the psychological impact of the war would be most brutal. In September 1940, the colony was subjugated by the Japanese, who relegated the French to the role of simple foremen. The natives were shocked to see their colonizers "colonized" in their turn, all the more so as it was by other Asians.

This portrait, though very hastily painted, nevertheless allows one to imagine the state of mind of the colonized in the aftermath of the war. They wanted immediate compensation for their sacrifices: economic and social development, and equality. While the first demand was achievable in the middle to long term, the second was unimaginable, for it would have brought down the whole edifice. My impression is that the most pressing demand in the immediate postwar environment was equality, not independence. People had had enough of giving without getting anything in return. They wanted their dignity to be respected without discrimination by race, birth, or religion. But this would mean the end of the colonial order, for without separation and discrimination, there is no colonialism. Domination only exists because one side is superior to the other.

This time round, the clash of wills favored the colonized. For the first time since the nineteenth century, the balance of power was shifting. And for good reason: demography was on the natives' side; their population was growing by leaps and bounds while the European contingent remained diminishingly small. In 1947, for instance, there were 35,000 Europeans in Madagascar and 4 million Malagasy. A ratio of 1 to 100, a gap that would only widen with time.

With so few civilians and soldiers, there was good reason to doubt the staying-power of French domination.

Political Decolonization

It is not my intention here to retell the history of decolonization. The subject has been extensively covered by journalists and historians, often from a biased and strongly anti-French perspective, but with an abundance of information, images, and first-hand accounts. Our time will be better spent dismantling or at least qualifying certain received ideas relating to the process itself.

A "Consensual" Process in Most Colonies

The Empire's dissolution was not as painful an undertaking as we are given to believe. With the exception of Indochina and Algeria, decolonization was almost a formality. In reality, France abandoned its colonies in order to dedicate itself to Europe and its own modernization.

In Tunisia, a handful of protests sufficed to convince Mendès France to arrange for the orderly and consensual attainment of independence, which was finally granted on March 20th, 1956. No tragedies, terror attacks, or guerrilla fighting. In Morocco, the process was a little less peaceful. In Casablanca, bombs were set off in areas frequented by Europeans: the Central Market in 1953 and the Mers Sultan roundabout in July 1955. A few days later, the city of Oued Zem (250 kilometers from Rabat) was put through hell when, in the space of a few hours, a Moroccan crowd massacred forty-seven Europeans, including women, children, as well as the patients, nurses, and doctors of the local hospital. When reinforcements arrived, they are said to have fomented a dreadful campaign of reprisals. While the death toll is uncertain, it is said that several hundred people lost their lives. There is no way to verify this claim.

Despite this violence, Moroccan independence primarily played out on the political level, as part of a long and unpredictable tug of war between Sultan Mohamed V and the colonial authorities. Finally, after three years of confrontation, Paris "unplugged" the protectorate by completely disavowing the colonial administration, as well as some of France's most loyal allies, including El Glaoui. On April 7th, 1956, Morocco became independent.

In Sub-Saharan Africa, decolonization was a mostly peaceful affair. In 1960, from Dakar to Antananarivo, speeches were made, the tricolor was lowered, and the colors of the newly independent nation were raised.

Two shadows—one benign, the other bloody—nevertheless fell across this peaceful tableau. In Guinea-Conakry, miscommunication and outsized egos derailed the emancipation process. Sékou Touré, the nationalist leader, rejected the process of gradual emancipation proposed by De Gaulle, declaring his country independent in October 1958. He would pay dearly for this: in the 1960s, conspiracies, subversion, and other economic pressures awaited him at every turn. The case of Cameroon was much more serious, with intense fighting casting a pall over the country between 1960 and 1964. Formally independent from 1960, Cameroon immediately became embroiled in a civil war pitting government forces under the command of French officers against pro-independence guerrillas united under the aegis of the Union of the Peoples of Cameroon (UPC).

In both Guinea and Cameroon, however, the issue was never to maintain the colonial order, but rather to transfer power to political formations well-disposed towards France.

Why did the French grant independence so easily? Three complementary explanations can be advanced. The first is that the colonies cost much more than they brought in. This state of affairs existed well before the war but would become significantly more pronounced after the Brazzaville Conference (1944), where France promised the natives housing, medical care, education, and economic development. These promises, made in the context of a demographic boom, were enough to ruin France, which preferred to pull out while it still could. The second explanation resides in the urgent need to modernize France. Starting in the early 1950s, the idea gained ground that the colonies were squandering France's vital forces and hindering its industrial innovation (captive markets). The Dutch example was instructive in this connection: the Netherlands experienced record growth after it ended its colonial adventure in Indonesia (1949). Finally, the colonial dream was gradually eclipsed by the European one. Little by little, French elites lost their appetite for foreign lands and began to imagine the contours of a new Europe that would be unified, pacified, and prosperous. The great colonial vastness was abandoned in order to concentrate on what really mattered, namely drawing closer to France's peers. It is moreover notable that the Élysée Treaty, which once and for all ratified Franco-German reconciliation, was signed in January 1963, or barely six months after Algerian independence! It is as if a page had to be turned before a new one could be written.

Horror in Algeria and Indochina

What public opinion retains from decolonization are the absolute catastrophes that were the colonial wars in Indochina (1946–1954) and Algeria (1954–1962). These two conflicts were at once wars of liberation and civil wars between pro and anti-French forces. In Algeria, the FLN killed more Muslims than it did Europeans: 30,000 versus 3000, a ratio of 10 to 1. More Muslims sided with France than with the FLN: around 200,000 (regular and auxiliary forces), as compared to 30–50,000 guerrilla fighters at most. The same goes for Indochina: at the height of the conflict, the Vietnamese national army counted 168,000 native soldiers, as compared to 79,000 for the Viet Minh[1] (1949).

There is no civil war without fratricidal massacre. It is the old story of Cain and Abel, transposed onto the colonial context. In Indochina and Algeria, two, equally valid truths came to blows. They were not *collaborators* and *patriots*, *cowards* and the *courageous*. All loved their country; all risked their lives to defend it. The cowards were those who remained indifferent, the shirkers, those who kept score from the comfort of their café tables.

Both sides had valid arguments, both were legitimate. One side hoped that, by collaborating with France, they could shorten their country's path towards modernity; the other believed that, before dedicating themselves to the work of modernization, they had to rid themselves of colonization as one would rid oneself of an unwelcome parasite. Both sides were right in a sense but also wrong. The former failed to understand that France could no longer keep them on life support: development was just too costly. The latter failed to see that, in order to become rich and powerful, it was not enough to liberate oneself; one must also find the magic recipe that guaranteed development, a recipe that varies from one people to the next depending on its specificities.

The hyperviolence of the wars of liberation was also enacted against French civilians and soldiers alike. This leads me to consider that the former colonized and the former colonizers are now even. The match is a draw. Each side did great harm to the other, much more so than was necessary to defend their cause.

In Algeria, FLN guerrillas rampaged against French civilians, including women and children.

"The grandmother and the fifteen-year-old young woman were naked and tied to a chair in the kitchen. They had been raped and disemboweled. Their throats had been cut from ear to ear. In the adjoining room, there was a two-year-old boy whose head had been smashed against the wall, his brains splattered all over."[2]

---

1. On the methods and state of mind of the Vietnamese guerrilla fighters, I recommend the following study: Quartier, Vincent. "*L'armée Viet-Minh, vue par les Français en 1949*", *Revue Militaire Suisse* (online): https://cafi47.files.wordpress.com/2013/11/vietminh.pdf
2. Reported by Lieutenant-Colonel David Galula in *Pacification in Algeria*.

Did the struggle really require this? How is it useful to smash a baby's skull?

In August 1955, FLN militants killed French miners and their families by stabbing them with pitchforks in Philippeville. The massacre began at lunchtime and extended into the evening, when the alarm was finally sounded and the first reinforcements began to arrive.[3]

After the Évian accords were signed in March 1962, the FLN continued to abduct Europeans despite the ceasefire. They were never returned to their families, and no one knows what became of them. Some among them were drained of their blood in the underground clinics operated by the FLN. Try to imagine an innocent young woman being slowly drained of her blood until she dies.

Once independence was obtained, civilians continued to be massacred in violation of common sense and the most basic morality. On July 5th, 1962, the populace, supported and egged on by the army of the frontiers,[4] hunted down Europeans and any Algerians deemed close to the French in Oran. Despite the screams and calls for help from tortured civilians, French soldiers were ordered to remain in their barracks.[5] The police had been dismantled because, theoretically at least (and in keeping with the Évian accords), the business of keeping the peace was the responsibility of a mixed Franco-Algerian police force. This force never lifted a finger. It is estimated that round 700 were killed or went missing. The attitude of the French government was also deplorable: not content with forbidding soldiers from leaving their barracks, it never held the Algerians accountable for these events and failed to use the available resources to locate the hostages (dead or alive).

Horror struck Indochina, too. The Viet Minh committed war crimes against French prisoners, whose numbers exploded after the defeat at Dien Bien Phu (May 1954). By the thousands, they were dragged barefoot through

---

3. The FLN assassinated radio and switchboard operators first. The first reconnaissance flights took place in the middle of the afternoon, once the deed had already been done.

4. The army of the frontiers were FLN forces that did not fight on Algerian soil between 1954 and 1962. These soldiers were confined to Morocco and Tunisia on the other side of the defensive line (the famous Morice Line).

5. As is often the case in these dramatic episodes, some men disobeyed illegitimate orders and came to the aid of the civilians. Many French soldiers (including Muslims) organized the defense of certain buildings where civilians were able to find refuge on July 5th, 1962.

virgin forests, without proper clothing or first aid. Very often, the captive soldiers slept in the homes of natives, who were supposed to feed them a little
rice. Eventually, the Vietnamese communists constructed camps in the middle
of the forest, resembling FARC camps in Columbia. In such a hostile environment, there was no need for barbed wire or impassable moats, for to flee
them was too dangerous, if not impossible. The handful of prisoners who
tried to escape or merely disobeyed in one way or another were tortured. The
cruelest form of torture was being "put to the buffalo," in which the captive
was forced to spend the night with the buffalo, on bug-infested, excrement-
covered ground. Some lost their minds. Another form of torture was to lock
the captive in a 50 centimeter by 50 centimeter cage ("the Japanese cage"),
where, for days on end, he had to remain on all fours. It was impossible to lay
down or avoid soiling oneself.

The purpose of repeating these sordid details is to demonstrate that both
sides engaged in nameless cruelty. Both violated human dignity. Both gave
free reign to barbarism when limiting the use of force should have been the
rule. It is far from my intention to diminish French responsibility, especially
when it comes to torture or population displacement. Instead, I seek to show
that, by the time peace was signed, all debts had been paid. The page should
have been turned on the past, the better to build the future.

Yet Algeria has never wanted the war to end. It has continued uninter-
rupted since July 1962: in the declarations of FLN apparatchiks, in the curric-
ula taught schoolchildren, and in the minds of a not inconsiderable segment of
the diaspora that seems to live in France "despite itself." It is a curious mentality that forces one to live in a country one hates with all one's heart. It would
be so easy to simply return to Algeria or move to Dubai or Canada rather than
living alongside "war criminals."

Yes, once the war of liberation was over, France and Algeria were even.
Upon leaving, France gifted Algeria the Sahara—a godsend given the history
of the territory, which no force from Algiers, Oran, or Constantine had ever
succeeded in subduing. The desert tribes knew how to fight and loved their
autonomy.[6] Apart from its strategic depth, the Sahara also of course contains
immense hydrocarbon reserves, which have showered hundreds of billions of

---

6. It wasn't until 1905 that the French army succeeded in pacifying the desert, 35
years after the pacification of Kabylia and almost 60 years after the surrender of
Abdelkader.

dollars on Algeria since independence. One might also, as Bernard Lugan has admirably done, count the kilometers of railways and asphalt roads that the Algerians inherited from the French.[7] One can always retort that the French built this infrastructure for the benefit of the pied-noirs, to which I would respond that France could just as well have blown it all up once a million pied-noirs were sent packing between March and July 1962.

The FLN's primordial error was to have expelled the pied-noirs, thereby depriving themselves of a dynamic human resource, one adapted to Algerian conditions and with a stake in the country's future. The pied-noirs were not expatriates who had come to spend a few years in the sun. They were Algerians who had broken their backs to plough, build, and invest in the country. In the 1950s, their economy had begun to take off, dangling the promise of a radiant economic future for the entire country. But fanaticism and xenophobia deprived Algeria of the only Algerians with managerial and engineering skills. There is no point in accusing France of insufficiently training Algerians between 1830 and 1962 (I did this myself in the preceding chapters) if the FLN expelled the best personnel at its disposal. Recall that hateful slogan: the *suitcase or the coffin*. Well, the pied-noirs packed their bags and Algeria dug its own grave.

"With the pied-noirs and their dynamism—and I mean the pied-noirs, not the French—Algeria would be a great African and Mediterranean power today."[8] —Hocine Aït Ahmed, former FLN leader

The situation was different in Indochina, for reasons we all know. France's departure in 1954 was merely a pause in the process of decolonization. The French transferred control over this pearl of their empire to the United States, which immediately established a foothold south of the 17th parallel. Until 1975, the North (Hanoi) and the South (Saigon) would continue to pursue two interlocking wars: a colonial war against the white man (the American) and a civil war.

Despite these repeated traumas, one never hears Vietnamese leaders complaining about the colonial legacy or sees them parading around showing the

---

7. 70,000 kilometers of roads and 4,300 kilometers of railways in Algeria, as compared to 11,500 kilometers in Morocco on the eve of independence, and fewer than 1,500 kilometers of railways.

8. Extract from an interview with a Montpellier association review (*Association culturelle d'éducation populaire*): *Ensemble*, June 2005. I was unable to obtain a copy of the original.

world their scars. Perhaps they have no need to blame others for their failures. Instead, they work tirelessly to never again become a colonizable country. Perhaps this is the secret of success.

The British Anti-Model

The stubborn belief that British decolonization was somehow exemplary also needs to be put to rest. Nothing could be further from the truth: Indian independence was an absolute tragedy that cost the lives of hundreds of thousands of innocent civilians. The British contented themselves with setting a date for their departure, leaving it to the natives to fend for themselves when it came to inventing a new world. This led to the division of the ancient Indian Empire into three artificial entities: Muslim Pakistan, multiethnic but mostly Hindu India, and Muslim Bangladesh, a satellite state of Pakistan. The turmoil that followed their hurried departure was extraordinary. The exodus of refugees between India and Pakistan involved around 15 million people who had to leave their homes to reach Pakistan (for Muslims) or India (for Hindus). The Kashmir conflict, which continues to this day, is a consequence of this split and may one day lead to nuclear war between New Delhi and Islamabad. To the east, Bangladesh found itself colonized by Pakistan after having rid itself of the British. A terrible war involving mass rape and violence against civilians took place in 1970–1971 and resulted in the emancipation of Bangladesh from Pakistani control.

In Malaysia, decolonization was violent, if less traumatically so than in India. The British nevertheless had to fight communist guerrillas for twelve years (from 1948 to 1960).

In Africa, the record of British decolonization is far from a fairy tale. In Kenya, Mau Mau warriors were castrated. In South Africa and Rhodesia (present-day Zimbabwe), the departure of the British gave way to racist republics in which African communities were segregated and discriminated against. It was not until the 1990s that the page was turned on this chapter. In a certain sense, it was Mandela who brought the decolonization of South Africa to an end.

PART V:

THE EMPIRE STRIKES BACK
(1960S TO THE PRESENT)

THE MAGHREB:
INDEPENDENCE SQUANDERED

"Providence sometimes favors peoples, as it does individuals, by giving them an opportunity to grow up all at once, but this is only on condition that they know how to profit from it. Profit, then, from the fortune that is offered you. Your desire for independence, so long expressed, so often disappointed, will be realized if you show yourselves worthy of it."

NAPOLEON III

A book on colonization cannot stop at the threshold of independence. Leaving things there would miss the essential, that is, the real reasons for the passions currently roiling France, some immigrants, and several former colonies. If the post-colonial period had been happy, if independence had been a success, no one would be speaking today of reparations or the duty of remembrance.

Haiti, the first independent black republic, has completely failed as a state and society. The result is that many Haitian intellectuals still sing in unison their sad, stale chorus of France's eternal guilt. And, if only to make it rhyme, they add a line about the historical responsibility of the United States towards the Haitian people. If Port-au-Prince was the equivalent of Miami or Dubai, a prosperous city that exudes success, its inhabitants would be busier living their lives than blaming everything on the French and Americans.

In the Maghreb and, especially, Algeria, the post-independence fiasco has also fueled an obsession with victimhood that only grows by the year, as if the generations born after 2000 suffer more from colonial trauma than those who actually lived through it. It goes without saying that, if Algeria had managed to make its people a little less unhappy, if it had fairly distributed its hydrocarbon revenue, no one or almost no one would lend their ear to Anti-French diatribes. The man on the street's immense disappointment makes him vulnerable to *decolonial* propaganda, indeed complicit in its dissemination. It is always easier to blame others for one's misfortunes than to put one's house in order.

This is in cruel contrast to Vietnam, which has got down to work instead of worshiping its scars. And yet no other former French colony suffered as deeply for simply wanting to regain its sovereignty. Vietnam was twice devastated in quick succession by foreign powers (France from 1946 to 1954, the United States from 1965 to 1975). So many Algerians will blather on about France using napalm on Kabyle villages in the 1950s and yet feign ignorance of the fact that the Americans poured millions of liters of it on the Vietnamese countryside and in much greater proportions than what was used by the French military.[1] But still Vietnam advances, as Algeria goes backwards, one instilling hope in its youth, the other teaching it resentment. Two different attitudes to life, dictated by two unequal civilizations. The Vietnamese calls on man to take responsibility while the North African makes excuses for him.

The Second Decolonization: The Departure of the Jews and European Minorities

In Algeria, the pied-noirs were shown the door in 1962. In Tunisia and Morocco, they were given the choice to stay, but most decided to leave. In both countries, the young were the first to leave, driven away by the economic crisis that set in on the first day of independence, in contrast to the metropole, where "les Trente Glorieuses" were in full swing, ensuring jobs for all. There followed a series of political decisions that disgusted the Europeans who might otherwise have preferred to stay with their Moroccan or Tunisian friends. In 1964, Bourguiba abruptly nationalized farmland, de facto expelling the French families who represented the only Tunisian agriculture worthy of the name. In 1973, Hassan II launched the *Morocconization* program, which was nothing more than nationalization in disguise. Vexed by this development, many business and factory owners preferred to pack their bags and start from scratch elsewhere.

---

1. American forces dumped eighty million liters of napalm and other chemical agents on Vietnam. To measure the profound and lasting impact on the country, I recommend reading the geographer Amélie Robert's study (complete reference in the bibliography).

In the midst of this human floodtide, the Jews stood apart, quitting their traditional homelands in Fez, Meknes, and Djerba in droves, thereby putting an end to a presence that stretched back to antiquity. The Europeans' departure played a large part in this, the two groups having been partners in the enterprise of cultural and economic assimilation that began in the nineteenth century. The creation of the state of Israel of course also played an essential role, inspiring many but also fraying relations between Jews and Muslims. In 1973, the Yom Kippur War convinced the last holdouts to leave. This *second decolonization* was a tragedy, because it deprived North Africa of an ideal intermediary for its complicated dialogue with the West. The Jews represented a "third way" between progress and tradition. One only had to imitate them to access western modernity without ceasing to be oneself.

The Jewish and European Populations of Morocco 1960–1982

Year	Jewish population	European population
1960	162,000	396,000
1971	31,000	112,000
1982	10,000	62,000

Source: official data and censuses

Rid of its Jews and Europeans, the Maghreb would dig its own grave, its conscience clear. Behind closed doors, it would once again take up with its old demons, precisely those that had made it weak enough to be colonized by France in the first place . . .

The Old Demons Return

Maghreb civilization is not just Muslim, but also Arab and Berber.[2] It is the product of a rather primitive feudalism, in which the right to wage war is apportioned among lords, religious leaders, and tribes. The lives of men,

---

2. Also Jewish, although Jews were always physically and morally confined to the margins. For centuries, Jews inhabited the *mellah*, taking the jobs that were most scorned by Muslims. Hence the relative insignificance of their impact on the broader Maghreb civilization.

women, and children are punctuated by danger, flight, and combat: sooner
or later, these things will cross their paths.

At heart, this is a civilization rooted in its way of life more than its land,
whence its stagnation. It is a world in which the triad of inequality, tribalism,
and religious fanaticism provides the center of gravity.

Since 1970–80, these three elements have resurfaced like a crocodile taking advantage of its prey's momentary inattention to suddenly emerge from
muddy waters and devour it before it can cry out for help.

Of course, a civilization is much more refined than a common reptile. It
shows its teeth in roundabout ways, immediately recognizable to insiders but
forever inscrutable to the absent-minded. Some find themselves in the belly of
the beast without ever realizing they have been eaten.

Inequality, that old demon of the Maghreb mentality, was restored in all
its majesty, particularly at school, where it was decided to Arabize the lessons.
This was a catastrophe. On the one hand, teachers were not prepared to teach
in Arabic. On the other, scholarly publications in Arabic were rare or non-
existent, and continue to be so.

The insiders (members of the nomenklatura, bourgeois urbanites) immediately saw the danger and rushed to the French mission schools so that their
children could escape the great demolition taking place in the "native" education system. A two-tier school system thus emerged: one in Arabic, where
the poor were prepared for mass unemployment or under-employment, and
one in French, where sons of good families were handed the keys to success. A
great way to kick away the social ladder left by the French and which had allowed, while it still worked, young Moroccans, Tunisians, and Algerians with
nothing but their talent to offer to be saved from poverty.

In Algeria, Arabization got underway in 1965, in Morocco in 1978, and, in
Tunisia, it was gradually introduced around the same time.

With the passing years, there has also been an alarming recrudescence of
tribalism. It took advantage of the rural exodus to transpose itself upon cities,
bringing with it all of its shortcomings and few of its benefits. Of the old tribal
spirit, there remained only its disorder and indiscipline, no trace of the horse-
man's flair. Asphalt and concrete devoured the noble soul of the great lords.

Since the 1970s, Rabat, Algiers, Tunis, Fez, Constantine, and many other
cities have become miniature Calcutta's where rural life is perfectly at home:
there, it dictates the rules and influences ways of life. The peasant has imported his customs, which go well beyond food and dress, and are above all

synonymous with disorder. He refuses to pay taxes and throws himself into the informal economy, just as his father before him had hidden his harvests to deceive the caid, the sultan's tax collector. He insists on paying a *bakchich* to the emergency room nurse so that he can skip ahead of more serious cases (the principle of inequality). He pours scorn on the regime at every opportunity but will throw himself at the feet of the meanest local councilman to obtain a stipend. He will also do nothing to ensure that his children attend school and actually learn something, convinced as he is that one can succeed in life by simply kissing the right hand or kowtowing at the right moment. He behaves in the city as he behaved in his tribe, adjusting his moral sense to the interests of family and clan. He thus sees no great problem with crooks, thieves, and frauds; he is only moved when he or one of his own are victims. No one believes anyone else, trust collapses, and the capacity for collaboration within society is severely degraded. Yet a people can only pull itself out of poverty via intense collaboration among its members. A nation only progresses by virtue of common will and effort.

Religious fanaticism has managed to do even better than tribalism by transforming itself into something unrecognizable. The popular religiosity of the rural world reinvented itself on contact with the cities. Instead of collapsing and disappearing under the onslaught of modernity, it accepted codes from abroad, particularly the Middle East. It traded the *zawiya* for the *jamaa*, a place of study and socio-religious training. It abandoned the extreme reverence of the apprentice for the master and replaced it with a kind of servile veneration of the Islamist sheik by his followers. The French sidelined religious notables (like the *sharifs* of Bhalil), but, in the person of the Islamic fundamentalist, the North Africans invented a new religious nobility and gave it a say in politics.

Endemic corruption is merely the obvious logical result of these three decisive factors. It is unevenly distributed, because the capacity for corruption is concentrated in the hands of a minority. It is compatible with the tribal spirit, which sees life as an unremitting battle between men and which values victory over the means by which it is brought about. And finally, corruption is entirely compatible with Islam. As it is understood in North Africa, this religion does not seek to elevate man above himself. It is simply a means to instill a sense of the common good, and thus a principle of unity. Recall that the common good does not exist in the tribal world, where the general interest does not extend beyond the confines of clan and faction. Islam responds brilliantly to this shortcoming. Its intrinsic fanaticism brings together, around a higher goal, populations that would otherwise be mired in their own short-term selfishness. Jihad is invoked to mobilize enemy brothers, bitter cousins, and jealous neighbors. It represents the grammar of change in North Africa: most dynastic revolutions in Morocco were driven by Islamic fanaticism. It is excitement more than discipline that inspires action, for one is more *inflamed* than *convinced*.

The question of moralizing or civilizing the human being by making him more honest, gentler, and more educated does not arise. Islam is not Catholicism. It has not managed—or does not want—to create a new man. It leaves sufficient elbowroom to individuals for the purpose of harming one another. In the Maghreb, you can engage in corruption, lie, and go back on your word without shame. Religion has nothing to say about such things; it makes no effort to deeply cleanse souls and consciences. It prefers to devote itself to politics—that is, kingmaking and lawmaking—instead of to creating better beings.

Suicide

In the 1980s, the Maghreb began its long and painful encounter with the consequences of its errors: social crises, political bottlenecks, terrorism, despairing youth.

In Algeria, the military kept a tight grip on the reins of power, seizing the country's hydrocarbon revenues for itself, cleverly buying the loyalty of former combatants in the war of liberation for this purpose. In the 1980s, clientelism took off, with thousands of individuals and families fraudulently enrolling as beneficiaries of aid programs for the *mujahideen*.[3] Instead of shrinking with the passage of time, as would be expected, their numbers constantly grew . . .

In Tunisia, the economy faltered as Bourguiba grew ever older and more ill. In 1978, a standoff between the UGTT[4] and the government saw the capital set ablaze (an event that would come to be known as "Black Thursday"). On

---

3. Name given to the Algerian resistance fighters between 1954 and 1962. A *mujahid* (plural *mujahideen*) practices or practiced jihad against France. They numbered no more than 30,000 at the FLN's peak. Nowadays, more than one million Algerians are card-carrying *mujahideen* . . .

4. The Tunisian General Labor Union. Founded in 1946, it played a major role in the resistance to the French colonial presence.

January 26th, cars burned, windows were smashed, and official buildings were targeted. With the police overwhelmed, the army had to intervene. In the ensuing violence, dozens of people were killed. In January 1984, Tunisian cities were shaken by bread riots, casting a harsh light on the fiasco that twenty-five years of independence[5] had become: 143 people lost their lives.

Having nothing much to offer the country's youth, the regime became increasingly ossified. It professionalized the police and intelligence services and saw to it that social movements were infiltrated. At the same time, the system selected the bourgeoisie, or rather a segment of the bourgeoisie, to siphon up contracts and occupy economic niches sheltered from competition. Too bad for the entrepreneurs who had no contacts in the presidential palace . . .

In Morocco, the story was much the same. In the late 1970s, the left was shattered, its leaders imprisoned, exiled, or politically neutralized, forced to accept the established order and cheer on the official line. Following two attempted coups in (1971 and 72), the army was also sidelined. Superior officers were given the chance to do business rather than politics.

Born in 1979, I first opened my eyes in a country where generals farmed wheat, corn, and tomatoes, a country where army privates worked on their officers' farms . . . One fine Sunday in 1989 or 1990, my father took me to Ain Aouda, near Rabat, to visit a livestock fair. At the time, he had ambitions to make milk and cheese on his small farm. The master of the house, totally drunk, gave us a tour of the hangars and enclosures. He was an active-duty colonel . . .

This dysfunction was general. The mantra of the 1980s was "get rich and stay out of politics." The state was the master of ceremonies, favoring some and hindering others. The Minister of The Interior, Driss Basri (1979–1999), perfectly embodied the state of mind of this era, having at his disposal a veritable court of businessmen, senior officials, and informants. He certainly had his qualities (every state needs a top cop), but unfortunately occupied a space that did not suit him. In the mid-nineties, he launched a clean-up campaign, a sort of raid on employers, supposedly for the purpose of fighting smuggling and corruption. Business owners were roughed up and the broader economic community was appalled.

---

5. Under pressure from the IMF and World Bank, on December 31st, 1983, the Tunisian parliament decided to raise the prices of semolina and pasta (+70%), and bread (+108%).

The Algerian Civil War: When History Stuttered

Thirty years after independence, the FLN once again had an appointment with revolutionary war. This time, however, the roles were reversed; it was no longer the rebel but rather the embodiment of the established order. It was no longer the insurgent who promised the moon and the stars, but rather the party of the status quo and bad news (poverty, repression, injustice). It had to fight a vicious guerrilla force while simultaneously seeing to the day-to-day business of paying officials, maintaining public services, and preserving economic equilibria. All things considered, the FLN found itself in the same position as France in 1954. A striking reversal.

Even more striking was the thesis developed by the Islamic Salvation Front (FIS), the hardcore of the protest movement. What the FIS proposed was to once and for all decolonize Algeria. According to its leaders, Abassi Madani and Ali Belhadj, independence had been stolen in 1962. For, by choosing so-cialism, the FLN had refused to restore the Islamic laws and institutions that the French had suspended in 1830. Without them, the Algerian people were cut off from their historic tradition and true identity. Without them, coloni-zation continued. It had merely changed hands, the army and the FLN having picked up where the French left off. On this view, the struggle of the FIS was part and parcel of the war of national liberation.

Violence very quickly claimed the lives of innocent civilians, those who played no part in the conflict between regular and guerilla forces. Starting with the first skirmishes in early 1992, the dead already included teachers, journalists, artists, activists, and students. The Algerian people found them-selves on the front lines. In some regions, the state armed civilians and or-dered them to see to their own defense. In 1993, militias composed of volun-teer citizens (and, rumor has it, convicts) began to spread. In 1996 and 1997, there were horrific massacres of civilians, sometimes just outside the gates of Algiers. It was a true war of all against all.

In total, between 1992 and 2002, at least 100,000 people were killed and thousands disappeared. As much as the war of national liberation, this *black decade* was a foundational event for Algeria.

The similarities between the two conflicts are striking. First, in point of their character: both were at once revolutionary wars (pitting insurgents against the regime) and civil wars (pitting the people against itself). Second, in point of their location: the Islamists attacked Algerian police forces in the region Palestro at nearly the same spot where FLN guerrillas had decimated a column of French soldiers in 1956. In Chrea, forty soldiers were killed in an ambush in 1993, a stone's throw from where fourteen French soldiers had lost their lives in 1958. In both Chrea and Palestro, the mountainous and wooded terrain gave an advantage to the insurgents and favored ambush. In the Casbah of Algiers, the Islamists quickly found their bearings in the maze of narrow streets, allowing them to prevent the police from accessing it over the course of 1992. A cruel stutter of history: the French police before them had lost control of the Casbah in 1955 and 1956.

The Islamists, like the FLN guerrillas at the time of French colonization, sought to send two messages: (1) that resistance on the part of the regime was futile, hence the use of terrorism (cutting the throats of police officers in front of their families, for example); and (2) that the insurrection was on the threshold of taking power, with the capital surely to fall in a matter of days. To create the illusion that a new order was imminent, an Islamic counter-society was established in every area from which the police had withdrawn. In "liberated" zones such as Palestro in 1993, the state school was boycotted, the consumption of alcohol was banned, and women were obliged to wear the veil.

The moral order was completely overturned. The practice of "express" marriage, in which marriages lasting several weeks were permitted in order to satisfy the insurgents' sexual needs, was thus introduced. With the help of some carefully crafted fatwas, married women could be seized on the pretext that their husbands were "impious." Upon contact with such absurd and scandalous rules, dumbfounded civilians simply stopped asking questions: if they wanted to live, they would have to get used to obeying. They learned the value of cowardice. Had the Islamists succeeded in taking power, they would have kept their heads down and let the new regime do as it pleased, just as they had allowed a handful of terrorists to upend their daily lives.

They were not dealing with choir boys, needless to say. Indeed, the Islamists had a talent for persuasion. They mutilated the refractory, just as the FLN had sliced off the noses of cigarette smokers. And they saw to the security of those who collaborated, just as the FLN refrained from attacking civilians who had paid the revolutionary tax. One might say, though it is impossible to prove, that the Islamists took inspiration from the revolutionary practices of the *mujahideen* of the fifties and sixties. This extended to the domain of immigration, with the FIS infiltrating the diaspora in France and raising funds there. Sixty years earlier, it was the FLN that, by means of persuasion and intimidation, had targeted Algerian workers in France, extracting considerable sums of money from them.

In each case, the response of the regime in place was the same: after a period of denial, during which it treated the insurgents as outlaws, it ultimately recognized that there was indeed a war underway and responded accordingly. Under colonization, Toussaint Rouge (November 1954) was the tipping point. Under the FLN regime, the war was acknowledged following the attack on Algiers airport (August 1992). Immediately, security forces were endowed with extraordinary powers and the normal course of justice, with its various delays and guaranties, was suspended. Starting in 1993, special tribunals presided over by judges whose identity was kept secret were established. During the war of liberation, the French army completely bypassed civilian courts and saw to justice on its own, with its own interrogation and internment centers. Confronted with the Islamists, the Algerian regime did not hesitate to emulate French colonial practices. It opened interrogation centers that were inaccessible to the judiciary and corralled thousands of Islamists in centers located in the Sahara Desert. The mere mention of these truly lawless places was enough to make any Algerian tremble: the Cavaignac police station, the Châteauneuf barracks, the Serkadji prison. The recurrence of French names is to be noted: even Serkadji had formerly been a French institution (the Barberousse prison).

In these centers—which came dressed in euphemistic designations like *coordination* center, *research and investigation* center, and *operational command* post—there was of course torture. The worst torture, in fact: electric shock torture, waterboarding, nail-pulling, rape, torture of the suspect's loved ones, etc. All these horrors evoke the darkest hours of the battle of Algiers, proof that Jacques Massu's paras[6] did not have a monopoly on horror.

The issue of torture internationalized the conflict. Amnesty International, Human Rights Watch, and the UN called upon the Algerian regime to exercise restraint. This of course recalls the difficulties faced by the Fourth Republic, which, at every UN general assembly, had to convince the world that human rights were being respected in Algeria. History was repeating itself.

---

6. Trans. Jacques Massu (1908–2002) was a French general commanding the 10th Parachute Division at the time of the Battle of Algiers (1956–57). Dispatched to the city to put down the insurrection there, Massu's troops became infamous for their liberal use of torture to extract information regarding the FLN's organization and leadership. Massu's role in these events would be immortalized in Gillo Pontecorvo's 1966 film, *The Battle of Algiers*.

While the Algerian authorities extensively engaged in torture, they also understood that what was really at stake in the war was the population and only that. This was the only territory worth conquering. Whichever side managed to earn its sincere support or resigned obedience would win the war. Hence the regime's preoccupation with getting civilians involved in the conflict, prodding them into taking a clear position for one side or the other. One of its cleverest methods was to create the self-defense militia mentioned above. Membership in a militia constituted an ostentatious act of allegiance to the regime, committing both the militia member and his extended family. In this, the regime signally emulated the French Army in Algeria, which spared no expense in creating and organizing French-aligned self-defense forces: the famous *harkis*.[7]

After ten years of horror, what conclusion is one to draw? Who won?

The regime that had emerged from the struggle for independence held on to power, won a military victory, and managed to translate that victory into political action by staging a "return to normalcy." A policy of amnesty was instituted, allowing it to rehabilitate a large proportion of the insurgents, thereby granting a kind of impunity to the butchers as long as they were willing to admit their defeat.

In the war's aftermath, a new equilibrium was established in Algeria. The social domain, its mores and mentalities, was taken over by the Islamists. Politics and the economy remained in the hands of the military, which continued to plunder petroleum revenues. This original, permanent crime was drowned out by the increasingly mafioso aspect of Algerian society as a whole. Corruption infected every sphere, a culture of *après moi le déluge* spread, fraud was everywhere, as was hatred of work and effort. In this respect, Algeria was in step with its North African neighbors. In Morocco and Tunisia also, the state of mind of the masses was heading towards straightforward, unabashed nihilism: no harm seen, no harm done; the cult of emigration; ostentatious religiosity veiling the degradation of attitudes and aspirations, and so on.

So why was Algeria the only North African country to slide into civil war?

There is no final answer to this question, for war is the result of objective causes and contingencies that do not lend themselves to any straightforward

---

7. In the War of National Liberation (1954–62), the term *harki* encompasses several different realities: the Muslim militiaman of the self-defense forces but also the Muslim soldier affiliated with the French army.

224 A Counter-History of French Colonization

equation. At a given moment, an *invisible hand* lights the fuse or throws water on the embers.

It is nevertheless clear that Algeria had a lead on its neighbors and was much closer to the precipice than the Moroccan monarchy or the Tunisian republic.

The religious crisis was intense there. Society needed a replacement for the Sufi brotherhoods that had been the soul of Algerian Islam before colonization. Persecuted first by the French, then by the Algerian authorities, weakened by exodus, the brotherhoods were out of action by the early 1980s. That the population yearned to reconnect with a shared religiosity that valued the common good and solidarity between generations and regions only made it that much easier for the Islamists to impose themselves. The FIS responded to these needs by occupying all domains previously held by the brotherhoods: the spiritual, cultural, social, and political. From Tlemcen to Constantine, it "unified" Algeria, just as the brotherhoods had formerly federated believers despite regional and tribal divisions.

When civil war broke out in the early 1990s, Morocco and Tunisia lagged "behind" Algeria by perhaps ten or fifteen years: religious life was not in quite such a bad state, and a non-negligible part of the population was still rooted in peasant life. They would have time to see what was coming and prepare themselves accordingly.

Religious crisis is of course accompanied by acute social dysfunction.

In Algeria, there was intense social rage. The theft of the nation's petroleum revenues inevitably provoked tremendous indignation among the population. The plundering of the country's natural resources was compounded by a severe housing crisis. In the 1980s, it was common to see three Algerian families sharing one and the same apartment! The housing crisis transformed the daily lives of the Algerian people into a hell unknown to their Moroccan and Tunisian neighbors. In Algeria, the growth of the population (which had tripled since independence) was not accompanied by the creation of new housing. Under socialism, the private sector had been suffocated and the public sector neglected. The country's elite, meanwhile, had little empathy for the masses. It is easy to imagine the exasperation felt by young people, incapable of leaving the parental home, incapable of marrying, incapable of having sex.

This was a youth with nowhere to turn, for Algerian society lacked intermediary bodies capable of absorbing the shock and offering alternatives to violence. Indeed, Algeria had been shattered by reforms as brutal as they were misguided, with the result that the traditional elites who might have acted as a buffer between the FLN and the population were eliminated. Under colonization and revolutionary socialism alike, the class of village and tribal chiefs was systematically destroyed, pressure was put on populations to relocate to the cities, far removed from their natural leaders, and the religious brotherhoods, which acted as intermediaries between political power and the country's heartland, were marginalized.

And yet, with neither mediator nor mediation, violence is the only way to make oneself heard.

This violence was entrusted to the worst protagonists imaginable. On the one hand, the military regime, ready to do whatever was necessary to keep its privileges and accustomed to intrigue and abuse. On the other hand, the Islamists, with their apocalyptic vision of the world and total absence of scruple when it came to savagery and murder. Among them were many "Afghans," young Algerians who had been battle-hardened in Afghanistan in the days of the Soviet invasion.

Or to put it otherwise, nothing good could ever come from such a configuration, the interested parties both possessing a state of mind as cynical as it was depraved.

Of these two monsters, victory would belong to whichever was the most cunning, cruelest, and most determined.

In the course of their confrontation, certain repressed energies could be given free rein. Some descendants of the *harkis* thus avenged themselves against soldiers and the FLN, Islamism serving as a pretext for settling old scores with a regime that had been built on the mortal remains of their ancestors. An interesting hypothesis suggested by the historian Pierre Vermeren, and which deserves further exploration,[8] traces a connection between the civil war of the 1990s and that of the years 1954–62. In any case, it would be foolish to imagine that the massacre of the *harkis* would go without a response. To see one's father or uncle publicly tortured is enough to disinhibit anyone and legitimates taking action years later, whatever the cause. For some, the proximity of violence creates an appetite for violence. For such people, shedding blood is no calamity, but rather a tool like any other to bring about change.

---

8. See Pierre Vermeren, *Une Histoire de l'Algérie Contemporaine*, Paris, Nouveau Monde Éditions, 2022.

And Algeria is probably one of those societies where the recourse to violence is considered legitimate, as are also Mexico, Colombia, and Venezuela, all countries in which engaging in politics goes hand in hand with the eradication of rivals, countries of civil war where a bout of fever can sweep away an entire generation.

SUB-SAHARAN AFRICA: CRASH-LANDING

"Congo resembles an inexperienced adolescent who has suddenly lost a strict tutor. By himself, he must learn a liberty for which he has had so little preparation."

VICTOR PRÉVOT

"You'd have to be mad to keep your money in Africa."

FÉLIX HOUPHOUËT-BOIGNY

Independence did not make the African problem go away.

Africa's new leaders had to find the solution to the equation that France was never able to solve during colonization: bringing about economic and moral progress in the midst of an unprecedented demographic explosion.

Without capital, competent cadres, or any administrative tradition, this was a tall order indeed.

What to do? Where to begin?

At the time, there was no ready-made recipe available. Nor is there any today. Because no power on earth is capable of leading a civilization in one direction or another.

Many different experiments were thus tried, sometimes with enthusiasm and even some success. Many mistakes were also made, only to ultimately resign oneself to the perpetuation of carnivorous elites and their privileges, at the expense of peoples.

What Economic Model for Independent Africa?

Socialism, communism, or capitalism? Food self-sufficiency or the mechanization of industry?

So many fine ideas on glossy paper. So many disappointments, also. Reality is stubborn and resistant to the products of ideology, all of which—absolutely all—are ignorant of the most important thing, that is, human nature and civilization.

Even capitalism, which is thought to be aligned with human instincts, missed the mark in black Africa. It was not conceived to operate in a society where accumulation is not a cardinal value, where man is not the absolute master of nature, and where the prestige of the chief is based on what he distributes to his clients, rather than his compliance with the rules of the game (the much-vaunted *governance*). Capitalism did not recognize the importance of collective life and the extended family on the black continent.

Nor could Africa invent its own model of development, or indeed "their" own, since there were many Africas between the savannah, the Sahel, the forest, and the Great Lakes.

Between 1960 and 1962, some captivating experiments took place in Senegal to get the local economy, cooperative and interlinked, back on its feet. Unfortunately, members of the Senegalese middle class with experience of trade (international trade, peanuts exchanged for imported consumer goods) forced Sédar Senghor, President of the Republic, to dismiss the sponsor of this process, Prime Minister Mamadou Dia. To maintain the status quo and convert Senegal into a trading-post economy, the marabouts (well-versed in trade) and the urban coastal elites (Dakar and Saint-Louis) made common cause in torpedoing Mamadou Dia's efforts.

Further south, Houphouët-Boigny practiced a form of enlightened clientelism on the basis of cocoa and coffee. Between 1960 and the early 1980s, Ivory Coast experienced the *Vingt Glorieuses*, a gilded age where the single party[1] saw to it that the nation's financial windfall was redistributed to the various elements of society along regional, ethnic, and political lines. So long as export prices were consistently high, all went well. But when prices dropped, the house of cards collapsed. Starting in the late 1970s, the fountain began to run dry. In 1980, the IMF imposed its structural adjustment program on Ivory

---

1. The PDCI: Democratic Party of Ivory Coast.

Coast. The party was over: in its place, a chemotherapy regimen supervised by international financiers. Goodbye sovereignty, goodbye abundance, bonjour tristesse.

A few lucky countries, which can be counted on one hand, hit the jackpot with highly profitable oil wells. Gabon was one such. In the 1970s, it drew massive numbers of immigrants from the Sahel (Senegal, Burkina Faso, Mali), becoming a paradise for French petroleum interests, which gradually replaced forestry interests, the former kings of colonial Gabon. As we know, however, petrol is a "curse." From anglophone Nigeria to francophone Gabon, it established a monochromatic economy where the black gold was traded for food-stuffs and imported goods.

No one will contest that, in general, Africa was in terrible shape in the 1980s. With every passing year, Madagascar, for example, even succeeded in becoming yet more impoverished.

Desired Neocolonialism

Keep to oneself and get by as best one can, unite with one's neighbors, or instead seek out France's paternal aid?

With rare exceptions, the former colonies preferred to maintain ties with France, inaugurating a new relationship that the public would come to know as Françafrique. Few, by contrast, know that Françafrique was desired and built by Africans in collaboration with their former colonial power.

As we saw earlier, Sékou Touré's Guinea immediately said no to France. Starting in 1958, the Guinean leader kept to himself, isolating his country from its francophone neighbors and plunging society into the nightmare of dictatorship, torture, and arbitrary rule.

At the same time, between 1958 and 1962, Sédar Senghor did everything he could to federate the former colonies of French West Africa into a single political-administrative entity that might bring them some leverage at the international level. This project was torpedoed by France, Houphouët-Boigny's Ivory Coast, and the outsized egos of young African leaders, who preferred to be the "kings" of trifling countries rather than the viceroys of an ambitious federation. In 1960, the die was cast and the federation abandoned.

Similarly, many African nations pooled their resources to create the Air Afrique airline (1961). Staffed in its early days by enthusiastic and devoted employees, Air Afrique was a wonderful idea, but it never reached cruising altitude. Waste, lack of vision, resentment between member states . . . in the 1980s, the company collapsed.

That left France, the former colonial metropole, delighted to find itself once again in an asymmetrical and scandalously unjust tête-à-tête with its former colonies. Woe to the weak!

But could things ever have been otherwise, with young African leaders themselves openly wondering what was to be gained by independence?

As the future president of Ivory Coast declared before the United Nations in 1957: "We have every right to say that we have no future without France."

As Houphouët saw it, Africans were not ready to go it alone and had to join a "democratic and fraternal Franco-African community, founded on equality." Is this not a beautiful way of defining Françafrique?

Gabon's first president, Léon Mba, also had no desire for independence. Instead, he wanted Gabon to become a French department, after the model of Martinique or Guadeloupe. After De Gaulle bluntly refused this idea, Mba suggested that his country adopt the French tricolor! Once again, the French refused.

In Senegal, Léopold Sédar Senghor was himself convinced that Africa was in no condition to govern itself, asking Mamadou Dia, his fellow traveler and the nation's future prime minister, to wait twenty years before cutting the umbilical cord joining Senegal to France. Senghor was not a colonialist, he was simply clear-eyed: he wanted to replace colonization—an abject regime—with strengthened cooperation until Senegal was up to snuff.[2] Does that make a collaborationist of Senghor? Only a fool or a postcolonialist could think such a thing.

More seriously yet, many African presidents had no faith in their troops, secretly signing defense agreements stipulating that France would defend them in the event of a coup d'état.

Sixty years on, it would thus be unjust to downplay the genuine desire for Françafrique among these new countries. Africa needed help and implementing assistance always requires an institutional framework: agreements, steering committees, routines, and collaboration.

The CFA franc embodies this type of cooperation between parties that, while "equal" in point of rights, are unequal in that of power. Paris set up a

---

2. An anecdote recounted by Roland Colin, a former fellow traveler of Mamadou Dia and personal friend to Senghor.

financial community open to its former colonies as well as new newcomers enticed by the advantages of a stable and convertible single currency (the CFA was thus freely adopted by Guinea-Bissau, a former Portuguese possession, and Equatorial Guinea, a former Spanish colony).

The CFA was one less "problem" for its member states, which delegated management of their monetary policy to France. They should have taken advantage of this situation to focus all their energies on economic development and regional integration but plainly failed to do so. Is France to blame for this?

It is not racist to offer this assessment. To the contrary, it is a sign of respect, for only a true friend encourages you to seize hold of the opportunities offered by life and realize your potential, without excuse or delay.

From cooperation between unequal parties to neocolonialism, however, it is but one step, and it was blithely taken. The fault lies with both sides: France, possessive of its *turf* to the point of arrogance, and Africa, which failed to act responsibly at critical moments in its existence.

One example suffices to convey the downward spiral of Françafrique.

In August 1963, the Democratic Republic of Congo's president-priest, Fulbert Youlou, found himself faced with a military coup. In vain, he called upon France for help. Without specific orders from Paris, the French soldiers based in Brazzaville would not budge. It was mid-summer when the coup d'état occurred, and Jacques Foccart, the Élysée's Africa advisor, was on the high seas, where he could not be reached. Solicited by the Quai d'Orsay, De Gaulle relied on the advice of the French ambassador, who advised against any French involvement. Gossip had it that the General took a dim view of the president-priest, who he criticized for the multicolored cassocks that Christian Dior had designed for him.

So the priest was replaced by Marxist soldiers, ushering in a cycle of instability in Congo-Brazzaville, a country known for its abundant natural resources. In neighboring countries, Paris' inaction cast doubt on the solidity of the defense agreements that had been signed at the time of independence several years earlier.

At the Élysée, the mood was one of regret.

The following year, the same scenario seemed on the verge of being repeated in neighboring Gabon. On February 17th, 1964, soldiers took power in Libreville and locked up President Léon Mba in Lambaréné, 250 kilometers from the capital.

This time round, France responded swiftly. There was no question of repeating the mistakes of Brazzaville. A team of paratroopers was sent from Dakar. Soon thereafter, troops from Congo and the Central African Republic landed at the Libreville airport. Mba was restored to power. Blood was spilled: French soldiers killed a Gabonese officer and wounded three other rebel soldiers.

Several African countries, including Madagascar, Ivory Coast, and Chad, warmly welcomed the French intervention. It nevertheless constituted flagrant interference in the affairs of a former colony.

But the worst was yet to come. Between 1964 and 1967, France itself chose the replacement for Léon Mba, who was no longer "up to the job" and had fallen seriously ill. De Gaulle had Albert Bongo come to the Élysée for an interview. After passing this interview, Bongo was set on the path to power. From his hospital bed in Paris, President Mba was forced to modify the constitution to insert the position of vice-president. The "paperwork" was signed at the Gabonese embassy in 1966. Mba was then forced to hold a presidential election, where he would run on a "ticket" that included Bongo. Once reelected, Mba had the courtesy to die in November 1967, his mission completed. Bongo became president. The whole affair was scandalous.

Setting aside one's indignation, however, the question must be asked: who had allowed France to overstep the limits of decency and trample underfoot the sovereignty of a free nation? The answer is as simple as it is unpleasant: the immense weakness and irresponsibility of several African elites.

You already know what follows. From coups to palace revolutions, the former colonies sank into instability and destitution. Nor did the countries that held out, like Senegal and Ivory Coast, escape the fiasco of the development model. The 1980s, in this respect, were a brutal call to order: the IMF and the World Bank dictated how much African governments had the right to spend and how they were to spend it. This was the era of sinister Structural Adjustment Plans, which, despite their best intentions, ended up diverting the tiny trickle of life that still irrigated the schools and hospitals of Black Africa.

Since then, it has been every man for himself.

The Time for Predators

It's 1990. All illusions have been lost: communism is dead, along with Ivory Coast clientelism. There has been no development, societies have been cast off, with the rich on one side and the immense, miserable masses on the other.

People cut one another's ears off in Liberia and Sierra Leone. States collapse in a carnival of cannibalism and gang rape. Francophone Rwanda pulls off the feat of killing 800,000 innocent civilians by machete in less than three months. Congo-Kinshasa comes undone as the health of Mobutu declines.

Welcome to tropical hell.

In the jungle, it is essential to secure your place high in the food chain and not think too much about the fate of those below you. This is the mentality adopted by African elites: they no longer gave a thought to anything except preserving their hides, social justice, equality, and dignity be damned.

They gave up on governing, preferring to administer their fortunes, fiefdoms, and careers. The state fell into ruin, but the senior officials were all smiles, for they took a cut on every container landing at the port of Abidjan or Cotonou. The gendarmerie controlled nothing more than the capital and the road to the airport: no matter, a clique of senior officers lined its pockets by stealing the diesel and food meant for soldiers.

The country was no longer managed; society's decay was administered. And this was done while paying lip service to the proprieties and language of the day: human rights, democracy, pluralism, sustainable development, biodiversity . . . so many buzzwords to get a hearing in Paris or Geneva, cleverly concealing the hideous face of predation.

There was no longer any question of challenging the current world order, one need only swear allegiance to the dominant ideology. Everyone plays pretend. The African leader says the words that the Western decision-maker wants to hear and in turn listens to the admonitions of consultants and humanitarians as they trot out whatever happens to be the catechism of the moment.

Convinced of his rightness, the white man never stops giving advice. Obsessed with holding on to power, the African leader and his entourage listen and take notes. A fair price to pay for continuing to enjoy the delicacies of development aid.

"O, good morning, my Lord Crow!
How well you look! how handsome you do grow!
'Pon my honor, if your note
Bears a resemblance to your coat,
You are the phoenix of the dwellers in these woods."

At these words does the crow exceedingly rejoice;
And, to display his beauteous voice,
He opens a wide beak, lets fall his stolen goods.[3]
In your opinion, who is the crow?

---

3. Jean de la Fontaine, translated by Henry Wadsworth Longfellow.

THE NEW EQUILIBRIUM: FROM COLONIAL DREAM TO MULTICULTURAL DREAM

"The colonists cut us deep
We're gonna do it the other way round
We've come to take what we're owed
In your streets your pus will run
There's more than one terror attack to come
Here in France . . ."

> LUNATIC (RAP GROUP), SONG: *BO (BANLIEUE OUEST)*.[1]

"For in the first days of the revolt you must kill: to shoot down
a European is to kill two birds with one stone, to destroy an
oppressor and the man he oppresses at the same time: there
remains a dead man, and a free man; the survivor, for the first
time, feels a national soil under his foot."[2]

> JEAN-PAUL SARTRE

Françafrique is behind us. The era when Paris was in any position to impose its viewpoint on Africans has passed.

Today, there is a new relationship between North and South, much more balanced than one might imagine. The South has rediscovered its power, the power to harm the North and trouble its day-to-day existence. The North still

---

1. *Petite Anthologie du rap anti-français* by Christian Combaz. Source : https://www.lefigaro.fr/vox/politique/2015/10/05/31001-20151005ARTFIG00352-petite-anthologie-du-rap-anti-francais.php
2. Preface to *The Wretched of The Earth*, Paris, François Maspero, 1961. Tr. Constance Farrington.

holds formal power, whether economic, diplomatic, or military, but it has lost entire swathes of its sovereignty. It is still capable of dispatching paratroopers to Mali and Ivory Coast, but it no longer knows how many Malians or Ivorians are to be found on its own soil. They may include dangerous elements capable of committing impromptu terror attacks.

The Eiffel Tower and the Palace of Versailles, symbols of French grandeur, are surrounded by Mouride street vendors. The police are powerless.

Gone is the asymmetry. Africa and the Maghreb have ammunition to spare, no longer are they dominated.

The new equilibrium is in fact the result of collusion between the elites of North and South at the expense of their respective peoples. It is part and parcel of a global trend, wherein Western oligarchies overcome prejudices of race and religion so as to enter into partnership with their Arab and African counterparts.

This new deal has two victims: the people of France and the peoples of the former colonies.

It rests on two pillars: business and immigration. It hides behind two convenient screens: diversity and repentance.

The New Governance

Since decolonization, France has found the most advantageous and efficient way to serve its own interests in the Third World. No longer is there any need to invade, bombard, and administer millions of indigent natives; it is enough to see to it that their governments guarantee the rights of French business. Whence the fashion for "good governance" and the omnipresent notion of the "business environment." Since the early 1990s, the issue of compliance with certain rules of the game has constituted the better part of dialogue with Africa and the Arab world. States are called upon to scrupulously respect private property and guarantee investors the freedom to repatriate profit and dividends to the country of their choice. The reward for compliance is respectability, meaning a good reputation, as measured by the *Doing Business* ranking established by the World Bank and rating agencies. They take note of everything: macroeconomic and financial compliance, the legal system, environmental policy, social and sociocultural policy—all is fed into an evaluation that can open or close doors.

The recalcitrant run the risk of losing out on aid and financing. They are stigmatized on the international stage and their opponents celebrated as paragons of democracy.

On the ground, French humanitarians have taken on responsibility for the civilizing mission. They are to be found everywhere there are lepers, malaria patients, migrants. In general, they do remarkable work that, while certainly costly, would be exorbitantly so were it confided to the French state, with its unionized civil servants and endless red tape. Like them or not, the NGOs are better equipped than any government organization to promptly learn from their mistakes and adapt to a changing context. Of course, they are partly subsidized by the state, but their expenditures are also an investment in France's image and a vector of influence overseas.

France has good reasons to act in this way. Indeed, she might have thought of doing so earlier, instead of going to the trouble of colonizing Senegal, Morocco, and Ivory Coast. After all, it is easier to support the interests of the Bolloré Group in Abidjan or Libreville than it is to run schools and clinics in these two cities, where extreme poverty rubs shoulders with despair. Before, it was necessary to maintain a costly bureaucracy and large army to support the activity of French capitalists in Africa or the Maghreb. Now, it is enough to "brief" the ambassador and his economic bureau to get it done.

From the perspective of the elites of the South, this is a good deal, even a fair one: they can now participate in the "development" of their country, a process from which they were excluded during colonization. They have their seat at the table of many multinationals and launch joint ventures with foreign capital to construct water supply networks, tram lines, and office towers. Seeking a stable and predictable environment in which to do business, their French and European partners assess their political influence and "connections" at their true value.

All of this is normal, fair, desirable even. There is no law against making money. To the contrary, one must make a lot of it if one is to adequately redistribute it.

The hidden reality may be glimpsed when we examine the influence acquired by Southern elites over French domestic affairs. This influence has been made possible by the economic prosperity of the groups that hold power in Morocco, Algeria, Gabon, and Cameroon, to only name them. Like the Saudi prince who decides to buy French politicians by giving them a Rolex, Arab and African leaders can buy influence networks in Paris: in the press (which is dying of starvation and will do anything for a few pages of paid advertorial content), in academic circles (also starved for resources), in artistic and cultural circles (always on the lookout for patrons), and of course in politics.

There is no point in reeling off the names of everyone in France who has received bribes from the secret services of this or that former colony, you get the picture: French elites are partly under the influence.

In the 1980s, my father performed a service for Moroccan intelligence by taking a suitcase full of banknotes to a major French journalist, the head of a Paris newsroom, who was spending the weekend in Marrakech. My father met him in La Mamounia, where he was staying free of charge. And how many French presidents and former presidents have holidayed in Morocco "on the house"? Recall the escapades of Jacques Chirac in Taroudant at the Gazelle d'Or.[3] The same man spent the last years of his life in a Paris apartment owned by the Hariri family of Lebanon.

This influence does not a placidly flowing river make. It comes up against large rocks here and there, which prevent it from following its course to Paris, the seat of economic, political, and media power.

Thus, Hassan II and the Mitterrand's (Mr. and Mrs.) bickered over the Sahàra question and human rights. The winds were certainly more favorable to Moroccan entryism in the time of Giscard d'Estaing, but all was sorted out in the end with the arrival of Jacques Chirac: during his twelve years at the Élysée, Morocco did as it liked in the Parisian microcosm. The honeymoon carried over into Sarkozy's administration, the "accelerated" president having a passion for Marrakech and its palm grove, where he liked to jog, followed at a distance by Moroccan security personnel. Under François Hollande, relations were more strained after a complaint was filed in Paris against a senior Moroccan security official accused of torture. The two sides were eventually reconciled at a September 2015 meeting between Mohammed VI and Hollande in Tangier.

Behind these peaks and troughs there looms the growing reality of foreign interference in France, whether it be by Morocco, Algeria, Tunisia, the Gulf States, or Sub-Saharan Africa. Decisive issues for internal security partly depend on the good will of former French colonies. First and foremost, religious affairs: the governments of North Africa forcefully intervene to promote this or that imam and make life easier in the mosques frequented by their respective diasporas. Just as crucial are issues relating to organized crime and terrorism, where the fingerprints of the ex-colonies can be clearly discerned. Several

---

3. Trans. The Gazelle d'Or is a luxury hotel in the Moroccan city of Taroudant famously patronized by Jacques Chirac and his wife, Bernadette.

Islamist cells have been neutralized in France thanks to incredibly precise tip-offs from the Moroccan authorities, and it would be naive to imagine that the Moroccans came by such detailed information without a direct or indirect presence on French territory. Obviously, immigration is the vector of this penetration. Without the almost 1.5 million Moroccans who reside in France, the work of the Moroccan intelligence services would surely be less incisive.

Dual Sovereignty

For the Moroccan authorities, a Moroccan never stops being Moroccan, even if he is a naturalized citizen of France. Dual nationals are simply Moroccans living abroad. Similarly, their children born in France are considered prospective Moroccans with whom religious, political, and cultural contact must be maintained, while France (the butt of the joke) sees to the job of educating them, housing them, and finding them jobs.

As a consequence, Morocco "exercises" its sovereignty over the four corners of France, everywhere there are Moroccans or descendants of Moroccans. The consular network and a myriad of cultural and religious associations crisscross the territory, behaving with discretion and restraint so as not to upset the state. The whole thing is set to music by the Moroccan Ministry of Foreign Affairs and a Ministry (or Secretary of State) for Moroccans Living Abroad (*Marocains Résident à l'Étrager*, MRE).

What holds for Morocco holds for other countries, former colonies that have become "owners" of their own little piece of France thanks to their large and sometimes rowdy diasporas.

Such remote control of the diaspora allows decisive influence to be exerted over local, regional, and national politics. Dual nationals vote and get elected. And when they attain prominence, they are celebrated and encouraged by the Moroccan authorities, who extol the "success" of these Moroccans Abroad. Najat Valaud-Belkacem, former French Minister of Education, is received with full honors in Morocco, as is Rachida Dati, the former Minister of Justice. They have even been received by the king himself. It is simply naive to believe that such immigrant-origin figures do not feel beholden towards the country of their parents' birth or treat issues pertaining to these countries with the same neutrality as they do relations with the Dominican Republic or Norway.

Without the immigrant vote, the Socialist Party would have departed from history ages ago. Without the votes of the *banlieues*, Emmanuel Macron's party would never have achieved such total control over the National Assembly. People often underscore the high rates of abstention among immigrant offspring, but this hardly cancels out the considerable number of votes they cast for "right-thinking" parties. In several places, the demographic equilibrium has been lastingly transformed, guaranteeing fiefdoms and impregnable strongholds for certain political movements. Marseille is an illuminating (and depressing) example of the symbiotic encounter between immigration and clientelism, a cultural breeding ground that always favors the same political camp.

One must be extremely naive to imagine that Arab and African regimes forgo taking advantage of their tremendous leverage over French politicians. And their advantage only grows with the Islamization of the diaspora, a vital question for the country's future. On its own, however, France has no grip on Islam, a religion that is completely alien to the country. It "speaks" a language that is incomprehensible to it, arouses emotions and psychological needs with which France has no familiarity. Soon, France will have to rely (if indeed it does not already do so) on its Muslim former colonies as intermediaries with the imams, associations, and lobbies that trample underfoot its territory and its sovereignty. Power is on the side of the formerly vanquished, and it is they who are in a position to either attenuate or intensify the harms caused by Islam's irruption onto the French scene.

Since 2015, France has sent dual nationals to Morocco to receive training as imams. Spain, Italy, and Belgium are also studying this possibility. Overwhelmed by the radicalization of the diasporas, European governments have turned to Morocco to put some common sense and moderation into the heads of future imams. The Mohammed IV Institute for the Training of Imams and Morchidats (women preachers) promises to remedy this situation, and it certainly has the skills needed to do so, skills notably lacking in the West.

The French have the means to pay, and the vanquished of yesterday have the power to insist that they do so. Just consider the audacity of Turkey's Erdogan, who sends the Grey Wolves[4] marching through French cities whenever the mood strikes him. Other European countries suddenly find them-

---

4. Trans. The Grey Wolves are the youth wing of Turkey's Nationalist Movement Party. They are today a present, active, and sometimes violent fixture in every European nation with a large Turkish diaspora.

selves having to answer to countries that formerly counted for nothing. Spain is under constant pressure from Morocco in what concerns illegal immigration. It regularly sends cheques to the Moroccan authorities to reequip them (in jeeps, ships, radar systems) and persuade them to continue tamping down on potential illegal immigrants. Spain is paying to keep the peace.[5] The same holds for Italy and the European Union, which transfer funds to the Libyan authorities in the hope of curbing departures. Between 2017 and 2020, Italy alone transferred 220 million Euros to the Libyan coastguard. Who has the power here? The one who pays or the one who is paid? The one who cashes in or the one who operates the till?

Immigration is itself the best argument for transferring wealth from North to South. Even the far right subscribes to this idea in holding that development aid could be the alternative to immigration. This is a cruel misconception: immigration is less the product of poverty than it is of the disgust caused by mediocre elites organized along the lines of predatory mafias. The people who pay 5000 Euros to cross the Mediterranean clearly have the resources needed to start a small business or, indeed, buy some government job in their country of origin. Yet they prefer to spend this money to cross the sea because they can no longer stomach living under regimes that mistake oppression for governance and plunder for administration.

The immigrants who flood the streets of France are the best ambassadors for the cause. The more numerous and visible they are, the more public opinion allows itself to be persuaded that something must be done upstream to help their poor countries of origin . . .

Year in, year out, France thus pays a tribute to its former vassals. The magnificent power that pacified the Maghreb and Africa 100 or 150 years ago is now reduced to paying to avoid invasion. As good an example as any other of the extortion to which the vanquished have been subjected since the dawn of time.

Formerly, the slogan had been "the suitcase or the coffin"; today, it is "the suitcase or the wallet." The migrant's suitcase is an eloquent argument for persuading Europe's capitals to open their wallets.

There is big money at stake in the departures of these unfortunates. There is much talk of shipwrecks, but little of the bounty that awaits the lucky ones.

---

5. Thirty million Euros in July 2019, in addition to 140 million promised by the European Union to combat illegal immigration.

No sooner have they settled in France than they hit the jackpot. The immigrants start sending Euros to their families, thereby relieving their countries of origin of several mouths to feed. Every year, nearly ten billion Euros leave France for the South "aboard" Western Union and other such banking platforms. Two billion Euros wind up in Algeria, and 1.8 billion in Morocco. In Senegal, these remittances (all diasporas included) account for almost 10 percent of the country's GDP!

Alongside these legitimate transfers are to be found billions of Euros in social fraud. The social security system estimates that at least 2.4 million of those receiving benefits live abroad and have been fraudulently added to its rolls. It is nothing short of a razzia, the all-out plundering of wealth created by the labor of a foreign people, the French people in particular!

No one seems to be bothered by this tribute (development aid, remittances from the diaspora, social fraud). Otherwise, vigorous measures would have been taken to reduce migratory flows.

Immigration has not been stopped. Instead, it has been extoled and raised to the level of state policy and international consensus. The Pact of Marrakech is nothing less than a dramatization of the unreserved adherence of the states of North and South to the idea that immigration is a good in itself and must be encouraged.[6]

Immigration is financed by the public purse. It is enough to trace the subsidies paid out by the Municipality of Paris, the Loire-Atlantique department, and the region of Occitania to quickly grasp that the NGOs completing the work of traffickers in the Mediterranean are working "under contract" for the state. The region of Occitania prides itself in having alone transferred 210,000 Euros to *SOS Méditerranée* between 2017 and January 2021. The same local authority is committed to helping local councils and public institutions receive migrants in the following ways (quoting in full from the website of the Occitanie Pyrénées-Méditerranée region):

- For local councils and local council communities: **1000 Euro/per person** present on the territory for more than **6 months**, with a ceiling set at **50,000 euro**.

---

6. The Global Compact for Safe, Orderly and Regular Migration was signed in Marrakech in 2018.

- For reception centers and public institutions: a maximum of **60 percent of eligible project expenses**, with a ceiling set at **150,000 Euros.**[7]

Who Has an Interest in Boosting Immigration?

The oligarchies of the North and South cannot do without it. Immigration is their drug. Anyone who attempts to deprive them of it faces immediate reprisal.

The real aims of each party are tinged by cynicism and short-term thinking. The overall impression one gets is in my view best summed up by the adjective "shabby."

Ethical Purification

For the countries of the South, immigration only brings benefits. You do not have to work for the DGSE[8] to see how this works, starting with the fees imposed on illegal immigration mafias. No one crosses the Sahara with a column of jeeps full of drugs and migrants without paying "customs duties"[9] to the right people. Without digging any deeper, one can simply estimate the fees collected on official currency transfers through banks and financial institutions with branches in Bamako, Niamey, and Douala (a true windfall).

Mass immigration also rids Africa and the Maghreb of their revolutionary elements. These would-be sans-culottes are transplanted to Paris, London, or Berlin, far from the leaders who robbed and despoiled them.

Among the delinquents who make life hard for the French are some who might otherwise have given themselves over to riot, to invading presidential palaces, to bumping off the corrupt and incompetent. Instead of making themselves useful, these thugs prowl commuter trains to rob workers and other innocents, who on top of it all they call racists. Rarely has a generation so mistaken its enemy.

---

7. Link: https://www.laregion.fr/Soutien-a-l-accueil-et-a-l-integration-des-demandeurs -d-asile-et-des-beneficiaires-d
8. Trans. The Directorate-General for External Security, France's foreign intelligence agency.
9. In nineteenth-century Senegal, traders had to pay off the chiefs and marabouts in charge of the territories through which their goods passed by means of a "customary tribute". Colonization put an end to this practice, replacing it with other taxes.

Arab and African potentates snort with laughter at these misguided young people and thank France for siphoning up their dangerous classes.

Some will retort that France is also a brain drain for the South. This is true. There are more Beninese doctors in France than in Benin. But does anyone deplore their departure from Benin? That is the question that must be asked. The response is obviously no. No one cries over the departure of doctors, mathematicians, and artists. Good riddance! The intelligentsia is always a source of problems: it knows its rights, it is (generally) less gullible than the people, befuddled as they are by illiteracy and a media in the pay of power, and they want human rights. In short, they are a "pain in the ass." Do you really think Morocco misses Leïla Slimani[10] or Abdellah Taïa?[11] Not in the least. Back home, their eloquence and outspokenness would have made waves. In Paris, they are magnificent export products, excelling for their shrewd analyses of French society.

The countries of the South are thus emptied of their most upstanding and competent people: those who refuse to compromise with corruption and nepotism, those capable of proving their worth anywhere in the world.

And when there is a need for rare and valued skills, they are simply imported in the same way as smartphones or BMWs. There is nothing easier than signing a contract with McKinsey or the Boston Consulting Group, nothing easier than hiring Turkish or Chinese engineers to construct a dam, nothing simpler than calling up a foreign contractor to ask that he repair your vehicle registration system. He sends you the best grey matter available. It checks into the hotel, carries out its mission, and then gets on a plane and goes home. It is just a question of putting out a call for bids—a buyer's job. Nothing could be simpler.

The art of governing a country in order to save it from underdevelopment is something else altogether. But no one is interested in this south of the Mediterranean, surely not the existing oligarchies, for whom this would be tantamount to signing their death warrant. To the contrary, they cheer on the departure of their country's most virtuous elements and watch in delight as its political and economic landscape is reduced to a swamp infested with crocodiles and snakes. For this is the ideal ecosystem for remaining in power: mediocre hucksters floating above a people lost at sea and with hardly enough to eat.

---

10. Trans. French-Moroccan writer and journalist.
11. Trans. Moroccan writer and film director based in Paris.

Sometimes, the simple fact of turning on the television and listening to a government minister talk is enough to convince you that all is lost, that the country is screwed, that there is no longer any hope when a minister cannot even form a sentence with verb, subject, and compliment. The system wins because the people forfeit. Despair triumphant.

Thank God for emigration.

The American Dream

With immigration, French elites are like addicts placed in front of some crack cocaine. They simply can't say no.

The influx of undocumented labor is essential to the metabolism of whole swathes of the economy, including the construction industry (a sector with significant political influence), the restaurant industry, security services, and agriculture (grape harvesting, strawberry-picking, etc.).

A "fortuitous" consequence of injecting a vulnerable and thus docile workforce into the economy is the enervation of trade unionism. Does anyone still fear a general strike in France? Which CAC 40 board of directors still loses sleep over industrial action?

For a certain form of capitalism, immigration is a blessing. Immigration allows it to undermine the social fabric as a whole, the better to make it accept the unacceptable: the dismantling of the welfare state, the pauperization of workers, the degradation of the middle class, and the submission of political institutions to foreign, illegitimate, and non-representative powers. When they import immigrants, oligarchies know very well that they are importing the seeds of division and discord. The victims of this system lose sight of their real enemy. Employees thus no longer know if they are oppressed because they are employees or because they are black or Muslim . . . In a dislocated society incapable of giving as good as it gets, passing *reforms* (i.e., cutting entitlements and social spending) is like shooting fish in a barrel. Worse yet, immigrant populations tend to accept inequality because they themselves come from countries where injustice and the revolt of the elites are not up for debate—a godsend when the time comes to convince society to abandon all cohesion. The French society of the oligarchs' dreams is half-way between California and India: networked and hedonistic on the one hand, poverty-stricken and resigned on the other. And the cherry on top: once naturalized, immigrants tend to vote for the left and progressives, two groups that have

been allies of the oligarchy ever since they abandoned social justice and any
notion of sovereignty.

The Multicultural Dream

To make this scam easier to swallow, the virtues of multiculturalism are sung
in unison. Morning, noon, and night, the social body is cooked in a boiler that
slowly habituates it to desiring its own disappearance so as to make room for
a better world: the multicultural world, of course.

There today exists a *multicultural dream*, just like there was a *colonial
dream* 150 years ago: two bubbles, emptied of common sense and all contact
with reality, but nevertheless sacred in their emptiness, quasi-religions, their
purity guarded over by zealous ministers. Heretics beware!

A New Lobby

In times past, there was a *colonial party*—in fact, a colonial lobby bringing together capitalists, media moguls, journalists and opinion writers, politicians
from every camp, "associations," scholars in fields like geography and botany
(the backing of science), members of the clergy, and so on. The colonial party
led a tireless campaign to create a consensus regarding colonization, justifying its "revealed truth" on the basis of the trinity discussed earlier in this
book: the civilizing mission (never implemented), profit (a mirage from start
to finish), and international prestige (a goal achieved during the Second World
War thanks to the selfless sacrifice of native *goumiers* and infantrymen).

It is no secret that the ideological core of this colonial party was on the left.
It managed to recruit the right as an auxiliary in its propaganda campaign.
Even then, the French right bowed before the moral superiority of the left . . .

In our time, another lobby decides on behalf of the French without giving
a single thought to their democracy. It is the *multicultural party* that promotes
the *multicultural dream*. Though it was born on the left, it is of neither left nor
right, the socialists having had the good sense to enlist a large portion of the
right (the so-called "parliamentary right") in this adventure. Like its colonial
ancestor, this lobby operates as a trans-partite conglomeration, "connecting"
people who sometimes hate one another around a common "truth." They are
trade-unionists, employers, journalists, university professors, artists, athletes,
human rights activists, and so on. Some of them know what they are doing,

others just do "the job" blindly, from a spirit of mimicry and opportunism. Tomorrow, they will say that the earth is flat if it gets them into the good books of the *Centre National du Livre*[12] or invited to the César Awards.[13] Corruption, pure and simple.

The multicultural dream supplies our leaders with a doctrine. It consists of a shapeless pile of flabby consensus positions, the mediocrity of which can be summed up as a series of hashtags: #refugeeswelcome, #blacklivesmatter, #noborders, #inclusion, #diversity, #stopfascism. These commands, pathetic though they are, benefit from the immense prestige of those who proffer them: celebrity professors, movie stars, the CEOs of the Fortune 500 and the CAC 40, etc. They float in the air and people's minds as unquestionable beliefs, a form of sacrality built upon elements of language, subtly glued together to form a founding myth that forces people to lower their gaze in deference. Woe to those who would dare profane this myth, for to do so is to invite the wrath of the Gods.

To say no, call into question, swim against the tide—all can cost you dearly.

Stupefaction

The success of the multicultural dream is not solely to be explained by the fear of punishment. It is also fueled by repentance and diversity. The first rewrites the past, the second preempts the future. Neither is concerned with the present, and rightly so, because the present does not easily lend itself to storytelling.

Repentance travels back in time to the colonial past to put out the lights, great and small alike: from the feats of a Lyautey in Morocco to the eradication of the plague and smallpox in Madagascar.

For Southern elites, repentance allows the mass departure of young people for France to be legitimated. One emigrates to put right a colonial trauma one has never experienced. Instead of asking what these young people might

12. Trans. The Centre national du livre (CNL) is a publicly-funded branch of the French Ministry of Culture that supports, via grants, loans, and promotional activity, the entire chain of production associated with the book trade, including writers, publishers, and book stores.
13. Trans. Funded, like the CNL, by the French Ministry of Culture, the César Awards recognize excellence in the French film industry and are that country's answer to the Oscars.

have accomplished in their countries, their right to take their due and move abroad is glorified.

In the North, repentance saps the strength of any slight hope of closing the borders. The French have been convinced that the use of force is illegitimate, even when it is for the purpose of defending their own country. And for good reason: did not French men use excessive force during the colonial period, the pinnacle of their power? Violence is taboo for the French and only the French. Others may resort to it, no one will remind them of the crimes of their ancestors.

With the past neutralized, it is time to go after the future. Such is the mission of Diversity, the universal remedy to all problems raised by migratory invasion and the irruption of Islam. The idea is simple: "move along, nothing to see here, everything will sort itself out, let diversity get on with it." With each fresh terror attack, we are thus exhorted to celebrate diversity; with each horrific news item, we are urged to have faith in diversity; with every spike in unemployment, we are reminded that diverse youth are worst hit, that what is needed is therefore more diversity!

The present, for its part, is stubborn, a "pain in the ass" for everyone. When not scorned, it is ignored. An immigrant attacks a young woman, no one will report the story. The victim dares reveal her attacker's origin, and people cry xenophobia. A total inversion of values and priorities.

Colonization was not without its hiccups. The colonial lobby played these down. From the very beginning, Africa, the Maghreb, and Indochina said no to France. Instead of acknowledging this rejection, one underscored the "troubles" caused by "outlaws." Beginning in the 1930s, children and adolescents known as the *yaouled* roamed the streets of Casablanca and Algiers, stealing, begging, and swelling the ranks of the first nationalist riots. They were taken for "sickos" and "madmen." Twenty years later, they would supply the shock troops of the independence struggle in the slums and medinas. It might be argued that Unaccompanied Minors are today's *yaouled*: they have something to tell us, but we are too frightened (of the doxa) to hear it. Like the European colonists of the 1930s, we will ignore the weaker signals and let ourselves be surprised when a "war of liberation" erupts in the *banlieues*. When that day comes, it will be too late.

As we await Judgment Day, the final showdown, the multicultural party encourages us to play with cement, steel, and inaugural ribbons. Just like its ancestor, the colonial party, it confuses us by amassing libraries in the "projects," and guzzling through billions of Euros in urban renewal. Its accomplishments are scarcely superior to those of colonial governors boasting of how many kilometers of railway track they laid.

As in 1950s Algiers or Dakar, billions of Euros are pumped into a reality that evades, resists, and retaliates. The more France spends money it does not have to renovate stairwells, the worse things become in the *banlieues*. This is no accident, for civilizations are not bought with welfare benefits and scratching people's backs. They are deaf to *urban policy*, just as before they turned their back on the Constantine Plan. They are annoying that way, for they are unreasonable.

The consent of a population is not measured in tons of concrete poured. Men and women can allow themselves to be corrupted, but not civilizations. When they say no, it means no, and it is difficult to get them to change their mind.

But what is the multicultural dream all about? Nothing other than to bring French civilization face to face with two civilizations that are completely alien to it. One has hated it for 1400 years, the other barely knows it. I am of course speaking of Islam and Africa.

PART VI:

WHAT IS TO BE DONE? MOURN THE PAST OR SMILE UPON THE FUTURE?

WERE THERE ANY BENEFITS TO COLONIZATION?

"Colonialism was a grave mistake, a fault of the Republic."

EMMANUEL MACRON

One of the easiest ways of getting yourself ostracized from academic circles is to mention the possible benefits of French colonization. The current consensus rewards self-flagellators and the inquisitors of past crimes. In private, however, away from the cameras, quite a few intellectuals will tell you that colonization was useful for putting an end to such barbaric practices as slavery and other forms of human trafficking. They will even admit that colonization provided peoples formerly dug in behind their particularisms with a vector of unity and harmony. This was of course the French language, a heritage shared by millions of Africans and Arabs. Just as much as the metropolitan French, they are its legitimate owners. In the francophone world, all are equal, whether one is a bourgeois Parisian from the VIIth arrondissement, an Ivorian planter from Bouaké, or a Tuareg of Mali. We all belong equally to the same intellectual and spiritual community born of colonization. In public, all of this will of course be denied by the official intellectuals. Hypocrisy and false pretense.

This taboo must be broken, not from a desire for transgression, but because we must defuse the bombs that litter our shared past. One cannot share an explosive memory, or an ever-open wound. That is the surest way to attract the parasites and germs that infect bodies instead of helping them heal.

How shall we take stock of colonization?

It is essential that we act like adults and see reality for what it is, neither glorifying nor damning it.

Colonization was an act of rape. It would be indecent to celebrate its memory, just as indecent as it would be to deny a baby born of rape the right to life. Yet the world in which I was born, along with millions of other Africans and Arabs, is the product of colonization and it is out of the question to erase it just to please some disgruntled activists. The Morocco in which I grew up was shaped by Lyautey, who unified it and restored its hope. My own father was saved from poverty by French colonization. It gave him a rapid and peaceful route for using his talent to improve his social station. Once France had left, my father eagerly and enthusiastically set to work on behalf of Morocco. My mother, for her part, learned of women's rights while attending the Taza high school, which in the early 1970s still employed teachers from France. Her contact with a certain Madame Claire, a nun who offered reading lessons to young boys and girls living in the "Waters and Forests" district, helped shape her vision of the world. Madame Claire washed her laundry in the same fountain as my maternal grandmother. These two women, different in every way, came together each day to admire the spectacle of their differences. Madame Claire did not wish to convert anyone to Catholicism and my grandmother had better things to do (first and foremost, care for her eight children) than bother trying to Islamize her neighbor. Watching these two women do their washing, my mother lost any xenophobic inclinations and all distrust of the foreigner.

What right do I have to turn against my parents and demand that they hate their childhood and youth? To do so would be adolescent, irresponsible, and vain. What's done is done, my identity is forever marked by France's (shortlived) sojourn in Morocco. Behaving like an adult is more a matter of drawing upon the positive traces left by its passage than wanting to erase it all.

The so-called *decolonials* want to erase and dismantle the identities of millions of individuals who are the products of colonization. To the crime of colonization, they wish to add another.

How is one to decolonize Morocco, the Maghreb, and Africa? By banning the use of French, by rolling back progress for women, by prohibiting the use of vaccines, by reinstating corporal punishment?

Their *decolonization* is a ridiculous and dangerous idea. It carries with it the barbarism of vandals who wish to destroy a heritage built by others and have nothing to put in its place. If the Spanish had wanted to decolonize

Andalusia, they would have dynamited the Alhambra, smashed the azulejos, and purged the Spanish language of all the Arabic words that it had integrated over the course of the centuries. Only a madman would be capable of such nonsense.

Only a madman would deprive himself of the benefits of the colonial experience. And they are not trivial.

To start with, as a rule, colonization conferred territorial unity upon peoples who had none. Take the example of Algeria. In 1962, no Algerian questioned the fact that the tribes of Oran, Aurès, and the Sahara fell under the same political-administrative entity. Yet, before 1830, this was anything but obvious . . . If France had never unified Algeria, how much time would the Algerians have needed and how many lives would they have lost to establish a nation? No one can really say, but it is certain that the price would have been steep indeed. Everywhere France laid foot, it consolidated various members into a single body. Morocco owes its territorial unity to the protectorate: without France, Marrakech would have continued to disobey Fez. Vietnam is the child of French colonization, born of the (forced) junction of Tonkin, Annam, and Cochinchina. And all the better, for it is now a viable, dynamic country.

Second, France bestowed clear and definitive borders upon countries that had none. It can always be said that they are arbitrary, but where in the world are borders not arbitrary? All reflect a power that gave rise to one or more wars, all are the expression of one side's victory and the other's defeat. If they had been allowed, the Germans would have placed their western border along the Vosges, not the Rhine. Similarly, if they had free rein, the Mexicans would set their northern frontier well above the Rio Grande. Once this is understood, one grasps the great service France performed for its former colonies: by imposing a *fait accompli*, it spared them blood and tears. Consider the case of Morocco's border with Algeria: wherever France drew a border, all is well; wherever it did not or could not lay down a dividing line, however, conflict and misunderstanding reign. Despite its shortcomings, which include cutting in two the pasturelands of nomadic tribes, Moroccans and Algerians have never called into question the arbitrary line that runs from Oujda to Figuig. South of this line, by contrast, they have been at war with one another for fifty years, first in the Sand War of 1963 to delimit the border near Colomb-Béchar and then, since 1975, the Western Sahara War.

It is often said that the borders resulting from colonization do not take ethnic realities sufficiently into account. This is certainly true, but is it possible to take them into account without waging war or displacing populations? When India and Pakistan attempted to adapt their borders to ethno-religious realities in 1947, ten million people were displaced and hundreds of thousands of them died. For ethnicities and communities mix, live in the same villages, and it is extremely difficult to draw a line of demarcation that makes sense.

Lastly, it is impossible to deny that the colonial crime, odious though it was, produced an undeniably beneficial electroshock, awakening a long-dormant sense of mission and unleashing energy. By draining the Mitidja plain, the colonists showed the Algerians that there was nothing inevitable about their situation, that it was possible to produce abundance where there once had only been sterility. Similarly, the Arabs who tormented the inhabitants of Spain taught them new irrigation techniques allowing them to restore life to areas where once there had only been scarcity. Colonization opened the eyes of peoples blinded by centuries of stagnation. It set in motion populations that had resigned themselves to exiting history and come to terms with lives of destitution and illiteracy. The before and after is as clear-cut and precise as the difference between sleep and waking.

Unfortunately, it was not enough to be awake. Powerful forces once again anesthetized the people, preventing them from shaking off the yoke of underdevelopment and creating the conditions for human dignity. In fact, these civilizations had weathered the colonial shock much more effectively than is generally assumed. As well-meaning people who wished to modernize Africa and the Arab world, France's mistake was to underestimate the civilizational factor. Yet civilization, like the unconscious, always has the last word. Those who ignored mentalities and values invariably met with frustration. If Morocco did not take off, it was not for lack of capital or technology, but rather because it is corrupt and to this day scorns excellence. The same goes for Algeria, which has never managed to take advantage of its petroleum windfall due to its mentalities and behaviors.

What's more, the frustration generated by the failures of post-independence policy fuels the discourse of repentance. Fingers are pointed at colonization because people are incapable of identifying the real enemy, namely, persistent and stubborn civilizational deadlock. The less one succeeds in curing the moral sickness of African and North African societies, the more one insists on blaming Lyautey, Gallieni, and Faidherbe. It is easier to kick a dead body than to act and succeed.

Yet one need not be a sociological genius to guess what prevents former colonies from becoming countries where the living is good. It is so obvious no one sees it, an elephant in the living room of which no one is aware because all are myopic and hard of hearing. All the Marshall Plans in the world will never succeed in putting an end to the hardships that a society imposes upon itself: corruption, nepotism, arbitrary rule, scorn for scientific knowledge, censorship of curiosity and free thinking, and so on.

And here can be mentioned a dark stain on the legacy of French colonization: a certain way of thinking requiring one to shrug off civilization, to silence its voice and hold that progress is entirely a question of quantifiable factors: labor, capital, and technology. Under colonization, it became commonplace to confuse the construction of a bridge with the arrival of progress, the opening of a port with the advent of material well-being, the building of a school with the dawn of Enlightenment. But all depends on the men and women who will cross this bridge, pass through this port, teach in these schools. If they are backwards and obscurantist, there will be no progress; if they are modern (which does not necessarily mean Westernized), progress will come knocking. Having become independent, the former colonies persisted in this colonial error by continuing to practice "lazy development"—that is, they continued to solely count on the material indicators while neglecting the cultural, moral, ethical, and spiritual domains. It is the approach of a civil engineer who thinks that bringing about change is merely a question of pouring concrete and stretching cables. He forgets that the human being is made of material tougher than stone: civilization, which is sovereign and does as it will with him. It can sink him just as it can raise him above his condition. And it is to civilization that one must address oneself if one is to develop a country.

If colonization has bestowed a cursed inheritance, it is perhaps here that it is to be found. The notion that one might pretend men and women are interchangeable blank slates has its source in French colonization. It is a grave error.

REPENTANCE IS A SICKNESS OF THE SOUL

"Others could have struck me down, others could have put me in chains; but Louis-Napoleon is the only one who defeated me."

EMIR ABDELKADER

Repentance is an essential tool for greasing the wheels of the new postcolonial equilibrium. It allows the oligarchies of North and South to justify mass migration and sentence the French to silence. The latter endure their ouster as a "well-deserved" punishment for the crimes of colonization.

Yet there is nothing more absurd or out-of-place than this demand for repentance.

Zero Legitimacy

First of all, it is not legitimate to demand repentance in our time, the generation now in its thirties having had no direct or indirect experience of the trials and tribulations of colonization. To the contrary, it has seen only its positive repercussions. South of the Mediterranean: the (relative) moderation of mores, among other happy repercussions. To the north: the luck of being born in France and becoming French thanks to *jus soli*. Indeed, colonization and the bilateral accords that followed it allowed several hundred thousand Arab and African workers to come there legally and lay down roots.

And yet the generation that has experienced only the most beneficial aspects of colonization somehow manages to be more "bruised" and "traumatized" than those who actually lived through it. There is clearly something to be reconsidered about the moral education of our young, who manage to "appropriate" the suffering of others. Perhaps they are so afraid of life that they seek refuge in the (genuine) trauma of their grandparents, if only for an excuse to avoid giving life a try themselves. Fear of being a citizen, fear of being an adult, fear of being responsible and thus accountable. Fear of being in control of their own lives to such a point that they take refuge in the role of the malcontent, he who trashes the work of others, literally and figuratively. Either he throws rocks or he spews invective and indulges in conspiracy theories. The essential thing is to be busy with something other than looking after his own interests, the essential thing is to destroy the lives of those who live it to the full, the essential thing is to wreck the stage upon which the human comedy plays out so as not to have to participate in it.

A large segment of Arab and African youth is suffering from a disease of the will.

When they live south of the Mediterranean, many young people do nothing with their lives other than look forward to the moment they can cross it. They refuse to complete their studies or learn a trade. A whole life goes by in waiting and thereby in submission to the very regimes responsible for the deprivation that drives them to flee. When they live north of the Mediterranean, these young people refuse to stay in one place: they are neither happy to live in France nor keen to resettle in their country of origin. They are nowhere, always "passing through," always "in parenthesis": neither French, nor Moroccan, nor Algerian, nor permanent residents of a state that suits their sensibility, like the United States or the United Arab Emirates. For this reason, they are incapable of giving the best version of themselves, for they refuse to step into the arena and put their lives to the test: they are always bound for elsewhere, one foot in and one foot out. Imagine a professional footballer who hates the jersey he wears and only dreams of playing for the opposing team: will he give his best on the pitch?

By virtue of its apathy, this young generation reaps nothing but exclusion and failure on both sides of the Mediterranean. It thus suffers, even suffers a great deal. And when one suffers, one often behaves foolishly, for instance by living in a past one never knew.

These young people fleeing their responsibilities are in no position to lecture France. Maybe once they have done their homework, they will have won the right to sit in judgement over the past.

What could it possibly add to the words of Abdelkader, the Algerian emir who almost drove the French from Algeria? The same Abdelkader who addressed himself thus to Bismarck in August 1870, after the latter proposed that he once again raise his sword against France:

"He to whom you have addressed this offer to march against the most glorious and most generous France and lend you the support of his loyal sword should, from contempt and disdain, refrain from answering you.

"May all our Arab horses lose their manes before Abd el Kader ben Mahi ed-Din betrays his gratitude towards the very powerful emperor Napoleon III (may God save him!).

"May your arrogant and unjust nation be buried in the dust and may the weapons of the French army run red with the blood of the Prussians (may their pride be punished!)

"Such is the wish of God's servant"

What value-added does a postcolonial activist, or rapper, or comedian have such that he can today demand of the French what Abdelkader himself never demanded of them?

Those who were in their rights to demand reparations were named Cedar Senghor, Houphouët, Sékou Touré, Ho Chi Minh . . . And, for the Belgians, Lumumba. These great men did not degrade themselves with begging. They were too proud.

Mohammed V never demanded repentance from Lyautey. Indeed, six years after the latter was dismissed from his position as resident-general of Morocco, he paid him a visit in Nancy. Nothing obliged Mohammed Ben Youssef (the future king Mohammed V) to visit Lyautey in 1931 other than the respect and consideration he felt for him. In any case, how could a Moroccan statesman blame France for having rescued Morocco from fragmentation?

No, the current generation has no right to demand accounts of the past. They will just have to roll up their sleeves. Colonization is over. Henceforth, the issue is to defeat underdevelopment in the South and mediocrity (which besets a portion of the diaspora) in the North.

Unacceptable from Every Point of View

The duty of repentance does not stand up to even the most cursory inspection.

To start with, it is a basic principle of law that guilt does not pass from one generation to the next, in the same way that punishment cannot be collective. To seek to punish all French people for the crimes of their state (collective punishment), committed one hundred years ago (transmission of guilt), makes no sense.

As a people, what's more, the French never wholly subscribed to the colonial idea. It was an idea of the elite that had collected around the colonial party. The French people were not aware of daily life in the colonies, nor of the atrocities and apartheid reserved for the natives. The first great accounts of the abuses inflicted upon colonized populations came relatively late, mainly in the 1920s (Albert Londres, André Malraux and Andrée Viollis, etc.). And again, these accounts were buried under a much greater volume of fundamentally colonialist official propaganda.

If we accept that the French people be punished today for the crimes of the colonial administrations of the past century, must we expect our children and grand-children to be punished in thirty or forty years by the Libyans for the crimes committed by Sarkozy-BHL[1] in 2011? Such are the depths of absurdity plumbed by the duty of repentance.

Finally, what kind of society holds resentment as its cardinal virtue? There is nothing noble about keeping the social fabric under constant pressure, polarized between those deserving of reproach (whites) and everyone else, who enjoy a sort of *immunity* by birth. A respectable society practices forgiveness, not repentance. It is wise enough to forget. It is oriented towards the future, not buttressed by the past. It marches towards cohesion, solidarity, and glory, instead of pitching camp around its scars.

And between you and me, what is one to make of a society so ready to forgive rapists and murderers, but which gets irritated when you ask it to leave its ancestors in peace, whatever their crimes?

---

1. Trans. Former French President Nicholas Sarkozy and French celebrity intellectual, Bernard-Henri Levy (commonly referred to by his initials, BHL), both of whom were ardent supporters of the 2011 NATO intervention in Libya.

Repentance Is Dangerous

If the duty of repentance was extended to relations between states, there would be no more diplomacy. War would be the common lot of every country. Imagine a France that never forgave Germany—the effect would be fatal for the European construction, since "everything" began with Franco-German reconciliation.

The refusal to forgive (the other name for the duty of repentance) has already caused numerous wars in Rwanda, where the Hutu and Tutsi are hostages to the crimes committed by their ancestors. The genocide of the 1990s was the direct consequence of a conflictual memory that manipulators prevented from healing. The recent history of Libya and Sierra Leone is so bloody because the indigenous black people refuse to forgive the descendants of freed slaves for a century of oppression. The catastrophe of Haiti is partly due to the reciprocal hatred felt by mulattos and blacks. Recall how the appalling Duvalier (Papa Doc) practiced *noirism*, a kind of ethnic favoritism intended to repair the offenses committed by mulattos against blacks.

Extended to the entire world, the duty of memory could potentially blow every nation apart. It could pit the Riffians against other Moroccans on behalf of the rebels massacred in 1959.[2] It could shatter Algeria on behalf of the suffering endured by the Berbers at the hands of the Arabs. It could tear France itself apart should the Vendeans decide to hurl the gruesome death toll of the genocide carried out there by the Revolution in the face of Parisians.

Relations between France and Spain could founder in irreparable hostility if Madrileños were to acutely recall the horrors of the Napoleonic occupation. Similarly, Spain might cut ties with Morocco were it to throw itself into the painful memory of the atrocities committed by the Riffian soldiers sent by Franco to pacify Barcelona. Italy might feel it had grounds to quarrel with Morocco because of the rapes committed by the *goumiers* in 1944 (the famous *marroquinate*). And should Sub-Saharan Africa suddenly remember the Muslim slave trade, it might turn against the Arab world from Rabat to Baghdad and demand reparations.

---

2. After the departure of Spain, the Rif found themselves once again under the yoke of Morocco. After an attempted uprising, they suffered severe repression in the form of bombardment and mass arrests.

264 A Counter-History of French Colonization

And so on and so forth . . . Enough to sow discord everywhere. It would be the work of a demon, not a humanist.

An Unjust Idea

One must have a very peculiar idea of justice to limit repentance solely to relations between the West and its former colonies. Why not kneel before the 600,000 Germans who starved to death during the First World War as a result of the Franco-British naval blockade? Were not these men, women, and children just as innocent as the victims of colonial repression?

Ultimately, repentance must be applied universally or not at all. The Russians should apologize for the hundreds of thousands of rapes committed against German women in 1945. The Allies should pay reparations to Germany for the millions of Germans they forcibly displaced after May 1945 and who formerly lived in Ukraine, Belarus, Hungary, Romania, the Baltic countries, and so on. These same Allies should repent for Dresden, Hamburg, and Tokyo, cities martyred in firebombing that above all targeted at civilians. And what is one to say about the two nuclear bombs dropped on Japan?

Clearly, the world would come to a standstill and become one huge Wailing Wall where the snivelers could converge, those useful idiots of the apostles of war.

A Weak Idea

Postcolonial activists should thus be wary of their doctrine, for it can easily be turned against them. If some young man from the housing projects can demand the repentance of the French state, what prevents the son of a *harki* from demanding repentance from the Algerian consul in Paris? Absolutely nothing. After all, the *harkis* were disemboweled and burned alive after independence, despite the fact that the FLN had committed to guaranteeing their security.

In the same vein, nothing stops the descendants of the pied-noirs killed (like so many others) in Oran in July 1962 from insisting on an official apology from the Algerian authorities.

And while we are at it, why should we forget the injustice that France committed against the loyal *goumiers* and *tirailleurs*? These Arab and black soldiers were treated with ingratitude by the military bureaucracy after the war. My grandfather earned a pittance for the four years he spent in a Nazi *stalag*. Properly compensating these veterans would be a nice rebuff to the postcolonialists, reminding them that native populations were never unanimously opposed to France.

Let's treat the subject with the seriousness it demands. Let's stop joking around with memory and focus our efforts on today's atrocities. Before our eyes, the Libyan and Sinai mafias are torturing African migrants (as in the good old days of the Ottoman Empire). On our screens, the crimes of Boko Haram are shown in all their horror, and we do nothing. As I write this book, South African criminals are massacring white farmers in their sleep, is that not racism? Is this not a grave insult to the rainbow ideal bequeathed by Mandela? Instead of spitting on the dead and buried, let us confront the monsters who degrade humanity in the here and now.

THE TRUTH, THE WHOLE TRUTH, AND NOTHING BUT THE TRUTH

"One must not waste one's time making good faith arguments with people of bad faith."

HASSAN II

"Telling the truth is the beginning of change."

DENIS MUKWEGE, NOBEL PEACE PRIZE LAUREATE

France is on the defensive and it shows, it is felt, its enemies know it.

Well-mannered, the French people respond to hateful accusations with contrition. They kneel and extend a hand in peace to those who would like to burn down their house. Other peoples would respond with the back of their hand and put a stop to the moaning; the French take their beating and do not understand why no one comes to their aid. They are perhaps waiting for the state to put itself between them and their assailants.

But the state lets it happen and the elites are amused by the plight of the people. They delight in seeing the dangerous masses of yesterday be spit upon by little thugs imported from overseas.

The French are abused and the Powerful—oligarchs, senior officials, university mandarins, and leading journalists—cheer it on. The strong have forsaken the weak.

What is to be done?

Go on the offensive and only count on yourself.

Armed with what?

The truth, the whole truth, and nothing but the truth.

To the demand for repentance, one must respond with transparency: everything must be said, everything put on the table, the best as well as the worst.

The truth is an antidote to the venom of repentance. To those on their knees, it whispers: stand up, hold your head high, take pride in your ancestors and be worthy of them. From those doing the complaining, it tears away the only "spoils" of their war: the belief that France is the mother of all their woes.

Truth or civil war, that is the dilemma we are facing.

The Truth of Nuance

Like everything else in life, the form taken by colonization depends upon the people, place, and time.

Between 1954 and 1962, as napalm was being dropped on the FLN in Algeria, soldiers there were distributing vaccines, medicine, and flour to Muslim families. In a way unparalleled in the country to this day, the Special Administrative Sections worked to bring aid to the needy. Each unit was commanded by a captain (wearing a blue kepi), who was assisted by French non-commissioned officers and Algerian Muslim soldiers (*mokhaznis*). In his service and depending on the circumstances, the captain had nurses, doctors, midwives, schoolteachers, civilians, and soldiers. At the program's height (1960), there were 700 SAS in Algeria. Each of them came to the aid of roughly ten thousand individuals.

Yes, the French army took care of some Algerians even as the paras were torturing others. Such is life, complex and nuanced. There are only spoiled children who refuse to accept this.

Among the subtleties that escape postcolonial inquistors is the presence of a liberal, pro-native core in all French colonies. They would have us believe that there were two homogeneous blocs: the pied-noirs (or colonists) versus the natives. Nothing could be further from the truth. In Algeria, for example, the OAS fought Muslims as much as they did pied-noirs who supported the Algerians.

The Truth about Collaboration and the Complicity between Natives and Europeans

A portion of the population and its elites collaborated with France. Without them, the occupation would have been impossible, for the French administration was chronically understaffed. Without Moroccan police officers, without Algerian and Congolese tax collectors, without Senegalese *tirailleurs*, without Vietnamese mandarins, the system would never have worked.

Collaboration is an excessively loaded term. It would be better in some cases to speak of mutual respect and shared esteem. This is how Emir Abdelkader felt for Napoleon III, whom he admired as a benefactor. As he put it, and at the risk of repeating ourselves: "Others could have struck me down, others could have put me in chains; but Louis-Napoleon is the only one who defeated me."

What anti-colonial activist or university professor could claim to "know more about it" than Abdelkader? What right do they have to put France on trial?

Great men like Abdelkader know there is a time for mutual hatred and another for joining forces. They are obsessed by the purity of their action, not the purity of some pseudo-morality of the salon. A true chief knows when to admit the mission has changed and that yesterday's enemy is not necessarily today's threat.

This path was taken but in reverse by several of the FLN's founding fathers, including Krim Belkacem, who fought alongside France in the Second World War. After 1945, he had to revise his convictions, turning his rifle against the occupying power. Where great men adapt, activists cling to fixed ideas.

The Truth about the Civil War

The wars of liberation were immense, fratricidal bloodbaths. Natives against natives. Everyone had blood on their hands, including the independence fighters, who also raped, butchered, and tortured. This is true of Vietnam, Algeria, and everywhere that independence has required recourse to violence. Even in Morocco, where bringing about independence was largely a formality, acts of violence were committed by the Muslim mob against other Muslims suspected of sympathies with France: in Oued Zem in August 1955, but also in the days following independence in Marrakech, Casablanca, and Meknes.

In Algeria, civil war reached new heights. Between conscripts, active-duty troops, and auxiliary forces, the French army in Algeria contained roughly 200,000 Muslim soldiers and non-commissioned officers. These soldiers fought against other Muslims. Some FLN fighters joined the French ranks, where they served with distinction in the *Commandos de Chasse*.[1]

Among the independence fighters, there was bloody infighting for hegemony. On May 28th, 1957, the FLN massacred all the inhabitants of the village of Mellouza (347 people) in reprisal for their alleged support for its rival, the MNA (*Mouvement National Algérien*).

The FLN killed more Muslims than it did pied-noirs and French soldiers. It mutilated hundreds who dared smoke cigarettes or drink alcohol. It persecuted families who sent their children to school or visited the clinic. Collective and public punishment allowed it to maintain the revolutionary fervor of Algerians.

Some of the crimes committed against Muslims were truly despicable. In 1956, the brother of Saïd Boualam (a famous pro-French tribal chief) was caught unawares by an FLN squad at his home. He was dragged in front of his residence, beaten in front of his children, and disemboweled.

The Truth about the Ordeal of the Pied-Noirs

Alongside Algerian civilians, the greatest victims of the Algerian war were the pied-noirs. The French state, which owed them protection, abandoned them to their fate in March 1962 with the signing of the Evian Accords, the prelude to Algeria's independence (July 5th, 1962). In the course of this five-month interval, the FLN unleashed a wave of kidnapping and murder against the pied-noirs. Between the ceasefire (the Evian Accords) and independence, some 3000 Europeans are thought to have died or disappeared.

Driven back to France by the policy of "the suitcase or the coffin", the pied-noirs received a deplorable welcome from their fellow citizens. In Marseille, dockers belonging to the CGT, the country's largest leftwing labor union, insulted them, the mayor mistreated them, and the government wanted to distribute them around France to departments with falling populations, such as Nord and Pas-de-Calais . . .

The Algerians and FLN, in other words, have no monopoly on suffering.

The list of decolonization's victims is very long. It is not right to erase the names of some, while underscoring those of others.

---

1. Trans. The *Commandos de Chasse*—literally, Hunt Commandos—were a special forces unit raised by the French during the Algerian War. They specialized in clandestine operations, commando style-raids, infiltration, counterinsurgency, long-range penetration, and special reconnaissance.

The Truth about Historical Continuity

History did not begin with colonization and did not end with decolonization. The myth of a *lost virginity* is as nonsensical as the argument that colonial trauma persisted after independence.

Before France's arrival on the scene, native societies were already familiar with injustice, slavery, poverty, and discrimination (towards women, some ethnic groups, Jews, and so on.).

The Regency of Algiers, a Turkish possession, was hell for Algerians, a racial and tribal engineering laboratory: Kouloughlis were pitted against Algerians, Kabyles against Arabs, *makhzen* tribes against *raya* tribes.

Senegal was a reserve of domestic slaves and serfs in thrall to a caste of marabouts and warriors.

Once France had left the newly independent countries, power was seized by native elites, who generally carried over the unfortunate practices of the colonial years: torture, censorship, arbitrary arrest, and chronic underinvestment in society.

In Guinea Conakry, France was driven out and replaced by single party rule under the leadership of Ahmed Sékou Touré (1958), who systematically plundered the state. People from his ethnic group and familial clan held the main levers of the administration. A torture camp was opened to punish opponents (Camp Boiro), with control of it put into the hands of the president's nephew, Siaka Touré. It is estimated that 5000 people died of hunger and abuse in Camp Boiro. Is that, too, the fault of France?

In Algeria, the practice of torture continued under Ben Bella after 1962. The repression was to know its darkest hours following Boumediene's coup d'état in 1965, with a French prison in Algiers being reopened for the express purpose of holding political opponents.

In Morocco, the political police subjected Moroccans to harassment and indignities that were certainly more serious than those practiced by the colonial regime.

Bourguiba's Tunisia was also ruled in an authoritarian and arbitrary manner. Oppression had no need of France.

Nor did it need the state: in the 1990s, the Islamists of the FIS and GIA gorged on the blood of Algerians. The civil war caused 100,000 deaths, and yet no one rubs this in the faces of Islamist leaders in the name of repentance. They are clearly less "naive" than the French of today, who are so "decent" that they feel responsible for crimes committed sixty years ago.

Is it to relativize the crimes of France to write this? Yes, perhaps, but to relativize does not mean to excuse. France had no excuse for colonization. To relativize is simply to put the facts in historical order, as an investigator would do. To relativize also means inviting today's whiners to put themselves in the dock: they may be the grandchildren of butchers who in the past massacred their fellow citizens and innocent civilians. Finally, to relativize is to demand that he who would put France on trial do the same with Erdogan for the odious crimes of the Ottoman Empire, which was a colonial power in Algeria, Tunisia, and so many other Arab countries.

The Truth about Migration

If France had truly been the monster portrayed by the postcolonialists, how is one to explain the eagerness of millions of Arabs and Africans to settle there?

Immigration began with independence.

In the 1960s, Algeria was already sending between 30,000 and 50,000 workers to France each year. In 1972, there were 720,000 Algerians legally residing in France, or twice as many as at the time of independence. Were they forcibly deported to France or was this a voluntary migration? You know the answer.

The phenomenon is similar in Morocco, albeit less pronounced, as Algerians were given priority in accessing the French labor market.

Year	Moroccan workers leaving the country
1962	4,818
1963	7,219
1968	12,479
1969	23,519
1970	31,006
1971	30,764

Source: La Population du Maroc, INSEA, 1974

Most Moroccan workers leaving the country headed for France, with 91 percent of them choosing it as their destination in 1971.

African immigration began a little later, but also confirms this blindingly obvious truth: there was no ill will between these people and France in the

1960s and 70s. They had put the past behind them, and France was remembered in a generally positive, even fond, way.

Hatred and resentment only emerged following the 1980s, when the South understood it had missed its date with development. To justify this failure, it fell back (to varying degrees) on colonization: *it's not my fault, it's Gallieni and Bugeaud's fault.*

The Truth about the Colonies That Played Their Cards Right

While colonization was a genuine failure, it nevertheless remains the case that advances were made. They were halting, fragmentary, and inadequate, to be sure, but they were real all the same. Tangible and stubborn, they give the lie to all forms of determinism because they were the work of exceptional men and special circumstances. The human adventure of colonization was capable of the best as well as the worst. And when the best presents itself, we have no right to dismiss it.

In Morocco, the best could be seen, looming on the horizon.

The Protectorate (1912–56) revived Moroccan society, bestowing the health and color it needed to face the challenges of the twentieth century. Moroccan civilization jettisoned some dreadful traits that had long brought hardship upon its people.

To begin with, France taught the Moroccan state to serve its subjects. This may seem self-evident today, but it had no counterpart in the mindset of precolonial Moroccans. The Makhzen bullied the population and could not care less about their well-being. Their logic was purely that of domination: "Pay your taxes or I'll kick your teeth in." Zero social services, zero empathy for the needy. Charity was outsourced to religious organizations (Habous, zawiyas, and marabouts). Security itself was a decentralized prerogative of the caid, pasha, and khalifa, figures who often had a very peculiar conception of how to make justice and keep order: "If you regularly give me gifts, I will remember you when something bad happens. In the meantime, keep giving me gifts."

Since colonization ended, the Moroccan state has looked after the people. It continues to tax them, of course, but at least some of it is returned in the form of public works, sanitation, irrigation, and municipal services.

The Protectorate delivered the final blow to the tribes, those giants of Moroccan history. How many sultans came up against a brick wall faced with the resistance and indiscipline of the Zemmours, the Zaers, the Ait Mguilds, and the Riffians? Over the course of forty-four years (interrupted by two world wars), France rid the Makhzen of their main internal rivals. Since then, governing Morocco is much more straightforward since the population exclusively owes allegiance to the monarchy. Unhindered by local or regional competitors, the state may act with much greater efficacy. In the past, it had to constantly negotiate with volatile tribal powers jealous of their autonomy. Is this not progress? Could the Moroccans have reached this point by themselves in so little time? When one considers the tragedy of tribal Yemen today, one is more inclined to look charitably upon France's civilizing influence on Morocco.

And what would have become of Moroccan women if Morocco had kept its sovereignty? They would certainly have continued to live cloistered lives, reduced to the status of mere objects. Such is the fate of Arab women in countries that were never colonized—Saudi Arabia, for example. There is no doubt that the colonial shock made it possible for Moroccan society to break the shackles it had for centuries made women wear.

The French presence acted as a great catalyst for phenomena that would otherwise have required an eternity to come about. Society was placed in a microwave for forty-four years. Yes, it was violent, but it succeeded in burning away the cancer that had polluted mentalities and institutions.

France did what it could (perhaps without even realizing it), but Morocco should have profited from the legacy left by colonization. True opportunities do not present themselves every day, passing them up or frittering them away is a form of self-sabotage and self-hatred. Once again, a problem of civilization.

The Truth about Giants, Geniuses, and Courageous Men

The French should feel pride, not shame, for the great men who distinguished themselves in the course of the colonial adventure. Yes, some abused their power, but several showed outstanding courage and dignity in the face of danger. Among them were statesmen like Lyautey, who literally "rebuilt" Morocco on better foundations. But also Napoleon III, who wanted to confine Algeria's pied-noirs, not its Arabs. The French sovereign loved and admired the Algerian people, doing what he could to give them a political and administrative framework that would secure their dignity. Unfortunately, Napoleon III was constantly thwarted by colonist circles, who were assisted in this by the

Parisian left. His fall in 1870 removed the last impediment to the conquest-plunder of Algeria, unleashing all the ravenous dogs, who proceeded to seize hundreds of thousands of hectares for agriculture, pushing Muslims ever further towards the caves, steep slopes, and deserts.

At the time, few French people understood Napoleon's project. Among those who did was Ismaïl Urbain, an Arabophile ahead of his time. The mixed-race son of a black mother descended from Guyanese slaves, he converted to Islam and learned Arabic. Urbain served in Bugeaud's entourage during the conquest of Algeria. He spoke, denounced, advised . . . and was finally heard by Napoleon III (who had come to power by a coup d'état in 1851), who did what he could to save what could still be saved of Algerian Algeria.

If someone tells you that colonization was a crime against humanity, respond by citing the names of a few colonial doctors who managed to save Africa with only the most meager resources at their disposal. Speak to them about Alexandre Yersin, the colonial doctor who isolated the plague bacillus, or Paul-Louis Simon, who discovered the role played by rat fleas as its vector, or the military doctors Girard and Robic in Madagascar, who developed the plague vaccine in 1932 and tested it on themselves.

Talk to them about the colonial doctor Laigret, who created a vaccine against Yellow Fever in Dakar in 1927. Or Victor Le Moal, known as "Captain Mosquito," a colonial doctor who tirelessly fought the vectors of malaria in Guinea. As head of sanitation in Conakry from 1905, he had the swamps drained, and tree stumps and ditches filled in. His recommendations were adopted around the world.

Tell them of the epic travels across Black Africa of doctors Jamot and Dumaz, in their quest to eradicate sleeping sickness. There is much also to be said about Dr. Marchoux, who truly revolutionized the way in which leprosy patients are treated.

And if your interlocutor still insists on accusing the French of genocide, ask him if he has ever heard of the Alsatian doctor and theologian Albert Schweitzer, who was the "only doctor" available in Gabon between 1910 and 1930. Schweitzer dedicated himself to protecting black people in the interior of Gabon against dysentery, leprosy, and all the other tropical maladies, free of charge and at the risk of his life and family. In 1947, the American magazine Life designated Schweitzer "the greatest man in the world."

The truth, the whole truth, and nothing but the truth, even when it comes from anecdotes and personal histories. Take Léon Roches, a young Frenchman who landed in Algeria in 1832 and found nothing better to do than fall passionately in love with Khadija, a very beautiful married woman . . . Instead of renouncing his love, he abandoned the family plantation on the outskirts of Algiers, plunged into the rebel zone, and presented himself to Abdelkader as a French renegade who had converted to Islam and wished to serve the cause of the emir.

Léon Roches' conversion was insincere but extremely convincing, for he learned Arabic and was able to recite the Quran in its entirety. He told himself that, by becoming a member of the Emir's entourage, he would surely find a way to take Khadija from her husband. Abdelkader accepted him as a close assistant, allowing him to visit the emir's tent daily.

How could one not be proud of a gentleman like Léon Roches, who love made capable of such madness?

Léon de Roches left us a touching, invaluable account of his immersion in Muslim and tribal Algeria entitled *Trente-deux ans à travers l'Islam*2 (I should warn you that he never saw Khadija again . . .).

And how could one not be proud of Pierre Savorgnan de Brazza, who conquered Congo with nothing but his silken tongue? Such is the genius of the French. Brazza managed to convince Congo's petty kings to sign protectorate treaties without any display of force, something that was in any case out of the question, as he possessed no more than a few dozen soldiers and rifles.

To those who inveigh against Gallieni, one must respond with the full truth. The man could be cruel, it is true, but it also should be remembered that he was made of different stuff than the deconstructed, fragile men of today. Gallieni endured a year of captivity under Ahmadou Tall without cracking, thousands of kilometers from Paris (1879–1880). And the cherry on top: as his prisoner, Gallieni persuaded his jailer to sign a trade agreement.

This, too, was France: men capable of courage and resilience. The dwarves who now pass for our leaders can only hate them. The weak envy the strong, the wretched are jealous of the sublime.

The Truth about the Present

In France, there are 120 knife attacks per day. Riots, terror attacks, property damage whenever the Algerian or Moroccan football teams are playing, the

---

2. Trans. "Thirty-Two Years across Islam"—never translated into English.

Champs-Élysées ransacked on a regular basis, the image of France badly dis-figured by crime and disorder.

More than 25 percent of detainees in French prisons are of Muslim origin. A crushing majority of the crimes committed in the public transport system of the capital region are committed by foreigners, many of whom come from the former colonial empire.

Lives shattered, skulls crushed: Marin, Adrien, Timothée, Arnauld Beltrame,[3] and so many other victims of attack by members of the diasporas.

What if the French were to decide one day to hold Rabat, Algiers, or Kabul responsible for the woes wrought by their citizens?

This is also a truth worth stating. France, too, has the right to accuse. She, too, can complain of foreign invasion, true and brutal.

It is pointless to denounce the crimes of the past if one closes one's eyes to those of the present. Selective indignation and cynicism have never been virtues.

---

3. Trans. Arnauld Beltrame (1973–2018) was a lieutenant-colonel in the French National Police Force (Gendarmerie nationale). On March 18th, 2018, he was mur-dered by Redouane Lakdim, a terrorist professing loyalty to the Islamic State. Beltrame had volunteered to replace a woman hostage whom Lakdim was hold-ing in a supermarket in Trèbes, a small town in the Aude department of southern France, saving her life at the price of his own.

CONCLUSION
A BAD IDEA WITH UNEXPECTED RESULTS

"It is our most absolute duty to show the government of France our gratitude for all that it has done for us. And the first to fail in this basic duty would be unworthy of our ancestors and infringe upon the orders of the Creator, who imposed the duty of gratitude and that of separating ourselves from the ungrateful."

HIS MAJESTY MOHAMMED V,
ADDRESSING THE MOROCCAN PEOPLE IN 1939

Colonization is a bad idea which has had unhoped-for consequences. Brutal from beginning to end, as fruitless for France as it was for the colonies, it nevertheless resulted in the resurrection of Morocco, the rescue of Cambodia, and the creation of new nation-states such as Vietnam, Algeria, and Senegal. The crimes of colonization did not prevent the birth of sincere friendship between victors and vanquished, nor even of a sort of fraternity so wonderfully reflected in their joint combat against Nazism. This Franco-Arab or Franco-African friendship is steadfast. It is immunized against quarreling and dissension, legitimate or not. The use of the French language is one of its many manifestations. Tourism, immigration, trade relations: it is as if we cannot do without each other. We cannot go back in time to erase the past, we can only make the best use possible of the benefits of colonization. They are real, and they are numerous.

Success is within reach. The future is ours. It depends solely on the decisions we take in the here and now. But the situation is critical.

The first decision is of an intimate nature. Immigrants must stop play-ing the embittered victim who flaunts his wounds and demands reparations. Doing so holds them down and prevents them from succeeding; they must let go of it. To lay claim to suffering, especially when it is the suffering of others (in this case, their ancestors), impedes rather than inspires success and accom-plishment. Native stock French people, for their part, must love their country, not revile it. They, too, gain nothing from bitterness and facile criticism: since they have given themselves over to it, nothing they touch succeeds, starting with the economy and culture. Everywhere, France is in retreat; everywhere, France grieves.

The second decision concerns governance, or how France should be gov-erned now that it has become multiracial and multi-confessional. What can the history of French colonization teach us here? Surely that separation—and therefore separatism—is inevitably in the cards whenever civilizations with nothing in common come into contact with one another. Simply saying this is not enough. A solution must be put forward to prevent France from breaking into pieces.

Finally, the third decision is to become aware. A new colonization is under-way, placing us under the yoke of moneyed powers and transnational lobbies, for whom the cause of the people—of our people—is the last concern. Already, France has become their ward, her sovereignty purely theoretical, a nebulous idea floating high above the halls of the Republic and the National Assembly. Do the immigrants (among whom I number myself) wish to experience col-onization? Do my native stock compatriots wish to become natives whose af-fairs are managed by collaborationist elites on behalf of foreign powers? If anything must be resisted, it is these new forms of subjugation now being im-posed upon our country. In this struggle, I hope that Arabs, blacks, Asians, and Gauls can come together as brothers in arms.

Vive la France, Vive l'Indépendance!

BIBLIOGRAPHY

The Colonial Dream

Girardet, Raoul. *L'Idée coloniale en France: de 1871 à 1962*. La Table Ronde, 1972.

De Vogüé, Eugène-Melchior. "Les Indes noires: Le voyage de M. Stanley." L'Europe et la France en Afrique". *Revue des Deux Mondes* (1829–1971) 102, no. 1 (1890).

Bordeaux, Henri. *Nos Indes noires: voyage en Afrique occidentale*. Plon, 1936.

Deroo, E., and Lemaire, S. *L'Illusion coloniale*. Tallandier, 2006.

Brunschwig, Henri. "Note sur les technocrates de l'impérialisme Français en Afrique noire." *Revue française d'histoire d'outre-mer* 54, no. 194–197 (1967).

Brunschwig, Henri. *Mythes et réalités de l'impérialisme colonial français, 1871–1914*. A. Colin, 1960.

Ageron, Charles-Robert. "Gambetta et la reprise de l'expansion coloniale." *Revue française d'histoire d'outre-mer* 59, no. 215 (1972).

The Precolonial Era

The Arab World:

Ennaji, Mohammed. *Soldats, domestiques et concubines: l'esclavage au Maroc au XIXe siècle*. Ceres, 1994.

Mounir, Omar. Bou Hmara, *L'homme à l'ânesse*. Rabat: Marsam, 2009.

Djellali, Abderrazak. "Le caïdat en Algérie au XIXe siècle." *Cahiers de la méditerranée*, no. 45, 1 (1992).

Van Vollenhoven, Joost. *Essai sur le fellah Algérien*. Doctoral Thesis. Paris, 1903.

Émerit, Marcel. "L'état intellectuel et moral de l'Algérie en 1830." *Revue d'histoire moderne et contemporaine* 1, no. 3 (1954).

De Foucauld, Charles. *Reconnaissance au Maroc 1883–1884*. Société d'éditions géographiques, maritimes et coloniales, 1888.

Barbe, Adam. "Public debt and European expansionism in Morocco from 1860 to 1956." *Paris School of Economics*, 2016.

Cochut, André. "Les Khouan: mœurs religieuses de l'Algérie." *Revue des Deux Mondes*, no. 14, 1846: 589–611.

D'Estournelles de Constant, Paul. "Les sociétés secrètes chez les Arabes et la conquête de l'Afrique du Nord." *Revue des Deux Mondes*, 1884.

Lesne, Marcel. "Les Zemmour: essai d'Histoire Tribale." *Revue de l'Occident musulman et de la Méditerranée*, no. 2, 1966.

Africa:

Pétré-Grenouilleau, Olivier. *Les traites négrières*. Gallimard, 2014.

Ayache, Simon. "Pouvoir central et provinces sous la monarchie au XIXe Siècle." *Publications de la société française d'histoire d'outre-mer*, 1981.

Boulevert, Yves. *Explorations en Afrique Centrale 1790–1930*. Y. Boulevert, 2019.

Indochina:

Boudet, Paul. "La conquête de la Cochinchine par les Nguyên et le rôle des émigrés chinois." *Bulletin de l'École française d'Extrême-Orient*, 1942.

Emerit, Marcel. "Les tribus privilégiées en Algérie dans la première moitié du XIXe siècle." *Annales. Économies, sociétés, civilisations* 21, no. 1 (1966).

Villemagne, Claire. "Commerçants et colons français au Tonkin, les pionniers oubliés de la colonisation." *Outre-Mers* 90, no. 340–341 (2003): 213–232.

Dorigny, Marcel, ed. *Haïti, première république noire*. Société française d'histoire d'outre-mer, 2003

Conquest and Pacification

The Arab World:

Lyautey, Colonel. *Du rôle colonial de l'armée*. Armand Collin, 1900.

Roches, Léon. *Trente-deux à travers l'Islam*. Paris, 1884.

De Tocqueville, Alexis. *Premier rapport sur l'Algérie*. Paris, 1847.

Urbain, Ismaïl. *Du gouvernement des tribus*. Paris, 1848.

Bugeaud, Thomas. *De la colonisation de l'Algérie*. Paris, 1847.

Ideville, Henry d'. *Le Maréchal Bugeaud d'après sa correspondance intime et des documents intimes*. Paris, 1881–1882.

Aucapitaine, Henri. *Les Kabyles et la colonisation de l'Algérie: études sur le passé et l'avenir des Kabyles*. Versailles, 1864.

Africa:

Gallieni, Joseph. *Rapport d'ensemble sur la pacification, l'organisation et la colonisation de Madagascar.* Charles-Lavauzelle, 1900.

Lyautey, Hubert. *Paroles d'action.* Armand Colin, 1927.

Indochina:

Teyssier, Arnaud. *Lyautey.* Perrin, 2009.

Pavie, Auguste. À la conquête des cœurs. Éditions Bossard, 1921.

Life in the Colonies

The Arab World:

Christelle, Taraud. *La prostitution coloniale: Algérie, Tunisie, Maroc (1830–1962).* Payot, 2003.

Katan, Yvette. "Les colons de 1848 en Algérie: mythes et réalités." *Revue d'histoire moderne et contemporaine* 31, no. 2 (1984).

Gary, Romain. *La promesse de l'aube.* Gallimard, 1973.

Gide, André. *Retour du Tchad.* Gallimard, 1928.

Comité d'Action Marocaine. *Plan de réformes marocaines.* Paris, 1934.

Hoisington, William A. *L'héritage de Lyautey: Noguès et la politique française au Maroc, 1936–1943.* Perrin, 1996.

Hoisington, William A. *Jacques Lemaigre Dubreuil de Paris à Casablanca.* L'Harmattan, 2009.

Montagne, Robert. "La crise nationaliste au Maroc." *Politique étrangère*, no. 6 (1937).

Lefeuvre, Daniel. *Chère Algérie: la France et sa colonie (1930–1962).* Flammarion, 2005.

Viollette, Maurice. *L'Algérie vivra-t-elle?* Alcan, 1931.

Africa:

Mollion, Pierre. "Le portage en Oubangui-Chari, 1890–1930." *Revue d'histoire moderne et contemporaine* 33, no. 4 (1986).

Goulphin, Fred. *Les veillées de chasse d'Henri Guizard.* Flammarion, 1987.

Jeaugeon, R. "Les sociétés d'exploitation au Congo et l'opinion française de 1890 à 1906." *Revue française d'histoire d'outre-mer* 48, no. 172–173 (1961).

Zimmermann, Maurice. "Les Concessions au Congo français." *Annales de géographie* 9, no. 44 (1900).

Lauro, Amandine. *Coloniaux, ménagères et prostituées: Au Congo belge (1885–1930)*. Éditions Labor, 2005.

Londres, Albert. *Terre d'ébène*. Albin Michel, 1929.

Profizi, Vanina. "Les fonctionnaires d'origine corse en AOF (1900–1920) : approche prosopographique de l'identité régionale en contexte colonial." *Outre-Mers* 98, no. 370–371 (2011).

Sautter, Gilles. "Notes sur la construction du chemin de fer Congo-Océan (1921–1934)." *Cahiers d'études africaines* 7, no. 26 (1967).

Indochina:

Phan Le Xuan. "L'enseignement du Vietnam pendant la période coloniale, 1862–1945: La formation des intellectuels vietnamiens." Doctoral Thesis, Department of Education, University of Lyon, 2018.

Viollis, Andrée. *Indochine S.O.S.* Les Bons Caractères, 2008. (Reissue).

Monet, Paul. *Les jauniers*. NRF, 1928.

Legrandjacques, Sara. "Hanoi au cœur des mobilités étudiantes, 1880–1945." *Bulletin de l'Institut Pierre Renouvin* 43, no. 1 (2016).

Duras, Marguerite. *L'Amant*. Éditions de Minuit, 1984.

Lartéguy, Jean. *Le Mal Jaune*. Presses de la Cité, 1962.

Hô Chi Minh. *Le procès de la colonisation française*. Paris, 1925.

Douchet. *Métis et Congaies en Indochine*. Hanoi, 1928.

Dr Jacobus X. *L'amour aux colonies*. Isidore Liseux Éditeur, 1893.

Decolonization

The Arab World:

Thénault, Sylvie. "Tous les Algériens ne souhaitaient pas l'indépendance." In *Algérie: des "événements" à la guerre. idées reçues sur la guerre d'indépendance algérienne*, edited by Sylvie Thénault. Le Cavalier Bleu, 2012.

Bachaga Boualem. *Mon pays, la France*. Éditions France-Empire, 1962.

Mathias, Grégor. *Les vampires à la fin de la guerre d'Algérie, mythe ou réalité?* Michalon, 2014.

Morgan, Ted. *Ma bataille d'Alger*. Tallandier, 2016.

Branche, Raphaëlle. *L'Embuscade de Palestro: Algérie 1956*. Armand Colin, 2010.

Horne, Alistair. *A Savage War of Peace*. New York Review of Books, 2006.

Lacouture, Jean et Simonne. *Le Maroc à l'épreuve*. Seuil, 1958.

Galula, David. *Pacification in Algeria 1956–1958*. The Rand Corporation, 1963.

Africa:
Dedet, Christian. *La mémoire du fleuve*. Libretto, 1984.
Georgy, Guy. *Le petit soldat de l'empire*. Flammarion, 1992.

Indochina:
Galula, David. *Counterinsurgency Warfare: Theory and Practice*. Praeger, 1964.
Rignac, Paul. *La guerre d'Indochine en questions*. Indo Éditions, 2009.
Chesneaux, Jean. "Fondements historiques du communisme vietnamien." *L'homme et la société*, 1969.

Post Independence
Rocherieux, Julien. "L'évolution de l'Algérie depuis l'indépendance." *Sud/Nord*, vol. 14, no. 1 (2001).
Vermeren, Pierre. *Une histoire de l'Algérie contemporaine*. Nouveau Monde Éditions, 2022.
Levin, Daniel. *Nothing but a Circus*. Penguin, 2017.
Sédar Senghor, Léopold. *Ce que je crois*. Grasset, 1988.
Kourouma, Ahmadou. *En attendant le vote des bêtes sauvages*. Le Seuil, 1998.

Repentance
Lefeuvre, Daniel. *Pour en finir avec la repentance coloniale*. Flammarion, 2010.
Lugan, Bernard. *Pour en finir avec la colonisation*. Éditions du Rocher, 2006.

Identity and Civilization
Lévi-Strauss, Claude. *Tristes Tropiques*. Plon, 1955.
Braudel, Fernand. *L'identité de la France*. Flammarion, 2009.
Braudel, Fernand. *La Grammaire des civilisations*. Flammarion, 2014.
Braudel, Fernand. *La Méditerranée et le monde méditerranéen au temps de Philippe II*. Flammarion, 2017.
Huntington, Samuel. "The clash of civilizations?" *Foreign Affairs*, Summer 1993.

Other Colonizations: Arabo-Berber, American, Portuguese, Brazilian, British, Belgian, etc.
Sanchez Saus, Rafael. *Les chrétiens dans al-Andalus, de la soumission à l'anéantissement*. Éditions du Rocher, 2016.
Fanjul, Serafin. *La quimera de al-Andalus*. Madrid, 2004.

Laroui, Abdallah. *Historia del Magreb. Desde los orígenes hasta el despertar magrebí.* Madrid, 1994.

Ye'or, Bat. *Juifs et chrétiens sous l'Islam. Les "dhimmis" face au défi intégriste.* Paris, 1994.

Aillet, Cyrille. *Les Mozarabes, Christianisme, islamisation et arabisation en péninsule ibérique (IXe-XIe siècle).* Madrid, 2010.

Guéraiche, William. "Regards français sur la colonisation américaine aux Philippines (1898–1916)." *Guerres mondiales et conflits contemporains* 209, no. 1 (2003).

Robert, Amélie. "At the Heart of the Vietnam War: Herbicides, Napalm and Bulldozers Against the A Lưới Mountains." *Journal of Alpine Research | Revue de géographie alpine* 104, no. 1 (2016).

Ramsey, Robert D. *Savage Wars of Peace: Case Studies of Pacification in the Philippines, 1900–1902.* Fort Leavenworth, 2007.

Prévot, Victor. "L'Œuvre belge au Congo." *L'information géographique* 25, no. 3 (1961).

Piette, Valérie. "La Belgique au Congo ou la volonté d'imposer sa ville? L'exemple de Léopoldville." *Revue belge de philologie et d'histoire* 89, no. 2 (2011).

Pélissier, René. *Les campagnes coloniales du Portugal, 1844–1941.* Pygmalion (Flammarion), 2004.

Pelissier, René. "La colonisation portugaise en Afrique: aperçus sur quelques Mythes et certaines réalités." *Matériaux pour l'histoire de notre temps* 32-33 (1993).

Freyre, Gilberto. *Maîtres et Esclaves.* Gallimard, 1978.

Winter, Jay. "Migration, war and empire: the British case." *Annales de démographie historique* 103, no. 1 (2002).

Chang, Iris. *The Rape of Nanking: The Forgotten Holocaust of World War II.* Basic Books, 2014.